PREVENTION'S
Fight
Fat

THE BEST NEW WAYS
TO CUT FAT—
FROM YOUR
PLATE AND
YOUR WAIST

EDITED BY MARK BRICKLIN AND
GALE MALESKEY OF *PREVENTION* MAGAZINE

RODALE PRESS, INC.
EMMAUS, PENNSYLVANIA

This book is being published simultaneously by Rodale Press as *Prevention's Fight Fat 1997*.

Copyright © 1997 by Rodale Press, Inc.

Library of Congress Cataloging-in-Publication Data
Prevention's fight fat : the best new ways to cut fat—from your plate
    and your waist / edited by Mark Bricklin and Gale Maleskey.
        p.   cm.
    Includes index.
    ISBN 0–87596–420–6 paperback
    1. Low-fat diet.   2. Weight loss.   I. Bricklin, Mark.
II. Maleskey, Gale.   III. Prevention (emmaus, Pa.)
RM237.7.P733   1996
613.2'8—dc20   96–27692

Distributed in the book trade by St. Martin's Press

2 4 6 8 10 9 7 5 3 1 paperback

─────── OUR PURPOSE ───────
*"We inspire and enable people to improve
their lives and the world around them."*

Prevention's Fight Fat Editorial Staff

Managing Editor: Debora T. Yost

Editor: Gale Maleskey

Contributors: Mark Golin; Stephen P. Gullo, Ph.D.; Anita Hirsch, R.D.; Jayne Hurley, R.D.; Rosemary Iconis; Myra Karstadt; Bonnie Liebman; Patricia Long; Holly McCord, R.D.; Judith Mandelbaum-Schmid; Dawn Margolis; Michele Meyer; Marty Munson; Cathy Perlmutter; Curtis Pesman; Jennifer Rapaport; Stephen Schmidt; John Sedgwick; Carrie Silberman; Elizabeth Somer, R.D.; Maggie Spilner; Michele Stanten; Sharon Stocker; Dana Sullivan; Beth Tomkiw; Margo Trott; Therese Walsh; Elizabeth Ward, R.D.; Teryl Zarnow

Editor, *Prevention* Magazine: Mark Bricklin

Executive Editor, *Prevention* Magazine: Emrika Padus

Senior Copy Editor: Jane Sherman

Cover and Book Designer: Lynn N. Gano

Studio Manager: Stefano Carbini

Technical Artist: J. Andrew Brubaker, Kathryn Greenslade

Permissions: Anita Small

Director, Book Manufacturing: Helen Clogston

Manufacturing Coordinator: Melinda Rizzo

Office Personnel: Roberta Mulliner, Julie Kehs, Bernadette Sauerwine, Mary Lou Stephen

Rodale Health and Fitness Books

Vice-President and Editorial Director: Debora T. Yost

Art Director: Jane Colby Knutila

Research Manager: Ann Gossy Yermish

Copy Manager: Lisa D. Andruscavage

Contents

Low-Fat Know-How

Contents

Contents

PART TWO

Big Gains in Weight Loss

Contents

PART THREE

Low-Fat Recipes
of the Year

Contents

Make your grand finale lean and luscious with these
tempting recipes.

Introduction

Al and Adele Average still eat way too much fat. And they look like they do. Here's how to be less than Average.

Do you consider yourself an average American? If so, you could be in trouble.

Can you guess how much fat the average American eats in a year? Twenty-five pounds? Fifty? Try 81 pounds. That's about 100 grams a day (although it's closer to 75 grams a day for a woman). It translates into 36,500 grams of fat a year, or 2,147 beef hot dogs; 570 meals of a hamburger, french fries and a milk shake; 414 eight-ounce bags of potato chips; or 260 tablespoons of vegetable oil. It's enough to clog up the coronary arteries of some 1.5 million people every year, which is precisely what it does.

Compare that 100 grams of fat to the amount that health experts say we are better off consuming, which is no more than 30 percent of calories from fat. If you're eating a 2,000-calorie diet, that comes to 66 grams or less a day. You can see that, for most of us, it means cutting our fat intake by one-third, more or less.

As we've learned about the health risks of high-fat diets, we have worked to cut out fat. We've switched from whole to low-fat milk and from premium ice cream to frozen yogurt. We eat a bit less red meat. Certainly we have more low-fat foods than ever to choose among. But the fact is, most of us are still overshooting the 30 percent mark.

Why? Public health officials agree: People need both information and motivation to stick with healthy habits such as low-fat eating. And that's where this book comes in.

It provides the information you need to make smart choices in low-fat eating. It helps you to set up your kitchen and stock your cupboards for quick low-fat cooking. It guides you in selecting tasty low-fat foods when eating out, whether your restaurant choice is fast food or fancy French. It shows you how to nibble your way through the proliferation of new low-fat and nonfat foods.

Prevention's Fight Fat can also keep you motivated. It offers inspiring stories of people who made the decision to live healthier, leaner lives, then figured out just how to do that. Plus it tells you exactly what experts in preventive medicine research use as their top strategies for low-fat eating and healthy living.

For those who also want to lose weight, this book gleans practical advice from the latest research findings. It lists foods that are proven to axe your appetite for hours, suggests how you can use fiber-rich foods to lose weight and helps you minimize damage to your waistline after an occasional pig-out.

Our chapters on exercise help you make the most (and least) of your shape, whether you're top-heavy, bottom-heavy or just plain heavy. And our focus on the psychological aspects of weight loss will help you curb overeating and resist the misplaced intentions of friends.

Our selection of 50 no-fat recipes may be the best value in this book. Selected by *Prevention* health book food editors, they are a sampling from the best-selling low-fat cookbooks on the market today, and they are guaranteed to get you into the kitchen.

With *Prevention's Fight Fat*, you can be less than "average." And we think that's great!

—The Editors

PART ONE

Low-Fat Know-How

Cheatproof Your Diet

Our calorie and portion size guide won't let you get away with giant servings, and it could help you drop 25 pounds.

Something doesn't add up. You're eating fat-free pasta and pouring fat-free dressing on your salad. You've switched to the small, low-fat shake at the drive-in. Yet you're steadily losing the weight-loss struggle.

Join the crowd. Americans are more fat-conscious than ever, yet we're getting fatter every decade.

The trouble is, we're consuming more calories! We took healthy advice—"Eat as much as you want as long as it's low-fat"—a step too far. That advice is true only for naturally low-fat, high-fiber foods like veggies, fruits and whole grains. With those foods, calories head for the basement.

But with the flood of new processed low-fat products, that advice can lead to trouble. Many of these products have nearly as many calories as their fatty counterparts (and very little fiber, a key to appetite control). Eat lots of these foods, and your calorie intake rises skyward.

Another mistake: We've lost track of portion sizes. We don't realize that some naturally low-fat foods like pasta can dish up a load of calories—if we eat it by the plateful. Or what we think is only a small taste of a high-fat favorite like butter may have—oops!—that many calories.

There is an answer—and it's not starvation rations.

What's needed is mindful eating. That means getting back in touch with what you eat—and how much. To do that, you start with a short-term course in calorie counting. Based on what you learn from this, you pinpoint calorie cuts in smart, healthy ways that you can live with forever so that you may lose weight for good. Here's how.

Create a Calorie-Counting Lab

It's much easier to count calories if you're organized. Set yourself up with these tools, gathered in one spot on the kitchen counter.

- A set of measuring spoons and measuring cups. Keep these just for measuring portion sizes. If you have a designated set, you'll be less likely to blow off measuring because your regular utensils are in the dishwasher.
- A calorie-counting guide that you're comfortable with. You might like *Bowes and Church's Food Values of Portions Commonly Used* by Jean Pennington, a classic guide that lists thousands of foods. *The LEARN Program for Weight Control*, by *Prevention* adviser Kelly Brownell, Ph.D., professor of psychology and co-director of the Eating and Weight Disorders Clinic at Yale University, offers a complete guide for keeping records for weight loss and exercise plus a calorie-guide appendix.

   Since you may need to convert fluid ounces to cups or tablespoons to teaspoons, make sure that your guide has a conversion table.
- A notebook to record all the foods you eat and how many calories they have. Best choices: a standard-size loose-leaf notebook or an $8\frac{1}{2}" \times 11"$ lined tablet. Either will give you the space you need. (Always keep a small notebook with you to record meals eaten away from home. Then transfer your notes to your larger notebook.)
- Pens or pencils, plus a highlighter. Use your highlighter to mark foods

Step One: Keep Track

First, without changing your diet, for two full weeks record every food you eat and how many calories it has. (See "Create a Calorie-Counting Lab" above, for some easy tips to help you do this.) Creating a record like this lets you determine your current-weight calories—the number of calories your body requires to keep you as you are. (You'll need this vital piece of information for Step Three.)

Nope—just guessing at your calorie intake won't do. The fact is, most people underestimate how much they eat. In a survey at the University of Minnesota in Minneapolis, 140 men and women were asked to esti-

that you look up in your calorie guide. Chances are that you'll look up some foods often. If they're highlighted, they'll jump right out at you.

- A pocket calculator to add up your daily totals. This is indispensable, unless you're a math whiz and enjoy doing it yourself!
- A food scale. Many times you need to measure food by weight. Scales are available in the kitchenware sections of department stores or kitchen specialty stores, from $6 up. It's nice to have a scale that lets you weigh your dish, reset the dial to zero, then weigh the plate with the food.
- A pair of reading glasses, if you need them. You might even prefer a magnifying glass for deciphering the fine print on labels.

Now that you're organized, here's what you need to do: Start each day on a new page of your notebook. List all the foods you eat for every meal and snack, along with the amount. Then look up the calories on the food label or in your calorie guide. Be precise. Don't just say, "A roast beef sandwich." List two slices of bread (get calories from the wrapper). List how many slices or ounces of roast beef (for prepackaged beef, calories will be on the label; for deli beef, you'll need your calorie guide). Measure and list how many teaspoons or tablespoons of mayonnaise (get the calorie count from the jar) you spread on your sandwich. For a restaurant roast beef sandwich, you'll have to estimate portions and use your calorie guide to tally them.

mate the sizes of the portions of 41 foods. They made errors that could lead to several hundred extra calories a day in their diets. "Most people tend to be way off in estimating the caloric value of their foods," says Robert Jeffery, Ph.D., a weight-loss expert at the University of Minnesota Medical School in Minneapolis.

Keeping records for two weeks rather than for just a day or two can show you just where your lifestyle laps up calories. You may overindulge only on weekends, or you may down an extra 1,000 calories at a Wednesday night bridge game.

Once you've carefully measured every last morsel and tallied up your two-week calorie intake, divide that total by 14 to get your average number of calories per day.

Step Two: Decide How Fast to Go

Next, determine how many calories you want to cut back every day. To lose a pound a week (the maximum safe rate of weight loss), you need to eat 500 fewer calories a day (assuming your activity level stays constant). But many experts recommend slower weight loss, because it's easier to stick with your plan that way. To lose a half-pound a week, cut back 250 calories a day. In one year you'll lose 25 pounds! Even if you cut back only 125 calories a day (to lose a quarter-pound a week), in one year you'll lose 12 pounds!

Note: If you've gained five or more pounds in the past year, you've been eating more calories than required to maintain your weight; you may need to cut back a bit more. Start with dropping 300 calories a day to lose a half-pound a week.

Step Three: Set Your Target

Now figure out how many calories you should eat every day to reach your new, desired weight. Take your current-weight calories (which you

---

Portion Control for Busy People

If you simply can't bear the thought of weighing, measuring or recording your food intake, you may want to simply scale down your mental picture of reasonable servings. To help you keep what you eat in perspective, here are the pictures you want to keep in mind.

- One portion of meat or fish (2 to 3 ounces) is the size of a deck of cards.
- A portion of cheese (1½ ounces) is the size of three dominos.
- One portion of pasta, rice or mashed potatoes (½ cup) is the size of half a baseball.
- A portion of salad or beans (1 cup) is the size of a baseball.
- One portion of peanut butter (2 tablespoons) is the size of a table tennis ball.

Exercise Counts, Too

Without a doubt, exercise is still the determining factor in whether a person maintains weight loss. If you have trouble finding time to exercise or temporarily lose the motivation or the time to continue with 30- or 40-minute workouts, try starting with 10-minute walks. Work toward finding several 10-minute opportunities to take brisk, short strolls during the day.

determined in Step One) and subtract from that the number of calories you decided to cut back in Step Two.

Let's say you're a 175-pound woman and you want to lose 25 pounds. After keeping records for two weeks, you find that you're averaging about 2,500 calories a day to maintain your weight. You decide to cut back 250 calories a day to lose a half-pound a week, or 25 pounds in one year. Subtracting 250 from 2,500 gives you 2,250, which would be your daily calorie target. (*Note:* Never go below 1,200 calories a day without consulting your doctor.)

Step Four: Pinpoint Your Problems

Identify the biggest calorie "hits" in the records from your first two weeks of calorie counting. Where did you blow it? Is it low-fat foods like fat-free cookies that turned out to be higher in calories than you realized? Is it too many dollops of high-fat, high-calorie foods, like sour cream or margarine? Is it Goliath-size portions of healthy foods like pasta? These calorie "hits" show you where to make changes.

Step Five: Revamp

Finally, take the daily menus you've already recorded and cut back on enough calorie "hits" to reduce your total calories to your daily target. (Our Calorie Blasters on page 10 will help you do this without shrinking portion sizes or fretting over exotic recipes.) *Voilà!* You have a weight-loss meal plan tailored just for you. You'll also have the skills to develop additional "mindful" meal plans that hit your calorie target.

(continued on page 10)

Blimpy or Wow!

To demonstrate our Calorie Blasters at work, we first tallied the calories in three typical American dinners—pasta, steak and a burger and fries. What did we find? Blimp City!

Then, we tried our Calorie Blasters. This time? Wow! Even we were surprised at how abundant our low-calorie dinners of all-American favorites turned out to be. As a fabulous bonus, fat plummeted and fiber rose.

PASTA DINNER

The secret to our Wow! pasta dinner? Zeroing in on all that pasta—it's nearly free of fat, but it's not low in calories! We combined less spaghetti with plentiful veggies; shopped for fat-free, lower-calorie spaghetti sauce and used fat-free margarine.

Wow!

FOOD/PORTION	CALORIES	FAT (G.)
1 cup spaghetti	200	1
1¼ cups broccoli	25	0
1 cup mushrooms	40	1
¾ cup fat-free, low-cal spaghetti sauce	75	0
1 Tbsp. Parmesan cheese	30	2
1 slice French bread	80	1
1 Tbsp. fat-free margarine	5	0
5 oz. red wine	100	0
Total	**555**	**5**

BURGER, FRIES 'N' SHAKE

Okay, you can't buy our Wow! burger, fries and shake at the drive-in. But look what you get by making it yourself: drive-in-style food for half the calories! The tricks: Whirl a strawberry smoothie in your blender. Substitute a low-calorie soyburger and reduced-fat cheese. Bake your "fries" (cut a potato in strips, coat a baking sheet with nonfat cooking spray, spread the potatoes on the baking sheet, spray again, sprinkle with paprika and bake at 450° until golden).

Wow!

Food/Portion	Calories	Fat (g.)
Soyburger (2.75 oz.)	70	0
1 slice reduced-fat cheese	50	3
1 Tbsp. pickle relish	15	0
1 Tbsp. ketchup	15	0
Hamburger roll	115	2
Baked french "fries" (3.5 oz.)	110	0
Strawberry smoothie (10 frozen strawberries, 1/2 frozen banana, 1 cup skim milk; 3 cups)	165	0
Total	**540**	**5**

STEAK DINNER

The heroes of this Wow! steak dinner are all low-calorie substitutes: London broil for filet mignon, nonfat sour cream and fat-free margarine, our own baked onion rings instead of french-fried ones.

Wow!

Food/Portion	Calories	Fat (g.)
3 oz. London broil	150	4
8 baked onion rings	50	0
7-oz. baked potato	220	0
2 Tbsp. fat-free margarine	10	0
1/4 cup nonfat sour cream	60	0
3 cups mixed green salad	25	0
1/4 cup fat-free, low-cal honey mustard dressing	40	0
10 oz. unsweetened ginger-peach-flavored iced tea	0	0
Total	**555**	**4**

FAT STATS

How Much We Spend

- Amount Americans shell out each year on dieting: $32 billion
- Annual revenues of the top three weight-loss companies: Weight Watchers, $1.6 billion; Jenny Craig, $400 million; Nutri/System, $225 million
- Amount Americans spend annually on weight-loss-related products: $380.8 million
- Amount spent on low-fat, fat-free foods: $8.8 billion
- Amount spent on diet soft drinks: $3.5 billion
- Amount spent on over-the-counter diet medications: $84.7 million

It's important, as much as possible, to divide your target calories into meals and snacks spread throughout the day. A natural tendency—but a big mistake—is to skimp on breakfast and lunch to "save" your calories for dinner and evening snacks. (A study suggests that this is what many American women do.) You'll set yourself up to get so hungry that you wind up bingeing.

After you lose some weight, your body will need fewer calories. If you hit a weight-loss plateau, that's a signal that you may need to cut out another 125 calories or so.

Calorie Blasters Forever

Your best chance of losing weight for good is making realistic changes that you can live with—always.

So you have some options: You can cut calories simply by cutting portions, but could you live with what may seem like dollhouse-size portions? You can cut back by learning a dozen new recipes, but do you really have the time and energy? And do you really want to give up your tried-and-true favorite foods, the meals you're comfortable with? For many people, the honest answer to all of the above is, "Not a chance!"

Here, on the other hand, are Calorie Blasters you can live with—which means that they work! Why? (1) Because they are supereasy—no elaborate new cooking required. (2) They allow you to eat your favorite meals—the ones you'll eventually gravitate back to anyway. (Only now they'll be streamlined in calories and fat.) (3) They give you mucho munching, because the portions either stay the same or actually get bigger. And by the way, they're healthy!

Deploy veggies. To really slash calories, mix mini-portions of high-calorie favorites—like macaroni and cheese—with giant helpings of veggies—the lowest-calorie foods of all.

Example: Instead of eating two cups of rice pilaf (for over 400 calories), mix a half-cup of pilaf with two cups of green beans, chopped sweet red peppers and mushrooms (for less than 200 calories total). The result? You get to enjoy the pilaf, but you slash calories and load up on fiber-rich vegetables. (Every day you need at least three half-cup servings.) Use the same trick to slim down a plate of pasta.

More veggie ideas: If you love coleslaw, mix a half-pint from the supermarket deli with two eight-ounce packs of shredded carrots from the produce aisle. One cup of low-calorie carrot coleslaw has about 50 calories; one cup of plain coleslaw has 200 calories. In a diner, you might order one side dish of macaroni and cheese, one of broccoli and one of carrots, served together on one dinner plate.

Take advantage of low-fat foods with low-calorie price tags. Check supermarkets for low-fat versions of any high-fat products you use. Then check their labels. If a low-fat substitute offers significant calorie savings, give it a try. Even if you sacrifice a bit of taste or texture (not that you always do), you may decide it's worth it.

How much does this help? Sometimes the calorie savings are stupendous! A single tablespoon of fat-free mayo saves 90 calories. A low-fat hot dog can save over 100 calories, as can a half-cup of fat-free spaghetti sauce. Always check labels to make sure that "low-fat" really means "low-calorie." Don't assume anything.

Look for ringers—and replace them. Ringers are low-fat versions of foods that still have lots of calories. Chances are good that your calorie counting turned up a few in your menus. Especially tricky are low-fat or fat-free cookies, frozen yogurt, ice cream, crackers, salad dressings and cheese. By comparing labels at the store, you may find another low-fat version of the same food that's a good deal lower in calories than the one you're using. Switch.

If you've "just gotta have it," make what you can't buy. If there's a high-calorie food that stirs your passions, sometimes the only way you can enjoy a low-cal version is to make it yourself. And if the recipe is a cinch, why not? See the calorie-saving recipes for homemade french "fries" (page 8) and homemade french "fried" onion rings (page 43).

Satisfy your sweet tooth with fruit shakes. We've all been told that fruit makes a low-calorie, healthy dessert. But if you're like many people, a banana doesn't usually feel like dessert. On the other hand, if you freeze a banana and then whirl it in the blender with skim milk or nonfat yogurt, it's amazing how it turns into a big, creamy banana milk shake for less than 200 calories! Real shakes—small ones—start at about 350 calories.

As a low-calorie dessert mainstay, these shakes give you supernutritious fruit (we need a minimum of two half-cup servings a day), with lots of fiber and calcium. For variety, keep bags of frozen strawberries, raspberries, peaches and blueberries on hand. Add honey for extra sweetness.

Axe Your Appetite

New research pinpoints the world's most powerful weight-loss foods.

There are few things in life better than a good bargain. But getting more bang for your buck is not just a good shopping guideline, it's also a great weight-loss strategy. That's because to drop pounds, you have to eat less yet still manage to satisfy your hunger. And the only way to do that is to stretch every calorie you eat in the same way that you stretch every dollar you spend on a budget.

Enter the bargain foods. On a calorie-per-calorie basis, they have greater power to fill you up and satisfy your hunger than other foods. And the faster they fill you up, the less you have to (or want to) eat. By including more of these bargains in your diet, you can easily save enough calories to finally lose the 10, 20 or 30 pounds you want—without ever going hungry.

All Foods Are Not Equal

A rose by any other name may smell as sweet, but 240 calories of apple is two times sweeter to your appetite-control system than 240 calories of ice cream. That's just one surprise from research conducted at the University of Sydney in Australia.

In the study, students were asked to come in each morning and eat 240-calorie portions of a specific food. Then they rated their feelings of hunger or fullness every 15 minutes. At the end of two hours came the ultimate test of how satisfied the students really were: They were allowed to hit a buffet table and eat as much as they liked, while researchers took copious notes.

A number of foods were tested, and when the crumbs settled it was very apparent that equal caloric portions of different foods do not equally satisfy hunger. Basing their ratings on a scale that assigned white bread an automatic score of 100, the researchers discovered that some foods are only half as satisfying as bread, while others are actually three times as filling. At the bottom of the Aussie list (in the middle of a grease stain) were croissants. With a rating of 47, they were barely more satisfying than air.

> *The not-so-modest potato fills you up faster and on fewer calories than any other food tested.*

The star performer was the not-so-modest potato. With a way-out-in-front rating of 323, it gives you the most bang for your caloric dollar, filling you up faster and on fewer calories than any other food tested.

The Method behind the Magic

Before we take a longer look at which foods make your stomach the happiest on the fewest calories, let's look at how they work this minor miracle. "The whole question of what makes a food satiating (satisfying to the appetite) is a complex one, and there are still many factors we haven't sorted out," admits nutritionist Barbara Rolls, Ph.D., director of the Laboratory for Human Ingestive Behavior at Pennsylvania State University in University Park. "In some cases, a food satisfies because we believe it will satisfy. In other cases it may be the taste, how quickly it is digested or the hormones it triggers."

But there does seem to be one constant that we can take to the bank. "Foods with a low energy density are less likely to be overeaten than those with a high energy density," says Dr. Rolls. What's energy density? It's simply the scientific terminology for how many calories a food packs for its weight. So your favorite chocolate bar has a high energy density because it weighs very little but delivers a whole bunch of calories—much to your dismay. On the other hand, a piece of apple of the same weight has a lot fewer calories, giving it a lower energy density.

Looking back at the potato and the croissant, the mystery of why one is more filling than the other becomes a whole lot less mysterious once the weight of each is taken into account. The 240-calorie potato weighs in at about 13 ounces; the 240-calorie croissant is just over 2 ounces.

"The more weight or volume of food for a given amount of calories, the less likely you are to eat more calories than you need," says Dr. Rolls.

Weight-Loss Friends and Foes

Stomach growling? Here's how foods rate when it comes to satisfying hunger pangs. Choosing a food from the top of the list (high satiety-index scores) will let you fill up with the fewest calories.

Food	Satiety-Index Score
Potato	323
Fish	225
Oatmeal	209
Oranges	202
Apples	197
Pasta, whole-wheat	188
Beefsteak	176
Grapes	162
Popcorn	154
Bran cereal	151
Cheese	146
Crackers	127
Cookies	120
Bananas	118
French fries	116
Bread, white	100
Muesli	100
Ice cream	96
Potato chips	91
Peanuts	84
Candy bar	70
Doughnut	68
Cake	65
Croissant	47

"First of all, if you see more food on the plate, you automatically expect to be more satisfied. Second, it takes longer to eat, making the experience more substantial." A greater portion of food also stimulates various receptors around the gastrointestinal tract—receptors that eventually tell the body that it has had enough to eat.

And finally, eating more food distends the stomach, literally filling it until you need to either stop eating or unhook your pants. But the weight-loss trick here is to find the foods that accomplish all of this for the fewest calories.

Foods That Fill You Up, Foods That Let You Down

To find the foods that are big on bulk but short on calories, let's get back to that Australian study. The foods tested were arranged in six groups: bakery products, snacks and confectionery, breakfast cereals, protein-rich foods, carbohydrate-rich foods and fruits. Right off the bat, researchers found that certain food groups as a whole are more filling than others on an equal-calorie basis. Fruits are number one, with an average satiety index of 170. That means that a fruit calorie is 70 percent more filling than a bread calorie. Next come carbohydrate-rich foods and protein-rich foods, which tied in a close second at 166. The third most filling group at 134 is breakfast cereals, then snacks and confectionery at 100. The least satisfying of the bunch were baked goods, turning in a poor rating of 85.

But each group had its star performers, as well as a few duds. Apples and oranges came out on top in the fruit category. Their satiety-index scores of 197 and 202 make them twice as appetite-fulfilling as bread (which, if you remember, had a score of 100). That's not surprising, considering that a 240-calorie portion of orange weighs nearly 1½ pounds. Low on the fruit-basket totem pole were bananas, with a satiety index of 118—not much better than bread. Again, this is no surprise, since 240 calories of banana buy you less than half of the bulk you get with an orange.

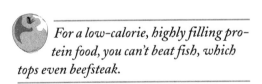 *For a low-calorie, highly filling protein food, you can't beat fish, which tops even beefsteak.*

In the carbohydrate category, we already know the winner—good old Mr. Potato Head, whose score of 323 mashed all competitors. The next best was oatmeal, with a very decent rating of 209. In last place was the potato again, but this time as french fries. Thanks to their swim in oil, fries contain about four times more calories than an equal weight of boiled tater.

FAT STATS

Top-Ten Filler-Uppers

These foods rate a high "satiety-index" score. That means a small amount can satisfy your appetite quickly with the fewest calories.

1. Potatoes
2. Fish
3. Oatmeal
4. Oranges
5. Apples
6. Whole-wheat pasta
7. Beefsteak
8. Grapes
9. Popcorn
10. Bran cereal

For a low-calorie but highly filling food in the protein category, you can't beat fish, which gets a healthy score of 225. Yes, it even beats beefsteak, which rates at 176. The fact that these protein foods are so satisfying is something that your own experience has probably taught you. And research agrees, says Dr. Rolls: Protein definitely knows which buttons to push in your appetite-control system.

The most filling snack you can reach for is a handful of popcorn. At a rating of 154, it's still 50 percent more satisfying than white bread. But from there, the whole snack category goes downhill fast. Ice cream rates only a 96, followed by chips at 91, peanuts at 84 and a candy bar at 70. The problem in this category is clear: Too much fat or sugar makes these foods so calorie dense that a few mouthfuls may blow your weight-loss budget.

Finally, you can forget about filling up without filling out when it comes to baked goods. The most satisfying food here is crackers at 127, followed by cookies at 120, doughnuts at 68, cake at 65, and the croissant, which came in dead last among all foods at 47.

The simple fact is that if you want to lose 10 pounds by this time next year, you'll need to cut about 100 calories a day (or 200 a day for 20 pounds and 300 for 30 pounds). The foods we've just explored can help, and here's how.

If instead of eating 300 calories of french fries you eat 100 calories of baked potato, not only will you feel just as full, you'll also have cut 200 calories right there. Reach for an apple at breakfast instead of a croissant and again you'll feel fuller but save yourself more than 100 calories. Or try oatmeal instead of a doughnut. It'll get you through the morning with fewer calories. For late-night munchies, opt for popcorn over potato chips. You'll feel more satisfied and slash nearly three-quarters of the calories.

And here's another bonus. These filling foods don't just satisfy you at the moment. They can continue to satisfy you for up to two hours after the meal. Remember the Australian experiment? At the end of two hours, the students could eat all they wanted from the buffet. But the ones who had earlier eaten the more filling foods ate less.

While the current research has only just begun identifying specific foods that fill you up for fewer calories, you can find some on your own. "Look for foods low in dietary fat," says Dr. Rolls. "They tend to provide more bulk for the calories. Also go for high-fiber foods like vegetables and fruits—again, they will fill you up for fewer calories."

What the Experts Eat

Do leading researchers in cancer and heart disease prevention practice what they preach? Their answers may surprise you.

Every week, it seems, there's a new scientific study telling you to do something different—sometimes 180 degrees different—with your diet. How low-fat should you go? Should you avoid margarine altogether? Are eggs okay? Chocolate? How many servings of fruits and vegetables do you really need? And what about wine? Should you make it red?

Here's how our nation's top nutrition researchers protect their own health in the midst of sometimes-conflicting advice.

William Castelli, M.D.

DIRECTOR OF THE FRAMINGHAM CARDIOVASCULAR INSTITUTE
IN FRAMINGHAM, MASSACHUSETTS

"I start every morning with a big bowl of rolled oats, to which I add an equal amount of applesauce or nonfat yogurt. It gives me a great dose of soluble fiber, which I hope will protect me from colon cancer. I also eat a lot of grilled fish and not much red meat (although I have had filet mignons that had less fat than a chicken breast), and I eat lots of vegetables and salads. I snack mostly on fruit. I love red wine—I generally buy a nice bottle and make it last one week. When I came to Framingham in the mid-1960s, my cholesterol was 270 and I had a terrible family history of heart disease. Now my cholesterol is under 200, and at age 64 I've outlived both my brother and my father by more than 20 years. I'm convinced it's because I've led a prudent lifestyle."

His Top Three Strategies

- Eat a low-fat, high-fiber diet.
- Jog for one hour, three times per week.
- Don't smoke.

I-Min Lee, M.D., Sc.D.

ASSISTANT PROFESSOR OF MEDICINE AT HARVARD MEDICAL SCHOOL

"My own research has most affected my exercise habits rather than my diet. Our latest data from the Harvard Alumni Study show that regular vigorous exercise can reduce one's risks of death dramatically—equivalent to comparing a pack-a-day smoker to a nonsmoker, or someone who is 20 percent overweight to someone of normal weight. In addition, I was raised on a traditional Chinese diet, where most of the calories come from grains and vegetables, and meat is used only in small amounts. I still hardly ever eat red meat, and most of the time I eat vegetarian meals. My one weakness is chocolate; I eat a small candy bar almost every day."

Her Top Three Strategies

- Run about 15 to 20 miles per week, and walk 1 mile each way to and from work.
- Eat a low-fat diet rich in fruits and vegetables.
- Don't smoke or drink alcohol.

Ronald M. Krauss, M.D.

HEAD OF MOLECULAR AND NUCLEAR MEDICINE AT THE LAWRENCE BERKELEY NATIONAL LABORATORY AT THE UNIVERSITY OF CALIFORNIA, BERKELEY, AND CHAIRMAN OF THE NUTRITION COMMITTEE FOR THE AMERICAN HEART ASSOCIATION

"When I was in medical school, I weighed 30 pounds more than I do today. I had a voracious appetite and was an aggressive eater—I had bacon and eggs nearly every day. But 25 years ago, when I started researching cholesterol and lipoproteins at the National Institutes of Health, I decided to make some changes. I cut back on eggs and started eating cereal and fruit. I lost the weight and have kept it off all these years. I rarely eat red meat, but I do eat chicken and fish, as well as plenty of fruits and vegetables and grains. I love chocolate, and I reserve that for special occasions. I think it's all right to indulge now and then."

His Top Three Strategies

- Jog three to five miles three times a week.
- Control weight.
- Consume a low-fat diet high in fruits and vegetables.

Jerianne Heimendinger, R.D., Sc.D.

DIRECTOR OF THE 5-A-DAY FOR BETTER HEALTH PROGRAM AT THE NATIONAL CANCER INSTITUTE IN BETHESDA, MARYLAND

"I make a conscious effort to consume at least five servings of fruits and vegetables a day, and often I go beyond that. The research into phytochemicals is so young that we really don't know which substances in fruits and vegetables are most protective against cancer and heart disease, so I consume a variety, eating a salad whenever I can. I start each day with a glass of orange juice and cereal topped with fresh fruit. I try to savor the natural flavors of fruits and vegetables rather than dousing them in high-fat sauces."

Her Top Three Strategies

- Eat more fruits and vegetables.
- Go to aerobics class or yoga at least twice a week.
- Dance for fun as often as possible.

Michael Jacobson, Ph.D.

EXECUTIVE DIRECTOR OF THE CENTER FOR SCIENCE IN THE PUBLIC INTEREST IN WASHINGTON, D.C.

"I'm not quite a vegetarian, but I'm moving in that direction. I eat fish, and occasionally I'll have poultry, but rarely red meat. I drink skim milk, and I generally eat whole-wheat bread. I don't have a salt shaker on the table. I don't eat out much, but when I do, I never order eggplant parmigiana anymore (which our studies show is one of the highest-fat dishes in Italian restaurants). And I've changed the way I order in Chinese restau-

Figuring Fat

The often-repeated advice to keep your daily fat intake at 30 percent or less of total calories makes sense in theory. None of the experts we interviewed said that they actually calculate their fat intake that way. "It's simply too complicated to try to figure your fat intake in those terms," says William Castelli, M.D., director of the Framingham Cardiovascular Institute in Framingham, Massachusetts.

His suggestion: Count fat grams instead. "The average American should have no more than 65 grams of fat per day (40 to 50 grams would probably be even better) and no more than 20 grams of saturated fat," Dr. Castelli says. Most of us consume 80 to 100 grams of fat per day, so read labels carefully; the fat grams are all there. When you've reached your limit, save those fatty indulgences for another day—or skip them altogether.

rants, too, avoiding the high-fat dishes. My wife and I like to cook at home, mostly low-fat meals; in addition to enjoying the food, we find that it's easier to clean up the kitchen because you don't have all that grease to contend with."

His Top Three Strategies

- Eat a low-fat, high-fiber diet.
- Don't smoke.
- Wear a seat belt.

Thomas Pearson, M.D., Ph.D.

PROFESSOR OF EPIDEMIOLOGY AND MEDICINE AT
COLUMBIA UNIVERSITY IN NEW YORK CITY

"I grew up in the Midwest eating steak six nights a week and roast beef on Sundays, and as a teenager, I'd down a half-gallon of whole Wisconsin milk in a sitting. Now my family eats red meat only once or twice a week, chicken and fish more frequently; the only milk we drink is skim. There's good epidemiologic evidence that animal fats—and not just saturated fats—may be linked to higher risks for heart disease. So we eat lots of fruits and vegetables—usually I've had five servings by lunchtime. I eat cereal and fruit for breakfast, and at lunch I've gotten away from eating sandwiches with mayonnaise, meat and cheese; now I just eat a couple of pieces of fruit and sliced vegetables. Often we'll have vegetarian dishes for dinner. Because there's good data that one or two alcoholic drinks per day can reduce heart attacks by as much as 30 percent, I do try to have a glass of wine or beer on evenings when I don't need to concentrate on work."

Our Top Three Strategies

Concentrate your healthy-living efforts in the following areas for the best payback. (Of course, if you smoke, quitting should be your number one health priority.)

Get regular exercise. Vigorous aerobic activity (at least three times a week) is still the best way to improve your cardiovascular endurance, gain strength and lose weight. But don't overlook the value of moderate exercise. Getting the most out of daily activities such as walking the dog, gardening or even attacking household chores with enthusiasm has a cumulative effect and can lower your risks of heart disease, high blood pressure, osteoporosis, stroke and cancer. Strength-training sessions are equally important; a couple of times a week is a good rule of thumb.

Eat less fat (especially saturated fat). You can do this by consuming smaller portions of red meat and limiting high-fat dairy products. Plan meals around fish, poultry, beans, lentils and grains. Cut back on the amount of added fat in your cooking and meal preparation, and use low-fat cooking techniques such as baking, broiling, grilling and steaming.

Get at least five servings of fruits and vegetables a day. Include at least one good source of antioxidant vitamins and beta-carotene daily in foods such as broccoli; citrus fruits; dark green, leafy vegetables; sweet potatoes and tomatoes.

His Top Three Strategies

- Reduce saturated animal fat by consuming only low-fat dairy products and less red meat.
- Eat more fresh fruits and vegetables.
- Drink an occasional glass of wine or beer.

Carolyn Clifford, Ph.D.

CHIEF OF THE DIET AND CANCER BRANCH OF THE
NATIONAL CANCER INSTITUTE IN BETHESDA, MARYLAND

"I don't exclude any particular food from my diet—I consume fish, chicken, red meat and sweets from time to time. But I try to eat generous amounts of fruits and vegetables every day, and I try to be aware of the hidden fats in foods, eating high-fat foods only in small portions. I rarely consume alcohol, but I do drink two or three cups of coffee per day. I don't take supplements."

Her Top Three Strategies

- Eat a low-fat, high-fiber diet.
- Exercise for 30 to 60 minutes three times a week.
- Get routine physicals and mammograms.

Stop Beefing and Eat Up

Is it possible that there's such a thing as low-fat steak? Yes. And low-fat pork chops, too.

For lots of us who grew up in the 1950s and 1960s, Sunday dinner invariably featured potatoes, rolls, string beans and roast beef, the meal's meaty main attraction. Seared to a crispy brown on the exterior, the roast grew pinker and pinker as it was carved into slender slices, until, at its heart, it reached that deep, juicy, thoroughly delectable red that has become the very color of dietary sin. Just thinking about those long-ago meals can make your mouth water.

Serious roast beef went out of fashion among the smart set years ago, along with all those other fat-laden cuts that make up what the food industry somewhat grimly refers to as muscle meats. Words like *steak* and *pork chops* and *veal tenderloin* have come to be synonymous with "heart attack" in the popular

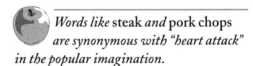

Words like steak *and* pork chops *are synonymous with "heart attack" in the popular imagination.*

imagination. But the truth is, the popular imagination, once again, has gotten a little carried away.

"There's nothing wrong with including meat as a part of your regular diet," says Chris Rosenbloom, R.D., Ph.D., professor of nutrition and dietetics at Georgia State University in Atlanta. "You just want to be sure that the cuts are lean and the portions aren't too big."

It's Fat Content That Counts

Given the current anti-meat hysteria, the idea that a little red meat here and there might be okay is close to heresy, but research has con-

FAT STATS

Get Real

To look like Barbie, the average American woman would have to grow two feet taller, add five inches to her chest and lose six inches from her waist.

firmed this startling truth. One of the better-known studies was conducted by Lynne W. Scott, R.D., director of the Diet Modification Clinic at Baylor College of Medicine in Houston. She prepared two diets that were virtually identical in fat and cholesterol content; one used beef and the other included chicken. She discovered that the group that ate the red meat did not all immediately roll off their chairs and die. In fact, the different diets did not appear to affect the blood cholesterol levels of the two groups at all.

The odd and unanswered question that this study raises is why anyone ever would have thought that there would be differences in cholesterol, given that the fat contents of the different meats were virtually identical going in. And Scott does not address the practical implications of her research. Is red meat as nutritious as chicken? That is, is the average beef dinner any fattier than the average chicken dinner? "That all depends," she says. "Is the chicken cooked with or without the skin? Is it fat-fried? Grilled? You probably don't cook your chicken the way I cook mine."

Since the early 1980s, the fat content of the average cut of beef has been slimmed down by 27 percent.

The U.S. Department of Agriculture (USDA) studies this sort of thing, however, and the information gleaned from its tables makes red meat look a good deal better than you might think. It's true that no red meat can equal the minimal fat content of skinless chicken breast, three ounces of which has just three grams of fat. Still, if all visible fat is trimmed from the leanest cuts of beef—eye of round and top round—they come surprisingly close to poultry, weighing in at just five grams of fat per three-ounce portion. (For comparison, a standard 1½-ounce doughnut has 11 grams of fat, and a tablespoon of a typical salad oil has 14.)

But not all chicken is skinless white meat. Three ounces of skinless dark chicken has 8 grams of fat, three ounces of chicken breast with the skin has 9, and if the chicken is fried, see you later. The fat count jumps to 13.

A New Breed of Trimmer Beef

Much of the credit for bringing red meat into the nutrition-conscious 1990s goes to the industry. With little fanfare, it has been mending its fatty ways. Since the early 1980s, the fat content of the average cut of beef has been slimmed down by 27 percent, and the average cut of pork has 31 percent less fat than before.

The changes have occurred at every stage of the business. Cattle ranchers have turned to scientists for help in identifying the genetic character-

The rule of thumb is easy enough: Buy the meat that comes from the rear end of the animal.

istics that produce slimmer cows and are using the information to breed leaner herds. They have fed their cows less fattening diets and taken them to market earlier, before they've had a chance to build up the bovine equivalent of love handles. (Age is critical to the fat content of meat; an important reason that chicken is relatively lean is that the bird you eat is a young chicken, not an old hen.)

New technology, such as the ultrasound developed for human medicine, has entered the business to determine more precisely the fattiness of the carcasses and reward those ranchers who have gotten the fat out. And meat packers are shaving that half-inch fringe of white fat that used to adorn most cuts of meat down to a quarter-inch, one-eighth inch or often nothing at all before the meats are shipped to retail stores.

The industry has also been toying with the meat itself, especially with its single most popular product, the hamburger, which accounts for nearly three-quarters of the beef consumed in the United States. The results have been mixed.

A few years ago, Dale L. Huffman, Ph.D., director of the Food Tech-

And the Meat Goes On

Meat used to be good for us, back when protein was king. Then came the big fat scare, and we gave up steaks and pork chops and hamburgers. Now we've learned that it's not the meat, it's the portion. And the cut. Hamburgers are still too fatty, but steak, lamb chops and pot roast are back on the list for healthy eating.

MEAT	FAT (G.)	CHOLESTEROL (MG.)
Beef		
Eye of round	5	59
Top round	5	71
Chuck arm pot roast, braised	6	89
Sirloin	6	76
New York strip steak	7	76
Choice tenderloin	9	71
Flank steak	9	57
Porterhouse steak	9	68
T-bone steak	9	68
Brisket, braised	13	77
Chuck blade pot roast, braised	13	90
Hamburger, extra lean, browned and drained	13	84
Hamburger, regular grade, browned and drained	17	89
Lamb		
Leg of lamb	5	76
Lamb chops	7	82
Leg of lamb, trimmed, with seam fat*	14	79
Lamb chops, with seam fat*	20	85

*Seam fat is the fat within the "seams" of the meat.

nology Institute at Auburn University in Alabama, produced a version of hamburger with approximately half the fat of the conventional variety.

He did it by beefing up his low-fat meat with carrageenan, a kind of

Just skim the following list, and you'll be amazed to learn that some cuts of meat are no fattier than a chicken breast. Except where noted, each of the entrée listings is based on a three-ounce portion that has been roasted or broiled and stripped of every bit of visible fat.

MEAT	FAT (G.)	CHOLESTEROL (MG.)
Pork		
Pork tenderloin	4	67
Cured ham	5	47
Pork top loin	6	66
Pork top loin, fried	13	66
Cured ham, with seam fat*	14	53
Hot dog	25	54
Poultry		
Chicken breast	3	73
Turkey, light meat	3	59
Turkey drumstick, with skin	10	76
Chicken breast, fried, with skin	13	83
Chicken thigh, fast-food, fried, with skin	26	121
Specialty Meats		
Elk	2	62
Ostrich	2	66
Squirrel	3	82
Veal		
Veal tenderloin	6	90
Veal cutlets, breaded and fried	8	95

seaweed, to keep it from tasting like cardboard, and by adding a generous pinch of salt. McDonald's introduced this concoction with some fanfare as the McLean burger, but the public was not particularly receptive. The

FAT STATS

How about Never?

- Most popular day of the week to start a diet: Monday
- Least popular: Thursday

Washington Post dubbed it the Flopper, and it is no longer available at most McDonald's restaurants.

A more promising approach to hamburger is provided by Donald M. Small, M.D., a Boston University School of Medicine biophysicist who, while tinkering in his kitchen, came up with a way to remove two-thirds of the fat and nearly half the cholesterol. He simply browns the meat in a saucepan with a small amount of vegetable oil for about ten minutes over high heat, then drains off the liquid and rinses away any remaining fat by showering the meat briefly with hot water. Dr. Small has described his technique for the general public in *The Healthy Meat-Eaters' Cookbook*.

Be Selective at the Meat Counter

Dr. Small's technique works only for ground meat, however. The best way to cut down the fat content of a slice of meat is to be selective at the meat counter. The meat industry has sufficient influence with the USDA so that, unlike every other food item in the supermarket, meat is not required to have labels that list nutritional information. Plus, there are enough different terms for all of the cuts of meat to fill a small dictionary. But the rule of thumb is easy enough: Buy the meat that comes from the rear end of the animal. As with humans, fat accumulates in a cow's middle regions. The key words to remember are *loin* and *round*. Sirloin, tenderloin, top round, eye of round—these are the cuts that tend to be lowest in fat. In meat lingo, *choice* means lean and *select* means leaner still. To be fair, it should be pointed out that the fat is the part that makes meat taste good, so you may not want to get rid of absolutely all of it.

For all of the improvements in the meat industry, it still has its drawbacks. It is prodigiously wasteful of land and grain. And, of course, it is not particularly kind to the animals it raises.

But vegetarianism certainly isn't a nutritional nirvana. "Look at Buddha," says Johanna T. Dwyer, R.D., D.Sc., director of the Frances Stern Nutrition Center at the New England Medical Center in Boston, referring to the most famous vegetarian of them all. "He was really fat."

Early fears that vegetarians might not get enough protein now appear overblown, but there is evidence that giving up meat can create deficiencies of vitamin B_{12}, which is found primarily in foods derived from animals, and iron. It seems that vegetarians, too, need to watch what they eat. "Just because your diet doesn't include meat doesn't mean it's healthy," says Dr. Rosenbloom. "I know students who live on french fries and Cokes and think they're doing themselves a favor. They'd be better off ordering a hamburger."

Meat eating does seem to be fairly well ingrained. Despite all the bad publicity, the average American still puts away 166 pounds of the stuff every year, a figure that shows no sign of declining, and the steakhouse is now one of the hottest components of the restaurant business. Chicken made serious inroads between 1976 and 1991, largely because of its perceived convenience and low price, but beef has been climbing back since then.

There is no question that Americans would do better to lay off the junk food and eat more grains and vegetables, two categories of food that, when sensibly prepared, are truly low in fat. But meat needn't be demonized. As with all things, it should be enjoyed in moderation, meaning no more than six ounces a day of the leanest cuts you can bear. Be a little choosier when you shop at the meat counter or place your order in a restaurant, and be aware that hamburger is probably not a great idea for now. As for that mouth-watering Sunday afternoon roast, make it top round or eye of round, or even leg of lamb, and you'll get a taste of the good old days with an acceptable amount of fat.

Eat the Rich

They're gooey, cheesy and chewy. And they're not bad for you. Thirty-three "fattening" foods that really, truly aren't.

Grab a napkin. We can see you drooling from here. We're going to tell you how to eat real beef stew, macaroni and cheese and a banana split with whipped cream—without gaining a single ounce or exceeding your fat budget.

Our extensive research, which involved hours of nutritional testing, day-long marathons of data calculation and several late-night staff gatherings punctuated by unseemly displays of unabashed gluttony, has revealed a joyous truth: When it comes to the conventional wisdom about what's good for you and what's bad, most of us have been misguided. Misinformed. Led astray. Duped.

Somewhere, somehow, while we were cruising along the food court of life, we were taught that the good-tasting stuff crowding the shelves is terribly fattening and chock-full of calories. We're talking about a lot of those greasy, gooey, cheesy and meaty meals we all crave from time to time.

Well, not all of them are that bad for you. Thanks to food science and some creative fiddling in the kitchen, there are loads of foods out there, from instant meals to snacks to full-blown recipes, that you'll swear are just laden with vats of fat, but aren't.

For example, you can eat real beef hot dogs, lobster and Italian sausage and peppers and not gunk up your arteries. No lie. Nothing on our list of 33 foods gets more than 30 percent of its calories from fat, the maximum percentage that many dietitians recommend for heart-healthy eating. Substituted for high-fat foods and consumed in normal-size portions, these tasty foods can making healthier eating a downright pleasure. So dig in!

1. Aunt Jemima Low-Fat Waffles. Two of these waffles have 18 fewer grams of fat than the ones you make from a mix, and they take a lot less time to prepare. Just pop them into your toaster. Look for Aunt Jemima low-fat pancakes and French toast, too.

2. Bacon, lettuce and tomato sandwich. Here's how to keep that smoky flavor and lose 16 grams of the fat: Use two slices of turkey bacon (a remarkable substitute for pork), low-fat mayonnaise, lettuce and tomatoes on a toasted whole-grain roll or bread.

3. Banana split with chocolate syrup and whipped cream. Sometimes laziness is a virtue. For example, let's say you took the time to make your own whipped cream. What you've just whipped up has as many as 22 grams of fat. But if you're lazy like us and buy one of the commercial whipped toppings, such as Cool Whip or the ones that come in squirt cans, you're getting only a few fat grams. Now use it to make a banana split that looks like it would harden your arteries but is actually healthy: Plop two scoops of low-fat ice cream or yogurt into a dish and sandwich them between the halves of a banana. Top with fresh cherries, strawberries, pineapple and kiwi chunks. Finish with whipped topping and chocolate syrup (also naturally low in fat). Total fat grams: nine. That's about half of what you'd get from a regular split. (For more guilt-free desserts, see "New in the Marketplace: The Scoop on Frozen Desserts" on page 34.)

4. Barbecued ribs. A plate of country-style ribs or spareribs can weigh in with more than 50 grams of fat. But you can make a lean boneless rib dinner by using pork loin or a boneless chop and slicing off the visible fat. Cut it into thick strips and slather it with all the barbecue sauce you want—a quarter-cup has only a gram of fat. Grill the ribs over hot coals for 20 minutes, turning occasionally.

For Oriental-style ribs, mix a few pounds of meat with 1 tablespoon each of onion powder, garlic powder, dry mustard, ground ginger and red pepper. Also add 1 teaspoon five-spice powder and 1½ teaspoons black pepper. Grill as above.

5. Beef stew. Some stews pack nearly 40 grams of fat into one serving. So make your own, using 12 ounces of lean round roast and one 14-ounce can of defatted beef broth. Add onions, garlic, carrots, peppers and potatoes and you'll have a fine feast with only 9 grams of fat per serving.

6. Breakfast sandwich. If you stop at your local fry pit for an egg, bacon and cheese sandwich, you'll start your day having bagged more than half of

(continued on page 36)

The Scoop on Frozen Desserts

Diving into something cool, creamy and delicious is a great way to delight your taste buds and lift your spirits. And when the dish is low-fat as well, and maybe even low-calorie, there's no reason to feel guilty about an occasional treat of ice cream, frozen yogurt or sorbet.

These days, the frozen desserts section holds a wondrous, baffling array of products. So read labels before you buy. Compare grams of fat and calories per serving of products. And while you're at it, double the serving size to one cup, unless you're one of the few people who eat only a half-cup of ice cream at a sitting.

FOOD	PORTION	FAT (G.)	CALORIES
Healthy Choice Low-Fat Praline Caramel Cluster Ice Cream	½ cup	2	130
Turkey Hill Nonfat Frozen Mint Cookies 'n' Cream Yogurt	½ cup	0	110
Edy's Fat-Free Black Cherry Vanilla Swirl Ice Cream	½ cup	0	100
Häagen-Dazs Fat-Free Raspberry and Vanilla Sorbet 'n' Yogurt frozen bars	1	0	90
Breyers Fat-Free Strawberry Frozen Yogurt	½ cup	0	100

For a frozen dessert to be labeled ice cream, it must contain at least 10 percent fat. If it has less, it is labeled as reduced-fat or "light" ice cream. Frozen yogurts have no fat requirements, and some contain more fat than certain ice creams. (One soft-serve brand we saw had six grams per serving.) Sampling different products may prove fruitful, too. The peach melba sorbet that your husband dumps into the garbage may prove to be *your* favorite.

Here's what we thought of the newest tastes in the low-fat frozen dessert field. All are available in supermarkets or convenience stores.

COMMENTS

Our favorite! Extremely good, with a great melt-in-your-mouth texture, plus crunchy nuggets of praline and caramel.

Extremely good, with a mellow, minty taste and big chunks of cookies.

Smooth texture, with nice pieces of whole fruit. Add some fat-free chocolate sauce and you have an elegant dessert fit for health-conscious company.

A hefty-size frozen pop with a tasty combination of tart, fruity sorbet and creamy yogurt. The other flavors in this line—Strawberry Daiquiri, Chocolate Sorbet, Banana and Strawberry, Wild Berry, and Chocolate and Cherry—are equally satisfying.

Creamy and light, with true strawberry flavor.

(continued)

The Scoop on Frozen Desserts—Continued

Food	Portion	Fat (g.)	Calories
Dannon Fat-Free Light Cherry Vanilla Swirl Frozen Yogurt	½ cup	0	90
TCBY Nonfat Raspberry Cheesecake Frozen Yogurt	½ cup	0	120
Ben and Jerry's Cappuccino No-Fat Frozen Yogurt	½ cup	0	140

your recommended daily intake of fat. Now if you make one of those sandwiches yourself, you can save 20 grams of fat. Simply fry three egg whites in a pan coated with no-stick spray instead of butter. Serve them on a toasted English muffin with Canadian bacon and low-fat American cheese.

Dress your kids up like giant Oreo cookies, then send them out to beg for food.

7. *Candy corn.* Dress your kids up like giant Oreo cookies, then send them out to beg for food. When they come home, steal their candy corn. Thirty pieces have only one gram of fat. Isn't adulthood great?

8. *Chef Boy-ar-dee Beef Ravioli.* It's Italian, it has beef, and it comes in a can. You'd swear that it has to be fatty. Not in this case. Chef Boy-ar-dee Beef Ravioli (as well as the cheese variety), Beefaroni and Tortellini all get less than 25 percent of their calories from fat.

9. *Chicken nuggets.* You can save 12 grams of fat compared with the McDonald's variety by making your own. Cut up chunks of chicken breast and roll them in bread crumbs seasoned with ground red pepper, herbs, Italian seasoning or taco seasoning. Add the coated chicken nuggets to a heated pan coated with no-stick spray. Flip them around

COMMENTS

Surprisingly tasty, considering that it's not only fat-free but sugar-free as well. (It's made with NutraSweet.) This line includes other flavors, too.

We enjoyed this dessert's rich, full flavor. "Tastes like premium ice cream." was one comment.

We usually like Ben and Jerry's, but this one needs some tinkering with both flavor and texture. Plus, we think 140 calories per half-cup serving is too high for frozen yogurt.

until the bread crumbs are brown and the chicken is fully cooked.

10. Chocolate milk. Nestlé Quik delivers only 0.5 gram of fat per two tablespoons. The key is to use skim or 1 percent milk instead of whole milk. Chocolate syrup is just as low in fat.

11. Clams, oysters and lobster. You always thought that these seafoods were bad for you? That's because you usually see them swimming in a sea of drawn butter. Keep them out of the dip and they are low in fat, registering between one and two grams per serving. Instead of butter, use cocktail sauce or a drop of hot-pepper sauce on each bite. If you're planning to dump your clams over pasta, prepare a light tomato sauce instead of the fatty oil-and-clam-juice white sauce.

12. Crab cakes. Sure, if you fry them in a half-inch of oil, they're fatty. But they don't have to be. By using no-stick cooking spray instead of oil and egg whites instead of whole eggs, you can cut the fat from 12 to 2 grams per serving.

To make them, coat an unheated skillet with nonstick spray. Add chopped celery, onions and parsley and sauté.

In a medium bowl, beat six egg whites. Add ¾ cup unseasoned bread crumbs, two teaspoons Worcestershire sauce and one teaspoon dry mustard.

(continued on page 42)

MARKETPLACE

Burgers, Hot Dogs and Cold Cuts

Not so long ago, serious fat fighters could forget about ever sinking their teeth into a juicy burger, grilled hot dog or thick ham sandwich. Those foods were so loaded with grease, you could practically hear your arteries slam shut after the first bite.

Now, however, people can indulge their desires with trimmed-down versions of these favorite foods. Health food stores are more likely than supermarkets to carry a good variety of these foods, but with a little detective work, you can find tasty low-fat or fat-free substitutes for ground beef, hot dogs and all sorts of cold cuts. Some are

Food	Portion	Fat (g.)	Calories
Hot Dogs			
Hormel Light and Lean 97% Fat-Free Beef Franks	1	1	45
Hormel Light and Lean 97% Fat-Free Pork Franks	1	1	45
Healthy Choice Low-Fat Franks	1	1.5	50
Soy Boy Not Dogs	1	4	100
Ground Meat Look-Alikes			
Ready-Ground Tofu: The Vegetarian Hamburger Substitute	3 oz.	4	60

made with soy protein, and thus help shift your diet toward vegetarian. And they offer big savings on fat.

Compared with three ounces of extra-lean ground beef, for instance, which has 218 calories and 13.9 grams of fat, a 2.5-ounce soy-based Boca Burger has 110 calories and only 2 grams of fat.

These foods are a snap to prepare, and cleanup is easy, since there's no greasy splattering.

Here's what we thought of the newest top contenders in this field.

COMMENTS

We rated these hardwood-smoked, honey-flavored franks "extremely good."

These also rated extremely high. "They taste like the real thing."

A turkey-and-pork combination that we rated "good," despite its strange pale color.

We liked the garlicky flavor of these franks but found the texture a bit mushy.

Mixed with spaghetti sauce, this soy product made a "meaty" dish that we rated as extremely good. It could also be used over rice or as taco filling.

(continued)

Burgers, Hot Dogs and
Cold Cuts—Continued

FOOD	PORTION	FAT (G.)	CALORIES
Ground Meat Look-Alikes—Continued			
Morningstar Farms Ground Meatless All-Vegetable Burger Crumbles	½ cup	0	60
Green Giant Harvest Burgers	⅔ cup	0	90
Deli Meats			
Healthy Choice Turkey Breast Variety Pack	1 slice	1	30
Hillshire Farm Deli Select 97% Fat-Free Honey Ham	6 slices	1.5	60
Oscar Mayer Free No-Fat Honey Ham	3 slices	0	40
Burgers			
Morningstar Farms Better 'n Burgers	1	0	70
Boca Burger: Chef Max's Favorite	1	2	110
Soy Boy Okara Courage Burger	1	5	130

COMMENTS

In texture and consistency, this is a lot like meat. "With soy this good, who needs meat?"

We rated this prebrowned crumbled burger mix "good." We liked the flavor but not the large chunks.

We liked the flavor and texture of this product but preferred the smoked varieties in this pack to the baked turkey.

A serving is six slices, but you could use less of this very thinly sliced ham. It's a little chewy but flavorful.

Great taste; a bit salty but very low in calories, with no fat. We liked the resealable package.

We rated these "very good," with the look, texture and smoky taste of real grilled burgers and not one smidgen of fat!

These are prebaked, so they can be heated quickly in the microwave. We thought they were very good, with a texture and flavor similar to that of beef. Other Boca Burger flavors have even less fat.

We thought these were "pretty darn good" considering they are made with a fibrous by-product of tofu-making. They're a little bland, but if you add relish, ketchup and chopped onions, you'll have a great meat alternative.

Stir in the celery mixture and 12 ounces drained crabmeat. Shape into ½-inch-thick patties and coat with bread crumbs. Coat the pan with no-stick spray and cook the patties over medium heat until brown. Turn and cook for three minutes more.

For low-fat tartar sauce, combine nonfat mayonnaise or yogurt, chopped pimentos and minced garlic in a food processor or blender and puree until smooth. Stir in red-pepper flakes to taste.

13. Frog's legs. Like everything else that's cooked down on the bayou, they're fatty, right? Not so. A serving of frog's legs contains less than a gram of fat. To prepare, sprinkle them with seasoned flour, then sauté for two to three minutes in a pan lightly coated with olive oil.

14. Fudge. Go ahead. Indulge. One ounce (a good-size cube to you) has 112 calories and 3.4 grams of fat. That's 10 grams less than a Snickers bar. (For more low-fat ways to indulge your chocolate cravings, see "New in the Marketplace: Guilt-Free Chocolate Treats" on page 60.)

15. Garlic bread. The kind they serve down at your local Italian spot is usually soaked with a butter spread. When eating out, ask to have your bread served plain with a little olive oil in a dish on the side, and sprinkle some garlic salt on top. At home, make your own: Mix three tablespoons olive oil with four cloves minced garlic and brush the mixture on both halves of a loaf of French or Italian bread. Toast under the broiler for three to four minutes.

16. Italian ice. What you're tasting is the sugary syrup; there's no fat. Beware, though, because a cup of Italian ice carries 247 calories. Ice pops are also fat-free.

17. Kraft Macaroni and Cheese. You lived on this stuff in college, re-member? And you loved it. But you haven't touched it since you read the box and found out that one serving packs more than 16 grams of fat. Well, here's a way to prepare a low-fat bowl of the creamy noodles without giving up any flavor: Simply leave out the three

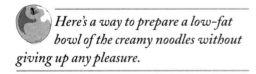

Here's a way to prepare a low-fat bowl of the creamy noodles without giving up any pleasure.

tablespoons of margarine that you're instructed to use. That orange pow-dered stuff, or "cheese sauce mix," as Kraft describes it, is so potent that you won't need the margarine for flavoring. And now you're down to just 4.5 grams of fat.

18. Low-Fat Pop-Tarts. The low-fat strawberry Pop-Tarts we tried were sweet and flaky, and whether you choose one with icing or not, you still get a low-fat treat. Each one contains three grams of fat.

19. Onion rings. The trick to making crispy onion rings that won't drip grease on your khakis is to keep them out of that deep fryer: Bake them. In a large bowl, beat two egg whites until foamy. Cut two peeled sweet onions crosswise into

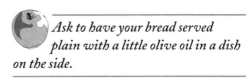 *Ask to have your bread served plain with a little olive oil in a dish on the side.*

$^1/_4$-inch slices. Separate the rings and toss them with the egg whites to coat. Roll the coated rings in a mixture of two cups cornflake crumbs and one teaspoon chili powder, then place them on a baking sheet coated with no-stick spray. Bake at 375° for 15 minutes. Only 94 calories, and 2 percent calories from fat, per five-ring serving.

20. Oscar Mayer Fat-Free Bologna. We couldn't believe this stuff had no fat and just 20 calories per slice. It tasted like the real thing between two slices of white bread. Oscar Mayer's Healthy Favorites Honey Ham, with 1.5 grams of fat per four slices, also scored well in our taste test. (For more skinny sandwich fixings, see "New in the Marketplace: Burgers, Hot Dogs and Cold Cuts" on page 38.)

21. Oscar Mayer Free and Hormel Low-Fat Hot Dogs. Hot dogs are the worst of the fatty foods. A typical dog contains nearly 15 grams of fat. But Oscar Mayer and Hormel have created fat-free and low-fat franks, respectively, that taste more than semi-authentic. Oscar Mayer's fat-free hot dogs are made of a mixture of beef and turkey, but they taste surprisingly like all-beef franks, although the skin is a bit rubbery. We liked the Hormel low-fat beef franks better because, with two grams of fat per hot dog, you still get a little taste of grease.

22. Parmesan cheese. A tablespoon has less than two grams of fat. If that's not low enough for you, Kraft makes a nonfat version, but it's not nearly as good as freshly grated cheese.

23. Pizza. Whether you make it at home or whether you order takeout, you can trim eight grams of fat and more than 100 calories by using less cheese. When you place your order, request the pizza with one-third less cheese.

24. Potato chips and hot beer dip. Sound like the recipe for a heart attack? Not when they're fixed our way. First, make your own low-fat potato chips by cutting potatoes into thin slices and microwaving them on a rack for about four minutes. To make hot beer dip that contains only one gram of fat, coat a saucepan with no-stick spray. Add green onions and garlic and sauté. Then, in a medium bowl, combine 1 cup each of shredded fat-free and reduced-fat sharp Cheddar cheese and sprinkle with 1 teaspoon cornstarch. Stir ³/₄ cup nonalcoholic beer into the saucepan and bring to a low boil. Slowly add the cheese mixture and stir until melted. Remove from the heat and blend in 1 cup nonfat yogurt. You're ready for dipping.

25. Potato skins with melted cheese. Prick a few baking potatoes with a fork and bake them at 425° for 45 minutes, or until tender. Cut the potatoes lengthwise into quarters and scoop out three-fourths of the potato pulp. Place the skins on a baking sheet coated with no-stick spray and bake at 425° for 10 to 15 minutes, or until crisp. Sprinkle some reduced-fat Monterey Jack and Cheddar cheese on the potato skins, then bake for 2 minutes, or until the cheese is melted. Each skin has only 42 calories and one gram of fat.

26. Pudding. Rice and tapioca puddings look bad for you because they're so thick and rich. But one serving of either contains under five grams of fat and less than 200 calories.

27. Refried beans. For some reason, we tend to think that all refried beans are made with lard. That might be the case across the Rio Grande, but it's not true for most canned beans. A half-cup of refried beans has only 135 calories and 1½ grams of fat. For a lean but filling taco, spoon some beans, chopped tomatoes, lettuce, salsa and nonfat sour cream into a soft flour tortilla.

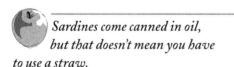

Sardines come canned in oil, but that doesn't mean you have to use a straw.

28. Sardines. They come canned in oil, but that doesn't mean that you have to use a straw. Pour the oil out, then rinse the sardines under the tap to reduce the fat, calorie and sodium content. A can of sardines prepared this way delivers just three grams of fat.

29. Sausage-and-pepper sandwich. Use spicy Italian turkey sausage and garlic, peppers, tomatoes and onions sautéed in a little broth to skim the fat off this one. In fact, one hoagie-size turkey sausage sandwich delivers just 344 calories and five grams of fat.

30. Shrimp. A serving of steamed or baked shrimp, a great source of protein, has only 84 calories and less than a gram of fat. Our favorite shrimp recipe bakes the little guys in a marinade of lime juice, Worcestershire sauce, hot-pepper sauce, some thyme, oregano and ground pepper and a drizzle of olive oil.

31. Twinkies. Have you tried the new low-fat version? We did, and we loved them. They're almost as creamy as their classic counterparts, but two have only 3 grams of fat, as opposed to 9 grams in regular Twinkies. Hostess also makes low-fat cupcakes and brownies.

32. Vanilla milk shake. As long as it's vanilla, a milk shake from a fast-food restaurant gets only about 24 percent of its calories from fat. If you go where they make their own from scratch, you can get the shake even leaner by requesting it with 1 percent milk and low-fat ice cream or frozen yogurt.

33. Veal Parmesan. Although veal is a relatively lean cut of meat, preparing it Parmesan-style is what gives it its hefty reputation. Instead of frying the breaded patties in oil, simply bake them. Coat a veal cutlet with egg white, then bread crumbs. Top with spaghetti sauce, oregano, black pepper and reduced-fat mozzarella cheese. Bake at 350° for 30 minutes. This version gets less than 30 percent of its calories from fat.

Dieter's Dream or Marketer's Ploy?

Reduced-fat foods do have a place in a low-fat diet. But they're not a magic wand for weight loss.

Weight Watchers ads claim that their reduced-fat desserts offer "total indulgence, zero guilt." That's typical of what marketers would like you to believe about low-fat or nonfat foods. While such foods can help you reduce the fat in your diet, they will not necessarily help you lose weight. And under certain circumstances, they may even lead to weight gain.

Why Fat Is Yummy

Fat imparts a variety of tastes, textures and aromas to food. It makes steak flavorful and tender, pie crust flaky and ice cream creamy. Most fatty foods are high in calories, so the body digests them more slowly than leaner foods, with lower calorie content. That's why you feel full longer after eating a well-marbled steak than you do after eating a lean piece of fish. The taste of fatty foods lingers in the mouth, since the chemicals in fat that provide flavor emerge gradually as you chew.

Just knowing that they're eating a low-fat food may make some people feel that they're entitled to indulge their appetite later.

The most widely used fat replacements are carbohydrates, which show up on food labels as dextrins, maltodextrins, modified food starches, polydextrose, cellulose and various gums. These add bulk to replace the lost fat, hold up 100 times their weight in water to provide moistness, and thicken the ingredients, making them creamier.

FAT STATS

Who's Lightest in Flight?

Healthiest low-fat and vegetarian food, by airline.

1. United
2. TWA
3. Continental

4. USAir
5. American

Fat can also be replaced by protein. Microparticulated protein, for example, is made by heating and blending proteins to create tiny round particles that slip and slide over the tongue to simulate the feel of fat.

Neither carbohydrates nor proteins capture the elusive flavor and texture of fat. Carbohydrates, for example, keep baked goods moist but not necessarily light or flaky. And neither carbohydrates nor protein can be used during cooking methods that require high temperatures, such as frying.

Where Reduced-Fat Foods Fall Short

Eating less fat is clearly a good idea. Studies have linked dietary fat with an increased risk of numerous health problems, including obesity, coronary heart disease and certain cancers. And cutting fat intake, even without cutting calories, does seem to help people lose weight, apparently because the body creates stored fat much more readily from dietary fat than from dietary protein or carbohydrates.

But calories still count. Research has confirmed that people who cut calories as well as fat lose more weight and body fat than those who cut fat alone. While foods that are naturally low in fat tend to be low in calories, the same is not true of many foods that are manufactured to be low in fat. Fat-Free Fig Newtons, for example, have almost as many calories as regular Fig Newtons, in part because the nonfat cookies contain more sugar. Light-N-Lively Strawberry Free Yogurt has no fat, but it contains

(continued on page 50)

Low-Fat Cheeses with Pizzazz

Especially for people trying to stay away from meat, cheese is a handy, tasty protein alternative. But regular cheese is loaded with fat, especially artery-clogging saturated fat.

Your best bet? Poke around in the dairy case the next time you're at the supermarket. You'll find a selection of fat-free and low-fat cheeses that offer substantial savings in fat. Check the labels—you won't often want one with more than three grams of fat per serving, which is usually one ounce. In comparison, a one-ounce serving of regular cheese can have up to nine grams of fat.

Food	Portion	Fat (g.)	Calories
Jarlsberg Lite	1 oz.	3.5	70
Kraft Reduced-Fat 2% Milk American Singles	1 slice	3	50
Polly-O Lite Shredded Reduced-Fat Mozzarella Cheese	¼ cup	3	60
Kraft Fat-Free Mozzarella singles	1 slice	0	35

Try a variety of cheeses. Some are definitely better than others, and some melt poorly. You may need to combine several cheeses to get the taste, melting qualities and fat content you want. Perk up low-fat cheese sandwiches with a slice of sweet onion and a dab of spicy mustard, or sprinkle paprika on an open-face melt.

Watch the sodium content, too. Cheese loses flavor when fat is cut, so sodium is added to make up for that. Stick with brands with 300 milligrams of sodium or less per serving.

We tasted the newest additions to the fat-free and low-fat cheese product line. All are available in supermarkets nationwide. Here are

COMMENTS

"Looks, tastes and has texture close to real Swiss." Got rave reviews.
Technically a bit higher in fat than low-fat, but worth it.
Available at supermarkets and delis, where you can ask for it
to be thin-sliced. Melts well.

Creamy. "Tastes like regular American." With 150 milligrams of calcium per slice, two slices of this cheese make a healthy, low-calorie snack.

The best-tasting of the mozzarellas we tasted, and a decent melter.

A little bland and rubbery, but you can really pile it on with this nonfat cheese. We rated it "fair."

(continued)

Low-Fat Cheeses with Pizzazz—Continued

Food	Portion	Fat (g.)	Calories
Alpine Lace Healthy Choice Fat-Free Shredded Skim Milk Cheese for Mozzarella Lovers	¼ cup	0	45
Healthy Choice Fat-Free PasteurizedProcess Cheese American Singles	1 slice	0	30
Fleischmann's Fat-Free 10-Calorie Spread	1 Tbsp.	0	10

63 percent more sugar—and 9 percent more calories—than Stonyfield Farm's full-fat strawberry yogurt.

Sticking with low-fat products that do have fewer calories doesn't guarantee effortless weight loss, either. Studies suggest that people tend to compensate for lower-fat, lower-calorie meals and snacks by eating more at other times. In part, that's because the lack of fat and calories simply makes them hungrier. But a study from Pennsylvania State University in University Park demonstrated another reason: Just knowing that they're eating a low-fat food may make some people feel that they're entitled to indulge their appetite later.

The researchers gave volunteers either of two different yogurts—one low in fat and the other high in fat—that contained the same number of calories. Only half of the volunteers knew which yogurt they were eating. Among those who did not know, the type of yogurt they ate made no difference in the number of calories they consumed at a subsequent lunch. But among those who did know, the ones who had eaten the low-fat yogurt consumed significantly more than those who had eaten the high-fat item.

The best way to lose your "fat tooth" may be to retrain your palate to acquire a taste for naturally low-fat foods.

People who stick with low-fat foods, without frequent lapses of disci-

COMMENTS

Tastes more like a salty Cheddar than a mozzarella. It doesn't melt, but it does offer 200 milligrams of calcium per serving.

Less texture and salty compared to Kraft's reduced-fat sliced singles, but that may be the price you pay for no fat. Offers 150 milligrams of calcium per serving.

If you won't eat broccoli without cheese sauce, you may like this fat-free Velveeta-like cheese, though it is somewhat runny.

pline, may eventually start losing their "fat tooth"—the lust for fatty foods. But one study has raised the possibility that the best way to retrain your palate is to acquire a taste for naturally low-fat foods, not the artificial versions. Researchers at the Monell Chemical Senses Center in Philadelphia divided 27 people into three groups. One group cut their fat intake by eating a diet that included reduced-fat substitutes for foods such as salad dressing, butter and desserts. Another cut their intake by the same amount without those fat substitutes. The third group stuck with their usual diet. After three months, only the group that had avoided all fat substitutes rated fatty foods less tasty than they had at the start of the study.

Whether or not further research confirms that finding, a diet rich in naturally low-fat foods, notably fruits, vegetables, grains and beans, does have one clear benefit: It provides a wealth of vital nutrients. In contrast, many of the new reduced-fat snacks and desserts offer little except empty calories and an increased risk of tooth decay from the extra sugar.

Where Reduced-Fat Foods Fit

While the ideal diet should be based on naturally lean foods, reduced-fat products can still play a significant role. Eating an occasional low-fat snack or dessert may help people stick with a low-fat regimen. Switching from regular salad dressing to low-fat or nonfat dressing can substantially

The New Fake Fats

Food engineers try to reproduce the taste and texture of fat without all the calories and other unhealthy features by changing the chemical structure of fat itself. The Food and Drug Administration (FDA) has allowed manufacturers to market products made with all four of the altered fats described below, Caprenin, Salatrim, Appetize and olestra. Here are descriptions of these "mystery ingredients."

Caprenin. This fat substitute is designed to simulate the rich taste and feel of cocoa butter without all the calories. Since Caprenin is made from fats that the body absorbs poorly, it supplies about 40 percent fewer calories than cocoa butter, although you get roughly the same amount of saturated fat.

Salatrim. Nabisco makes this product from various fats that either have fewer calories or are harder to absorb than other fats. For both reasons, Salatrim, like Caprenin, supplies about 40 percent fewer calories than unaltered fats do. The main drawbacks: Salatrim is high in unhealthful saturated fat, and it doesn't stand up to frying.

Appetize. Manufacturers combine vegetable oils with hydrogen gas to make them more solid and more stable, a process called hydrogenation. But hydrogenation creates trans-fats, which can raise blood cholesterol levels. To create a healthier solid shortening, researchers at Brandeis University in Waltham, Massachusetts, removed the choles-

cut both fat and calories. (See "New in the Marketplace: Low-Fat Salad Dressings" on page 142.) And reduced-fat dairy products provide the calcium that would be lost to the body if you merely cut dairy products from your diet. (Among reduced-fat foods, many low-fat dairy products taste unusually good. See "New in the Marketplace: Low-Fat Cheeses with Pizzazz" on page 48.) You'll even find low-fat and nonfat alternatives to such meat products as lunchmeat, sausage, hot dogs and ground beef, although they may contain even more sodium than their full-fat counterparts. (See "New in the Marketplace: Burgers, Hot Dogs and Cold Cuts" on page 38.)

Not all reduced-fat products taste as good as their high-fat counterparts, but you'll probably miss the fat least in products with strong flavors.

terol from animal fats and combined the fats with vegetable oils. In theory, the modest amount of saturated fat in that combination may be less harmful for the arteries than the fats in either margarine or butter. But Appetize contains as many calories as regular fat, so it's not better for the waistline.

Olestra. The best-known of a group of compounds known as sucrose polyester, olestra seems to mimic fat better than any other product developed so far. The fat in olestra is firmly bound to molecules of sugar, so it travels through the body undigested. What you get is essentially a nonfat fat than can be used for all types of cooking. Researchers who have tasted fat-free potato chips made with olestra say that they taste like the real thing.

Olestra has won limited approval from the FDA, so it's now available in some snack foods. The FDA is concerned, however, that the nondigestible fats could cause gastrointestinal problems or trap fat-soluble vitamins and drugs in the gut, preventing the body from absorbing them. Therefore, the FDA requires a warning label on all products containing olestra, alerting customers to the gastrointestinal problems that could develop and also that it is fortified with vitamins. (See "Olestra: Procter's Big Gamble" on page 54.)

In fat-free ice cream, for example, chocolate may taste richer than vanilla. (See "New in the Marketplace: The Scoop on Frozen Desserts" on page 34.) Likewise, you probably won't notice a difference between reduced-fat and regular ground meat when you use it with other ingredients.

Olestra: Procter's Big Gamble

Do you want to cut back on fat *and* stay healthy? Then here's what you need to know before you devour that bag of fake-fat potato chips.

It's an ingredient of every dieter's dream: potato chips and other greasy snacks that won't make you fat. And it's part of every public health expert's nightmare: an uncontrolled experiment on 200 million people using a dubious food additive.

It's the new fat substitute olestra.

When the Food and Drug Administration (FDA) gave Procter and Gamble the go-ahead to start using olestra in potato chips, tortilla chips and crackers, it did so over the opposition of dozens of public health and nutrition experts.

The fake fat, the experts argued, robs the body of carotenoids. Those pigments make many fruits and vegetables orange, yellow or green and may help explain why diets high in fruits and vegetables seem to protect against cancer, heart disease, stroke and blindness.

The FDA rejected concerns about olestra's impact on a diet that may prevent life-threatening illnesses, but the agency did require that foods made with olestra carry a warning, at least about "loose stools" and "abdominal cramping." Ironically, olestra's tendency to wreak havoc on your gut may be the best thing about it—if it discourages would-be eaters.

Olean—that's olestra's trade name—is now found in Pringles and a few other foods. So if you're considering including these foods in your diet, you have to decide whom to believe—the independent researchers who have spoken out passionately against the fake fat or the paid-consultant scientists whom the manufacturer has trotted out to defend its $200 million gamble.

Carotenoid Concerns

Here are the main arguments for olestra—and the reasons that they're flawed.

- As long as you don't eat olestra together with carotenoid-rich foods, there's no problem. "You don't eat carrot sticks with potato chips," Procter and Gamble apologists are fond of saying. They point out that olestra washes more carotenoids out of the body when both are eaten at the same meal. True. But millions of people eat potato chips with their sandwiches or crackers with their soup. If those foods contain lycopene-rich tomatoes, lutein-rich romaine lettuce or beta-carotene-rich carrots, for example, olestra will drag those carotenoids out of the body.

  And then there are the millions who snack on chips between meals. If Procter and Gamble's test results from studies on the absorption of certain vitamins are any guide, between-meal snacking may wash away up to a third of the carotenoids from a previous—or subsequent—meal.

- There's no proof that carotenoids do us any good. High-dose beta-carotene pills have clearly failed to prevent lung cancer in smokers. But "over 50 studies have found, with remarkable consistency, that diets rich in carotenoids are associated with lower risk of cancer at many sites," wrote Harvard Medical School epidemiologists Walter Willett, M.D., Dr.P.H., and Meir Stampfer, M.D., Dr.P.H., in a letter to FDA commissioner David Kessler.

  Nor does the beta-carotene failure mean that it's safe to deplete people of carotenoids. "There is a causal relationship between the ingestion of fruits and vegetables and decreased risk of various cancers and other degenerative diseases," says Norman Krinsky, Ph.D., a carotenoid expert at Tufts University School of Medicine in Boston. "Depletion of carotenoids may be accompanied by depletion of those factors in fruit-and-vegetable diets that are protective."

  So even though there is no absolute proof that carotenoids prevent disease, it's foolhardy to add something to the food supply that steals them from the body.

  And olestra is one heck of a thief.

  Eating eight grams a day of olestra—about 16 chips—with meals for two weeks led to a 20 percent drop in lutein levels in the blood

Look for It on the Label

Any food that contains olestra (Olean) must carry this warning label: *This Product Contains Olestra. Olestra may cause abdominal cramping and loose stools. Olestra inhibits the absorption of some vitamins and other nutrients. Vitamins A, D, E and K have been added.*

Olestra's makers are lobbying for a less stringent warning, while some nutrition researchers want an even harder-line one.

"Olestra's warning label should also alert consumers that the fake fat may increase the risk of cancer, heart disease and blindness," says epidemiologist Walter Willett, M.D., of Harvard Medical School.

---

of volunteers, according to Procter and Gamble's own study. Lutein, along with its close cousin zeaxanthin, is found in green leafy vegetables like spinach. Johanna Seddon, M.D., associate professor of ophthalmology at Harvard Medical School, has reported that people who ate higher levels of lutein and zeaxanthin were 43 percent less likely than people who ate lower levels to develop macular degeneration—an irreversible deterioration of the retina.

"Anything that lowers blood levels of lutein or zeaxanthin may contribute to this serious cause of blindness," point out Dr. Willett and Dr. Stampfer.

- Olestra will be used only in a few snack foods, so it won't have much impact. Olestra is the only fat substitute that can be used at high temperatures.

  So if the FDA ever expands its approval to cover deep-fried foods like french fries, all bets are off. Fast-food fans—many of them youngsters—aren't exactly the world's best fruit and vegetable eaters, so they probably start out with low levels of carotenoids in their blood. Anything that depletes them further could be disastrous.

- If carotenoids turn out to be important, olestra can be fortified with them later. Procter and Gamble is already adding vitamins A, D, E and K to olestra. Why? Because these vitamins are fat-soluble, and olestra appears to rob the body of anything that dissolves in fat.

  So even if Procter and Gamble later decides to add carotenoids to olestra, how would it replace the dizzying array of promising phyto-chemicals that scientists are just beginning to discover in fruits and vegetables? Many will be washed out of the body by olestra.

"The first law of tinkering is that you save all the parts," says consumer advocate Joan Gussow, Ed.D., professor emeritus at Columbia University in New York City, who was one of only five members of the FDA's food advisory committee to vote against olestra's approval. "With carotenoids and other phytochemicals, we don't even know what the parts are, let alone how much would be needed to restore the status quo to olestra."

What's more, by the time Procter and Gamble adds carotenoids and phytochemicals, it may be too late. "The odds are that olestra's adverse consequences would not be detectable for at least several decades, during which time enormous harm could have been done," contend Dr. Willett and Dr. Stampfer.

- Olestra causes digestive problems only when eaten in excess. About a third of the volunteers in Procter and Gamble's own studies got diarrhea when they ate 20 grams of olestra a day. That's about how much you'd get in a two-ounce single-serving bag of potato chips. And in one study, levels of diarrhea were troublesome even when people ate just 8 grams (16 chips) a day.

  Diarrhea wasn't the only problem. Since olestra isn't absorbed as it travels through the gut, it can leave the body as a greasy liquid. Procter and Gamble claims that this anal leakage has been eliminated by a new, "stiffer" version of olestra, but the company's own data show that it's not so.

  What's more, people who ate moderate amounts of olestra also had to contend with stained underwear and "greasy feces" that give a whole new meaning to the term *snack attack*.

- Olestra's digestive discomfort is no worse than that caused by eating a high-fiber diet. When people switch to a high-fiber diet, they may experience gas, bloating and cramps. But the symptoms usually subside within several days, after "good" bacteria in the gut adapt to the extra fiber. With olestra, the only way to end your tummy troubles is to stop eating it.

- Olestra will help people lose weight. While snacks made with it will be lower in calories, it won't mean a thing to the national waistline if people end up eating more chips and other snacks. And they will, if

FAT STATS

What We Eat

- Amount of time a normal person spends eating each day: one hour
- Percentage of people who leave some food on their plate when eating at someone else's house: 6
- Average number of gallons of diet soft drinks consumed per person per year: 14, or 149 cans of cola
- Average number of pounds of sugar and corn syrup consumed per person per year: 142
- Average number of pounds of artificial sweetener: 25
- Amount spent by the average American per year on fresh fruit: $68
- Amount spent on potato chips: $59
- Percentage of people who eat no fruit: 20
- Percentage who eat no vegetables except potatoes: 15
- Number of Americans who eat Spam regularly: 60 million

our experience with sugar substitutes is any guide. Following the explosion of artificially sweetened foods in the 1980s, sugar consumption actually rose, and obesity rates jumped by 30 percent.

"It is quite analogous to the cigarette smoker who, when offered 'low-nicotine' cigarettes, just smokes more of them," explains researcher Daniel Steinberg, M.D., of the University of California, San Diego.

Good-Bye, Mr. Goodbar

Having a love affair with Hershey's, Godiva and
M&M's? If you understand the chocolate battle,
you can win the weight war.

According to the scientific journal *Appetite*, the number one craving among women is chocolate—not exactly earth-shattering news. What's not to love about a sweet confection as satisfying in Oreos as in a soufflé? That's why chocolate is such a powerful "trigger food" for many women, meaning that it triggers eating and, frequently, overeating.

Speculation abounds as to exactly why chocolate exerts such a powerful influence on women's lives and body chemistry. One book, called *The Chemistry of Love*, noted that chocolate contains phenylethylamine (PEA), a chemical that's also found in the brain. PEA raises blood pressure and heart

(continued on page 62)

White vs. Dark: It's the Same Stuff

Think you'll get some dietary dispensation by eating white, waxy chocolate rather than the deep, rich, brown stuff? Think again.

White and dark chocolate have pretty much the same nutritional profile. One ounce of white chocolate has 151 calories and 8.6 grams of fat, while the same amount of milk chocolate has 145 calories and 8.7 grams of fat. So there are no real calorie or fat savings.

Semisweet chocolate does save you about 10 calories per ounce, because it contains less sugar than milk chocolate. But unsweetened baking chocolate has about the same number of calories plus a hefty 15.7 grams of fat. That's because it contains more cocoa butter per ounce.

NEW IN THE MARKETPLACE

Guilt-Free Chocolate Treats

Those of us with a taste for the stuff know that nothing else will do when it comes to appeasing chocolate cravings. So we're delighted that there are now so many chocolate treats on the market that let us indulge without all the fat (from cocoa butter) usually found in such goodies. Whether it's crunch, cream or slurp

FOOD	PORTION	FAT (G.)	CALORIES
Milky-Way Lite Miniatures	5	5	150
Hershey's Reduced-Fat Sweet Escapes—Triple Chocolate Wafer Bar	1	5	160
Häagen-Dazs Chocolate and Cherry Sorbet 'n' Yogurt on a stick	1	0	100
Edy's Coffee Fudge Sundae Fat-Free Frozen Yogurt	½ cup	0	100
Hershey's TasteTations Hard Chocolate Candies	4	1.5	70
Mori-Nu Mates Chocolate Pudding and Pie Mix	½ cup	1.5	150

you're after, you can find a great low-fat chocolate snack to satisfy your taste.

We scarfed down some of the newest low-fat chocolate products, and quite frankly, none of them flunked our taste test. Here are the ones we'd rate as tops.

COMMENTS

"Tastes like the real thing—extremely good," was one comment. And if you can limit yourself to three of these creamy little cubes, you'll have a great low-fat snack.

We loved all three of Hershey's Reduced-Fat Sweet Escapes—the Triple Chocolate Wafer Bar, the Toffee Crisp Bar and the Caramel and Peanut Butter Crispy Bar. They're reduced-fat, not low-fat, but they're still skinnier than the real thing. The wafer bar contains 5 grams of fat, compared to 11 grams in a regular bar of this type.

This very-adult ice pop combines tart cherry and rich chocolate sorbet in a concoction that belies its calorie count. And with absolutely no fat, it's a must-try treat.

"Great mouth feel. Love that gooey fudge." We found the coffee and chocolate combination to be a winner. "Doesn't taste like a no-fat product."

These delicious, low-fat, individually wrapped hard candies are long-lasting suckers. The candies are also available in caramel, butterscotch and peppermint.

Blend this powdered mix with a pound of extra firm light tofu and you have a surprisingly good low-fat, dairy-free pudding. A pleasant way to use healthful soy.

The Chocolate Cures: The Best Low-Fat and Nonfat Chocolate Treats

When you simply must have chocolate, try one of these all-time favorite low-fat treats.

- Alba Reduced-Calorie Dairy Shake Mix
- Canfield's Diet Chocolate Fudge soda
- Häagen-Dazs Chocolate Sorbet pop
- Jeff's Diet Chocolate Egg Creams
- Jell-O Free chocolate pudding cups
- Swiss Miss Diet Hot Cocoa Mix
- Wax Orchards Chocolate Sauce
- Weight Watchers Chocolate Mousse low-fat chocolate-flavored ice cream
- Weight Watchers Chocolate Treat Pop
- Weight Watchers Smart Options Chocolate Fudge Shake Mix

rate, making us feel much the way we feel when we're falling in love. Unfortunately, the theory that you could gain the same effects by eating chocolate—and other PEA-laced foods—wasn't borne out; the dietary version of PEA doesn't get far enough in the body to have an "I'm in love!" effect on the brain. In addition, the amount of PEA in chocolate is far smaller than the amount in some other, much less poetic foods, like salami.

 For the majority of women, there is no magic antidote for chocolate.

Theories on Cravings Abound

Another hypothesis suggests that chocolate stimulates the production of endorphins, the brain chemicals that produce pleasurable feelings, stop pain and cause addiction—possibly even chocolate addiction, says Stephen P. Gullo, Ph.D., president of the Institute for Health and Weight Sciences in New York City and author of *Thin Tastes Better, Con-*

trol Your Food Triggers and *Lose Weight without Feeling Deprived*.

Still another theory proposes that we crave chocolate because it is a carbohydrate that, after being shifted through the body's gears, enhances the production of serotonin, the neurotransmitter that quiets and soothes us. This last idea dovetails nicely with the fact that we know women crave chocolate more right before their periods start, when serotonin levels are markedly lower.

Chocolate may stimulate the production of endorphins, the brain chemicals that produce pleasurable feelings, stop pain and cause addiction.

Whatever the reason for your love affair with Mr. Goodbar, there are a number of ways that you can try to get a handle on it. It has been suggested that a magnesium deficiency may help trigger cravings for chocolate, which contains a modest amount of the mineral. It's difficult, however, to say whether any of the positive results sometimes seen with magnesium supplements are real or a placebo effect at work.

In addition, some psychologists who study eating behavior have suggested that "stimulus flooding" may suppress cravings; in other words, if you repeatedly give a person large amounts of the food she craves, she may develop an aversion to that food. But a substantial number of people haven't found a lifetime of eating chocolate, or other trigger foods, to be such a bore that they stop. In addition, by the time you get "flooded," you may find that you're also fatted.

So, for the majority of women, there is no magic antidote for chocolate. But there is a lot of help in the way of new food technology. The recent proliferation of low-fat and nonfat chocolate products allows chocoholics to indulge—provided that they don't use a fat-free label as an invitation to overeat. These treats have helped many chocolate lovers, men and women, enjoy both the taste of chocolate and the taste of being thin.

Put Your Diet to the Test

Is your diet on the low-fat track? This quiz will give you an idea by exposing problem areas and strong points.

Does the thought of having to count grams of fat, not to mention calories, each day, put you in a very, very bad mood? Well, there are simpler ways. This quiz can help you determine your diet's strengths and weaknesses without detailed record-keeping or advanced math.

For each question, simply circle the number of the answer that best describes how you eat on most days.

1. How many servings of grain foods do you eat each day? (Sample serving sizes: one slice of bread; a half-cup of cooked cereal, pasta or grain; one ounce of ready-to-eat cereal; three or four small crackers)
   1. Three or fewer
   2. Four
   3. Five
   4. Six or more

2. How many servings of fruit do you eat daily? (Sample serving sizes: one medium-size fruit; three-quarters cup juice; a half-cup cubed fresh fruit; a quarter-cup dried fruit)
   1. Less than one
   2. One
   3. Two or three
   4. Four or more

3. How many servings of vegetables do you consume each day? (Sample serving sizes: a half-cup chopped raw or cooked vegetables; one cup raw leafy vegetables; three-quarters cup vegetable juice)
   1. Less than one
   2. One
   3. Two
   4. Three to five

4. How many servings of protein foods do you eat daily? (Sample serving sizes: one ounce cooked meat, fish or poultry; one egg; a half-cup cooked legumes; two tablespoons peanut butter; one-third cup nuts)
1. Two or fewer   3. Three to five
2. More than seven   4. Five to seven

5. How many servings of dairy products do you eat daily? (Sample serving sizes: eight ounces milk or yogurt; 1½ ounces hard cheese; two cups cottage cheese; one cup frozen yogurt)
1. Less than one   3. Two
2. One   4. Three or more

6. In a typical day, how much total fat, including butter, margarine, oil, cream, full-fat salad dressing, mayonnaise and cream cheese, do you add to food in preparation and at the table?
1. More than four tablespoons   4. Two tablespoons
2. Four tablespoons   5. One tablespoon or less
3. Three tablespoons

7. How many times a week do you eat seafood?
1. Never   3. Two
2. One   4. Three or more

8. How many times a week do you consume dinners containing no meat, poultry or seafood?
1. Never   3. Two
2. One   4. Three or more

9. How many times each week do you eat meat (beef, pork and lamb)?
1. Four or more   4. One
2. Three   5. Rarely or never
3. Two

10. How often do you eat fried foods?
1. Three or more times a week   4. Once every two weeks
2. Twice a week   5. Rarely or never
3. Once a week

(continued on page 68)

NEW IN THE MARKETPLACE

Crackers Worth Their Crunch

Remember Melba toast, the original diet cracker? You could have Melba toast and cottage cheese for lunch and feel like you had done your waistline a big favor. Well, it's still around, and it's still a low-fat, low-calorie bargain, with 50 calories and zero fat per three-piece serving. (A serving of crackers is 28 grams, or one ounce.)

But Melba toast now has lots of competition. One of our favorite brands that has been around for a while, New York Flatbreads, is virtually fat-free, crunchy and full of flavor.

FOOD	PORTION	FAT (G.)	CALORIES
Keebler Reduced-Fat Sesame Toasted Crackers	10	3	120
Nabisco's Italian Herb Harvest Crisps	13	3.5	130
Quaker Fat-Free Monterey Jack Corn Cakes	1	0	40
Salsa Cheddar Snackwell's Snack Crackers	32	2	120
New York Style Bite-Size Bagel Chips (98% fat-free)	28	0.5	120
Venus Fat-Free Garden Vegetable Crackers	10	0	115

Most crackers, even the fat-free kind (and even those with microscopic bits of vegetables), aren't exactly nutritional powerhouses, so you'll still want to take it easy on portions. Some of the new crackers taste so good that you can easily eat more than a serving. Your best bet: Grab a handful and then hide the box!

We tasted the newest low-fat and fat-free crackers. Here they are, listed in order of preference. All are available in the cracker aisle or deli section of supermarkets nationwide.

COMMENTS

We really liked the rich, sesame flavor and crumbly texture of this cracker.

A tasty new addition to the Harvest Crisps line, with a hint of oregano and dried tomato. "A good bet to satisfy crunchy cravings."

"A nice light burst of cheese flavor." A new addition to the Quaker line of rice and corn cakes. Other flavors include blueberry, chocolate and caramel.

"A zesty flavor that would go well with low-fat cottage cheese dip." We liked the large serving size and the low calorie and fat-gram count, but some were suspicious of the two-inch-long list of ingredients in this cracker.

These tiny, garlic-flavored chips have a crisp texture, yet they melt in your mouth. "Good for mindless crunching or as a topping to soups or salads."

The green color and hard, dry texture didn't win any votes with us.

11. How often do you remove the skin from poultry before eating?
1. Never
2. Sometimes
3. Most of the time
4. Always

12. How often do you bake, broil, grill or microwave meat, poultry and seafood without adding additional fat?
1. Never
2. Sometimes
3. Most of the time
4. Always

13. How many times a week do you consume vitamin C–rich fruits or vegetables, such as oranges, tomatoes or green peppers?
1. Two or fewer
2. Three or four
3. Five or six
4. Seven or more

14. How many times a week do you eat at fast-food restaurants?
1. Four or more
2. Three
3. Two
4. One
5. Rarely or never.

15. How many days a week do you eat breakfast?
1. Never or one
2. Two or three
3. Four or five
4. Six or seven

16. How often do you choose low-fat milk (1 percent or skim) or other low-fat and nonfat dairy products rather than full-fat dairy products?
1. Never
2. Sometimes
3. Most of the time
4. Always

17. How much water do you drink daily?
1. 16 ounces or less
2. 16 to 32 ounces
3. 32 to 48 ounces
4. More than 48 ounces

18. How many ounces of sweetened soft drinks do you drink each day?
1. 48 ounces or more
2. 36 ounces
3. 24 ounces
4. 12 ounces or less

19. Which describes your typical daily meal pattern?

1. One meal

2. Two meals

3. Two moderate meals and one or two snacks

4. Three meals, or three moderate meals and one or two snacks

20. How many times a week do you munch on foods like cookies, candy, chips, doughnuts and cake?

1. Seven or more

2. Six

3. Two to five

4. One

Scoring

Add up the numbers corresponding to your choices.

61 to 80 points: Very good. Chances are that you meet nearly all the requirements of a well-balanced, low-fat diet.

41 to 60 points: Good, but could be better. You probably don't eat the recommended number of servings from each food group. Also, you may need to eat a smaller amount of fat and fewer processed foods.

21 to 40 points: Fair. There's a lot of room for improvement. You short-change yourself by not eating enough fruits and vegetables and by feasting on too much high-fat fare.

20 points: Critical. You're in need of professional help. You consume dangerously small amounts of critical vitamins and minerals from food, way too much fat and possibly too many calories. See a registered dietitian for help in giving your diet a major overhaul.

Seven Easy Ways to Enjoy Soy

There's lots more to soy than tofu. Here's how to make the most of this health-packed food.

Finally, soy's so hot it's smokin'! After years of neglect, mounting studies now suggest that soy foods help us dodge the big ones—heart disease and breast and prostate cancer. It may also help prevent osteoporosis. And substituting soy foods for animal products helps us cut way back on saturated fat—the worst kind.

There's one little problem, though. Soy foods like tofu and tempeh, a fermented soy product, may be menu staples all over Asia, but in the United States, where we grow half of the world's soybeans and then feed them mostly to chickens, the idea of soy for dinner somehow doesn't cut it. Fear of tofu—a white, spongy soybean curd that most of us don't have a clue how to use in cooking—runs deep.

If this describes you, relax! We've discovered seven surprisingly gentle ways to get you started with soy. They're all delicious and super-easy techniques that even soybean sissies can relate to.

Beyond Beans

Mind you, no one is claiming that soy makes miracles. "You can't expect to wash down your cheeseburgers and fries with soy milk and come out even," says soy authority Mark Messina, Ph.D., former program director of the Diet and Cancer Branch of the National Cancer Institute in Bethesda, Maryland. "But when you add it to a healthy diet, one serving of soy a day makes too much sense to ignore." Here are our suggestions.

Pour soy milk on your cereal. This is probably the easiest step of all.

How Much Should You Eat?

How much soy do you need to enjoy its health benefits? Experts don't know yet. What's more, the level of soy protein and protective isoflavones in soy products varies, depending upon where the soy was grown and how it was processed. For now, soy authority Mark Messina, Ph.D., former program director of the Diet and Cancer Branch of the National Cancer Institute in Bethesda, Maryland, advises eating at least one serving of soy food a day (the average intake in Asia) without worrying about grams of protein or milligrams of isoflavones. The exception to this, he says, is if you're using soy to lower your blood cholesterol. (In that case, see "Why Soy Is Hot" on page 72.)

One serving of soy food equals:

- 1 cup (eight ounces) soy milk
- ½ cup (two to three ounces) tofu
- ½ cup rehydrated textured vegetable protein (TVP)
- ½ cup green soybeans (sweet beans)
- One three-ounce soy-protein-concentrate burger
- ½ cup Nutlettes cereal

Soy milk doesn't taste exactly like cow's milk, and it's sometimes beige in color. Never mind. Chilled and poured on your favorite cereal, it's terrific. Most soy milk comes in aseptic cartons; it's available in supermarkets or natural food stores. Look for nonfat or 1 percent fat versions, plain or vanilla-flavored. After opening the milk, you can refrigerate it for about one week if it's in the original container. (*Note:* If you replace cow's milk with soy milk, try to find a calcium-fortified brand.) One cup (eight ounces) has 80 to 120 calories and 0 to 2.5 grams of fat.

Whip up tofu blender smoothies. Try whirring tofu, juice and frozen fruit into healthy shakes so creamy that they seem sinful. Use Mori-Nu Silken Lite Firm Tofu (aseptic pack) or soft tofu packed in water and sealed in plastic (both are available in supermarkets). Breakfast becomes dessert with this Strawberry-Banana Smoothie: In a blender, combine one cup unsweetened apple juice, one cup unsweetened frozen strawberries, one small banana and one 10.5-ounce package of Mori-Nu Silken

Why Soy Is Hot

First of all, soy is low in saturated fat, cholesterol-free, high in fiber (unless processing zaps it) and packed with first-class protein. But wait, there's more! Inside this humble bean nestles a clutch of powerful phytomins—plant compounds that seem to help us fight disease. Soybeans happen to be our only good source of some of the most promising phytomins—the isoflavones.

Although scientists have yet to pin down why soy works, here's what they think it may do for us.

Cream high cholesterol. Research shows that replacing some animal protein in a low-fat diet with soy protein appears to dramatically lower high levels of "bad" LDL (low-density lipoprotein) cholesterol. A combined analysis of the 38 best-conducted studies in this area showed that—in people with total cholesterol levels above 250—eating 47 grams of soy protein per day lowered LDL cholesterol a whopping 13 percent without bringing down "good" HDL (high-density lipoprotein) cholesterol. And in some research, just 25 grams of soy protein was effective. The study's lead author, James Anderson, M.D., of the University of Kentucky College of Medicine in Lexington, thinks it's likely that the isoflavones in soy make the difference.

Before you try 25 to 50 grams of soy protein to lower your choles-

---

Lite Firm Tofu. Blend until smooth. This makes two 10-ounce servings, with 200 calories, two grams of fat and two grams of fiber per serving. (Keep unopened aseptic packages of tofu in your cupboard until the "best used by" date; after opening, refrigerate the tofu in a sealed container for two to three days. Keep unopened water-packed tofu refrigerated until the "best used by" date. After opening, keep it refrigerated and change the water daily; use within five to seven days.)

Make chocolate pudding no one can resist. You won't believe how easy or how luscious this is. Blend one 10.5-ounce box of Mori-Nu Silken Lite Extra Firm Tofu with one pack of Mori-Nu Mates Chocolate Pudding and Pie Mix (a brand-new product that's sold in natural food stores), then chill. Wow! Each half-cup serving has 150 calories and 1.5 grams of fat.

terol, check with your doctor, who may send you to a registered dietitian to determine how much animal protein you should omit. You'll need a concentrated source of soy protein, too, such as Nutlettes cereal or Take Care High Protein Beverage Powder (see page 74). Alternatively, you'd need about two to three servings of other types of soy foods to get 25 grams of soy protein.

May help beat breast and prostate cancer. Rates of these cancers are low throughout Asia. In Japan, for example, deaths from breast cancer are only one-fourth of rates in the United States, and from prostate cancer, they're only one-fifth of U.S. rates. Researchers think that the isoflavones in soy could help explain the difference, because they mimic the hormone estrogen—a breast-cancer promoter—but in a form 100,000 times weaker. By occupying limited spaces on breast tissue, called receptor sites, isoflavones may prevent the more powerful estrogen from "docking." Isoflavones may also prevent estrogen from promoting prostate tumors in men.

May help outrun osteoporosis. Although diets in Asia are lower in calcium, fewer women there suffer from osteoporosis, possibly because soy protein causes less calcium excretion from the body than does the animal protein in Western diets. Also, soy isoflavones may help slow down bone loss after menopause and relieve symptoms such as night sweats and hot flashes.

Add "sweet beans" to your repertoire. These pretty soybeans could be next year's star veggie. Sweet beans are about the size of plump baby limas but are brighter green, sweeter and firmer. They're picked before maturity, blanched and sold frozen in 16-ounce poly bags. Boil them for two minutes, then serve as a side dish with a squeeze of fat-free liquid margarine, as a main dish with pasta and chopped sweet red peppers and Parmesan, or in a salad with tomato and onion. Look for Sun-Rich Sweet Beans in health food stores or Yu Yee Frozen Soy Beans in Asian grocery stores. A half-cup serving has 60 calories, two grams of fat and eight grams of fiber.

Indulge in healthy Sloppy Joes. Here's a quick-to-fix comfort food that is basically fat-free if you make it with textured soy protein (often called textured vegetable protein, or TVP) granules. Rehydrate the TVP with hot water for five minutes so that it has roughly the consistency and flavor of ground beef. Add a can of Sloppy Joe sauce, heat and serve on a bun. Today's TVP will amaze you—it's great! You can find it in natural food stores and some supermarkets. There are 60 calories, 0.1 gram of fat and 11 grams of protein in a half-cup of reconstituted TVP.

Go Nutlettes! The only ready-to-eat soy breakfast cereal, Nutlettes (made from a type of TVP that you don't rehydrate) has the texture of crunchy nuggets, stays crisp in milk and boasts a wholesome, nutty flavor. Here's a best bet if you are looking for a concentrated source of soy protein (25 grams per half-cup). You can order it

Once you make friends with soy, you might be tempted to learn a few of the thousand different ways that Asians fix tofu and tempeh.

by phone (24 hours a day) from Dixie USA at 1-800-347-3494. The price is $5.99 for two pounds (18 half-cup servings), plus shipping. Each half-cup serving has 140 calories, 1.5 grams of fat and 9 grams of fiber.

Drink soy-protein beverages. Another best bet for a concentrated source of soy protein is Take Care High Protein Beverage Powder, the same product used in many cholesterol-lowering studies. Made from isolated soy protein, Take Care High Protein packs 20 grams of soy protein in each serving. It comes plain or in chocolate or strawberry flavor; you can mix it with water or juice or use it in shakes. Call Nutritious Foods at 1-800-445-3350. Price: $8 per 12 to 14 servings, plus shipping. A serving has 100 to 130 calories and 1.5 grams of fat.

You can also get regular soy protein isolate powder, which supplies somewhat less protein, in natural food stores. Blend unflavored varieties with orange juice. Or mix Spiru-Tein Chocolate Peanut Butter Swirl powder with nonfat milk; it's great! Per serving, it supplies 179 calories, 1 gram of fiber and no fat. And since both Take Care and Spiru-Tein have lots of added vitamins and minerals, you may decide that you don't need a multivitamin/mineral supplement.

Things to Consider

Supermarkets and natural food stores carry umpteen good soy products these days, including vegetarian hot dogs, cheese, yogurt and ice cream,

NEWS FLASH

Don't Blame
Hormone Replacement Therapy

If you've been avoiding hormone replacement therapy (HRT) be-cause you've heard that it will make you fat, forget what you've heard. A study indicates that, despite what women may want to believe, hor-mone therapy is not to blame for those added pounds after menopause.

The study, by researchers at the University of California, San Diego, compared 671 women over a 15-year span. Some had never used HRT, some used it continuously, and some used it on and off. The researchers found absolutely no association between hormone use and weight gain.

"We can only speculate why the weight gain commonly seen in postmenopausal women occurs, but from our data, hormone replace-ment therapy is not the culprit," says Donna Kritz-Silverstein, Ph.D., associate adjunct professor in the Department of Family and Preventive Medicine at the University of California, San Diego, and the study's main researcher.

Fear of weight gain is one of the major reasons that post-menopausal women won't use HRT, despite the protection it offers against heart disease and osteoporosis, Dr. Kritz-Silverstein says.

So how to explain the extra weight that so many women past menopause put on? Blame it on the more sedentary lifestyles and slower metabolism that often accompany aging, says JoAnn Man-son, M.D., co-director of women's health at Brigham and Women's Hospital of Harvard Medical School.

To combat those unwelcome pounds, try an easy aerobic exercise such as brisk walking to burn calories and fat. And do some muscle-building weight lifting. The more muscle you have, the better you burn calories, even in your sleep, says Dr. Manson. Just don't blame HRT for those "love handles" and "saddle bags."

and many of them taste just great. So why didn't any of these foods make our shopping list? Dr. Messina's advice, at least while you and soy are still making friends, is to avoid soy versions of foods that you love. A direct comparison between the two is likely to make the soy product seem second best just because it's different from what you're used to.

But that caution doesn't apply to scrumptious veggie burgers made from soy-protein concentrate. These really do mimic a beef burger's taste, with jumbo health advantages. (See "New in the Marketplace: Burgers, Hot Dogs and Cold Cuts" on page 38.)

Be aware, too, that many soy products are higher in price. Dr. Messina's advice is to buy in bulk or order by the case if you can. Stock up at sale time, too. "My favorite soy milk," he says, "is whatever is least expensive when I'm shopping."

Who knows? Once you make friends with soy, you might be tempted to learn a few of the thousand delicious ways that Asians fix tofu and tempeh. "To people in the Far East," says *Prevention* staffer Yun Lee, who was raised on traditional Korean foods, "life without tofu is unimaginable!"

Fat-Fighting Tips
from around the World

Best-bet strategies for low-fat living
with an international flair.

We live in a big country full of big people. "In my experience, virtually every foreign visitor comments on the number of overweight people he sees here," says Mona Sutnick, R.D., Ed.D., a nutritionist and spokesperson for the American Dietetic Association. "When visitors walk the streets of our cities, they find it very striking."

International data support the observation. "Americans are among the most obese people in the world," confirms Theodore VanItallie, M.D., professor emeritus of medicine at Columbia University College of Physicians and Surgeons in New York City. Only Eastern and Southern Europeans come close to our bulk.

Yes, as incredible as it seems, even the French—inventors of the croissant—are considerably thinner than we are. Steak and kidney pie notwithstanding, so are the British. And Northern Europeans, famous for their love of ham and cheese, are even thinner. In fact, they're the slimmest people in all of Europe.

But when it comes to slenderness, no one does it better than the Asians. The Japanese weigh less than people of any other industrialized nation in the world, even after taking into account smaller body frames. According to a study by Dr. VanItallie, the average five-foot-four-inch woman in Japan weighs 126 pounds. She's a shadow of the average American woman of the same height, whose weight soars over 150 pounds.

Why are other countries doing better in the thinness department? When we talked with international experts—doctors, epidemiologists, food writers, diplomats and multinational citizens—they told us about healthy habits that are unique to certain countries. And they suspect that it's mostly these habits that are having an impact on weight control. But there were also common threads among these—slimming factors that popped up in country after country. These are lessons we need to take to heart, lessons that we could incorporate into our way of life, the experts say (for more on these, see "Lessons of the World" on page 80.)

So here's a rundown on some of the healthy habits that seem to be making a difference—a catalog of just exactly what the rest of the world seems to have going for it.

China

- The people in China carbo-load, on principle. The principle is *fan ts'ai*, and it describes the ideal balance of a Chinese meal. The *fan* (grain)—rice, noodles, steamed wheat or millet, or bread, depending on the region—dominates the meal. The *ts'ai* is the complementary food meant to flavor the grain; it's usually a green vegetable, sometimes stir-fried in a little plant oil. Meat is used in small amounts, if at all, as a condiment. "That's the way they typically eat, three times a day," says Banoo Parpia, Ph.D., project nutritionist for the Cornell-China-Oxford Project at Cornell University in Ithaca, New York, a comprehensive study of the diet and health of 10,800 families across China. Only for special occasions, like festivals, is the principle reversed, so there's more of the richer *ts'ai* and less of the grain. "What we get in Chinese restaurants in the United States is really festival food," says Dr. Parpia.
- They eat more calories but less fat. With so much grain in their diets, the Chinese actually eat more total calories than Americans—about a third more. Yet their fat intake is much lower, averaging 14 percent of calories from fat in rural China, compared with an average of almost 35 percent of calories in America.
- They bike everywhere. Rural Chinese tilling the fields obviously burn many more calories than a typical desk-bound American. But so do Chinese urbanites. "We compared Chinese office workers with Westerners. There, most of the office workers walk or bicycle to their jobs, so they get a lot more exercise," says Colin Campbell, Ph.D., a nutritional biochemist who heads the Cornell-China-Oxford Project. Cars are still a luxury, available only to the wealthy.

With less fat and lots of activity, it's no surprise that obesity rates are much, much lower in China than here. A bare 0.4 percent of Chinese men and 1.5 percent of women are overweight, compared with almost 35 percent in the United States today!

Japan

- Rice and vegetables are the focus. Steamed or boiled rice (without added fat) dominates most meals. In 1990, the average Japanese ate nearly a half-pound of rice a day. They also eat lots of preserved vegetables and moderate amounts of potatoes, fruit, beans (especially soybeans) and seafood.
- Meat, dairy products and oil are eaten sparingly. Dairy and meat products, although increasing in popularity, are not a traditional component of the Japanese diet. In fact, the average Japanese ate only about 23 pounds of beef and veal in 1993, compared with a hefty 94 pounds of cow consumed by the average American that year. It's a matter of economics as well as taste: Beef costs about three times as much in Japan as in the United States. The result is an ultra-low-fat diet. In all, only around 11 percent of calories in a traditional Japanese diet come from fat, compared with about 35 percent in the United States, says Dr. VanItallie, who lived in Japan for more than a year. "But their fat intake is on the rise, with the increasing popularity of American-style fast food," he notes.
- Small is beautiful. Small is not just a necessity, it's an aesthetic. The hallmark of a Japanese meal is minuscule amounts of different foods, each tidbit exquisitely arranged on its own dish. You don't get the American-style towering heaps of food—the Japanese consider that grotesque.
- Public snacking is rude. Eating in public, while walking down the street or riding on a subway, is frowned upon. "Even chewing gum is very bad, though some younger people do it nowadays," says Masako Kinoshita, who grew up in Japan and returns frequently to visit her family.
- Dessert is rare. "We customarily don't eat dessert," says Kinoshita. "Or some people eat a small sweet bean cake after a meal. Even after 40 years in this country, I still have no need for dessert. Sometimes, when

(continued on page 82)

Lessons of the World

Why are Americans so fat? Obesity is extremely complex, and scientists say that many factors are involved. But if you're tempted to credit foreigners' genes for their slenderness, forget it.

While genes often play some role, they generally do so through an interaction with an obesity-promoting environment, says Theodore VanItallie, M.D., professor emeritus of medicine at Columbia University College of Physicians and Surgeons in New York City. "Studies of Japanese who moved to Hawaii or to the West Coast show that these people gained a lot of weight—maybe 15 to 20 pounds over their brothers and sisters back in Japan."

The fattiness of the cuisine alone doesn't account for all of the international differences, either. Yes, the ultra-low-fat Japanese diet helps them keep their status as the thinnest affluent people in the world. But in other countries, the relationship between fat in the diet and fat on the people is sometimes contradictory.

In Europe, for example, epidemiologist Lawrence Kushi, Sc.D., associate professor of epidemiology at the University of Minnesota School of Public Health in Minneapolis, says the Northern Europeans—who love meat and dairy products and have a higher fat intake—are actually thinner than Southern Europeans, who eat less meat, fewer dairy products and less total fat.

So what is the secret? Six recurring themes emerged during interviews with our experts.

1. It's the motion. "Physical activity is the key," says Dr. Kushi. "Other people move more than we do."

    In the developing world, the reasons are obvious: They can't afford to be lazy. "Most people in poorer countries don't have the vacuum cleaners, food processors or any of the other time-saving, labor-saving devices that we have," says Norge Jerome, Ph.D., nutritional anthropologist at the University of Kansas in Lawrence. "Women especially are involved in food production. That means they work hard in the fields and the kitchen all day long." They also walk many miles each day just getting to and from the fields and the market.

Even in affluent countries, people get more exercise than Americans. The big reason: Old World towns and cities are, well, old. They predate Henry Ford by centuries. Streets are narrow and thus encourage walking and biking. Adding to the incentive to hoof it is the sky-high cost of driving in other countries.

2. Snack time isn't all the time. Foreigners tell us that in their countries, either they don't snack or they limit their noshing to certain appointed times, like the British midafternoon tea.

3. There's less focus on fatty foods. Europeans and Asians alike commented on how expensive food is in their countries relative to the United States—especially fat-packed meats, restaurant meals and processed foods.

4. The portions are smaller. Only in America can a fast-food chain name a product "The Really Big Chicken Sandwich." "A humongous steak served to one person in an American restaurant would feed a family of four in Sweden," says Maria Rosenberg, a Swedish-born teacher from Massachusetts.

5. Grains star on their plates. While we tend to make meat or cheese the centerpiece of our meals, healthier cuisines mandate that the largest serving on the plate be a filling, low-fat grain or starch. In Asia, for example, it's rice; Swedes emphasize potatoes, Europeans eat a lot of bread, and corn flour stars in Mexico.

6. Dessert's not their religion. Elsewhere, people don't pout if a gigantic chocolate cake doesn't appear at the end of a meal. They're more likely to enjoy fruit for dessert—or skip dessert entirely.

While people in most of the world are slimmer than those in the United States, the trend may not last: World obesity is on the rise, says K. Dun Gifford, president of the Oldways Preservation and Exchange Trust, a Boston-based nonprofit organization dedicated to promoting traditional foods of many cultures. "As societies get richer, people become more sedentary. They eat more calories, more meat and more American-style fast food. American fast food combined with a sedentary lifestyle is making the citizens of the world fat."

I eat at American friends' houses and they offer me a homemade dessert, I almost have to force myself to eat it—I think declining is not polite here."

- Public transportation keeps them moving. In Japan, public transportation is convenient and reasonably priced compared with cars. "When you take subways and buses, you end up walking a lot to and from the station," says Kinoshita. "And every train station has long, high stairs. You're always running up and down them to catch the trains."

- Bike racks are packed. What's the difference between a subway station in suburban Tokyo and one in suburban New York? In Tokyo, instead of cars, there are hundreds of bikes parked outside the station. In 1989, more than three million bicycles converged on suburban railway stations each day.

Myanmar (Burma)

- They sip soup. Forget soft drinks—the Burmese delight in sipping clear, lukewarm broth with meals, says Copeland Marks, renowned author of cookbooks on international cuisine, including *The Burmese Kitchen* (with Aung Thien). "If you're in a restaurant in Burma and the waiter sees that your soup bowl is half empty, he comes around with a teapot full of soup and refills it," says Marks. Studies in the United States suggest that soup has a unique ability to satisfy the appetite.

- They eat rice plain. Boiled white rice is at the center of most meals, says Marks.

- They can't afford meat. "Meat is money," says Marks. "If you're poor, you fall back on healthy foods—grains, vegetables, seafood and plain rice."

- Salads are exciting, filling and low-fat. "Complex, one-dish salads are the hallmark of Burmese cooking," says Marks, who writes his books by moving to exotic countries and rustling up meals alongside the locals. "My favorite, which I think is the healthiest, is called *Let-Thoat Son*. It includes three different kinds of noodles (egg noodles, rice noodles and cellophane noodles) along with rice, tofu, assorted vegetables and bean sprouts, and only a tiny amount of oil." (The recipe is included in his book.)

- Fried foods are garnish. The Burmese use bits of crispy fried garlic and onions for flavoring, "but you would drain them on paper towels for 15 to 20 minutes so you could see all the oil disappear," says Marks.

Korea

- They boil. "Korean food is the healthiest cuisine in Asia," maintains Marks, whose book on Korean cuisine is called *The Korean Kitchens of Korea*. The reason that it's so healthy? "While other Asians tend to cook with oil, the Koreans cook with water," he says. Boiled white rice and noodles are staples, but Koreans also enjoy boiled vegetables and meats.
- Squid is a favorite. Many Americans think barbecued beef is classic Korean cuisine, but it's not. "Koreans never had any money to buy that beef until recent years, when they became affluent," says Marks. "Their country is a little thumb surrounded by water, so they're big seafood eaters. Perhaps their favorite protein dish is squid, which is low in fat."
- Kimchi is their Baskin-Robbins. The Koreans savor more than 200 varieties of pickled vegetables called kimchi. No meal is complete without it, says Marks. It can be made from all kinds of vegetables, ranging from cabbage and cucumbers to eggplant and turnips. The vegetable is fermented with garlic, red chili peppers and little or no oil. (Some experts in the United States believe that spicy foods may have a unique ability to quell appetite.)

Sweden

- They follow *mat och potatis*. Translation: Food and potatoes, which implies that there's a lot of potato on the plate. Potatoes are included at most lunches and dinners, and they're often served just skinned and boiled. A little fish or meat, bread and a salad balance out a meal.
- Swedish meatballs aren't so big. "Meat is much more expensive in Sweden, so portions are much smaller," says Swede Maria Rosenberg, a Massachusetts teacher and mother of two daughters, who is married to an American. Similarly, cheese is popular, but servings are scant by American standards. "We cut slices with one of those cheese shavers,

so each piece comes out ultra-thin," says Rosenberg. "You might put just one or two slices on a piece of bread."

- There's a time for treats. Ask any Swedish kid, and she'll tell you about *Lordgas Godis*, or "Saturday goodies." "Children know they can have candy only at a certain time on Saturday. They save it for that time, gulp it down, brush their teeth, and then they're done eating candy for the week," says Rosenberg.
- Society invests in fitness. In the same way that the United States provides public libraries, most towns in Sweden offer a clean, inexpensive *simhall*, which translates as "swim hall" but offers much more. Along with a pool, there's typically table tennis, weight lifting, volleyball and other athletic options. Also, some towns are crisscrossed by well-maintained pathways for walkers and cyclists, so it's possible for people to walk or ride to the store without ever encountering automobiles.
- They walk. "In the wintertime, there may be fewer than seven hours of sunlight daily," says Rodale Press health writer Margo Trott, whose husband is Swedish and who has researched health habits in her in-laws' nation. "Seasonal affective disorder (a form of depression that appears to be related to a lack of sunlight) is not a joke there—people know that they have to get out while they can to keep their sanity. They typically may walk for 1 to $1\frac{1}{2}$ hours during midday."

The Netherlands

- They eat their veggies. "We don't have all the fast foods that are available in the United States," says Jacques Van Berkel, economic officer at the Netherlands' consulate in New York City. "And people consume a lot of vegetables—practically every vegetable grown anywhere is available in Holland."
- Restaurants are pricey. "The portions in restaurants are smaller and more expensive. In Holland, restaurant visits are usually reserved for special occasions," says Van Berkel.
- There are few ranch homes. For a short period of time in the seventeenth century, Dutch houses were taxed according to their width. So a few clever citizens built tall instead of wide—with plenty of stairs to climb. "In general, most people in Holland live in houses with at least two floors, so they have to walk up and down lots of stairs every day,"

says Van Berkel. And old buildings, of course, aren't usually equipped with elevators.

- They really do cycle past tulips and windmills. "It's normal for people to cycle to their offices, if it doesn't take more than 45 minutes," says Van Berkel. That's hardly surprising, given the astronomical cost of driving in Holland.

England

- The evening meal is light. It's true: The British diet often gets two thumbs down. But the Brits do some things right. Supper, for instance, is traditionally light in England.

  "The evening meal was usually just salad, salad and soup, or toast and soup," says Wahida Karmally, R.D., director of nutrition at the Irving Center for Clinical Research at Columbia Presbyterian Medical Center in New York City, who did an internship in London. (Research in this country suggests that a light dinner might help prevent fat accumulation.)

- Walking paths are protected. The English countryside is laced with hundreds of miles of government-protected footpaths. Where they cross private land, owners are responsible for maintenance. These paths are so popular with walkers, cyclists and horseback riders that a major environmental issue in England is how to preserve the countryside from damage inflicted by millions of eager feet.

- They love dogs and gardens. These renowned British interests burn calories. "They're always walking their dogs and working in their gardens," says *Prevention*'s Home and Family editor, Susan Flagg Godbey, who has led tours of the United Kingdom.

France

- Water's the uncola. Bottled water is the beverage of choice during the course of a busy day in France. It's far more popular than calorie-packed fruit juices or even soda.

- Bread is big. "People eat a lot of bread with every meal," says food writer Judith Olney, author of six cookbooks and a frequent traveler to France. "Bread is nearly fat-free, fresh and made with unbleached flour. They just rip off hunks and eat them."

Italy

- Pizza is light! Fulvia Castelli, a Milanese philosophy student now living in Los Angeles, explains: "A real Italian pizza fits inside your dinner plate. It's dotted with a little tomato, basil and oil. It's not loaded with lots of toppings and usually has less cheese."

- There's no ice cream at home. "We don't usually keep a big pack of ice cream in the freezer," says Castelli. "If we want gelato (the Italian version of ice cream), we have to go out for it. Compared with the United States, you get a tiny serving. And it's very expensive—maybe $2 for a very small cone. It makes me crazy every time I go back!" A more typical Italian dessert is fruit.

- They do the *passeggiata*. "In many areas of Italy, people spend the evening walking back and forth in the town center, visiting and chatting," says anthropologist Peter Brown, Ph.D., of Emory University in Atlanta. "It's a pleasant way to get exercise while they see their friends." (Spain has a similar tradition, called the *paseo*.)

- Streets are narrow. "In Italy, the roads are small, narrow and clogged," says Olney. "So people walk a lot. They have strong legs. Even very elderly people haul wheeled baskets around town to shop."

Mexico

- Corn is the foundation. "Corn is at the base of the Mexican food pyramid," says *San Francisco Chronicle* food columnist Jacqueline Higuera McMahan, author of *Healthy Mexican Cookbook* and six other cookbooks on Southwestern cuisine. "They eat a lot of it, in the form of tortillas. These are usually prepared with cornmeal and water, with no added oil. Those hard-fried taco shells that they sell here in America—we don't have that in Mexico. A typical meal might be a soft, warm corn tortilla heated on the griddle and filled with beans, salsa and a little shredded meat."

- Nonfat sauces add zing. Sauces, marinades and salsas put the zip in Mexican dishes, says McMahan, who lived in Mexico for five years. "Mexican sauces and salsas are usually based on several kinds of dried chilies, with water, garlic and onion and other seasonings. Some contain oil, but usually it's just a little. This is a very healthy cuisine."

- There's no cheese blanket. "Most of what you see in Mexican restaurants in the United States is not authentic," says McMahan.

"In the United States, someone got the idea to top Mexican dishes with a half-pint of sour cream and massive amounts of cheese. But when they eat an enchilada or tamale in Mexico, they use just a little bit of cheese. It might be a tablespoon of soft goat cheese or crumbly *queso ranchero*, both of which are lower in fat than many other kinds. Some regions of Mexico, like the Yucatán, use no cheese at all."

- Fruits and vegetables are their fast food. "When Mexicans do snack, they go for fruits and vegetables," says McMahan. "Street vendors sell jícama slices or roasted corn, sprinkled with chile and lime juice. Or they might carve beautiful little sections of watermelon, mango or other fruit—you see children walking down the street eating these flower-shaped slices. What could be better?"

Have It Your Way

Fast food is quick and cheap, and now it can be low-fat, too. Here's what we recommend.

Finding fast food that's nutritious and reasonably low in fat used to be a serious challenge. You would have better luck finding a counterperson with a clear complexion. A rubbery burger here. A lifeless bowl of iceberg lettuce there. A smidgen of a chicken tender under a glop of odd-tasting dressing. Meager choices, at best. But now it's possible—almost effortless—to get a low-fat fast-food meal that tastes pretty good and doesn't leave you hungry for lunch a half-hour after you've eaten it.

We hit the highway and sampled the stuff at the major fast-food chains. Unrecognized by the masses and wearing loose-fitting clothes, we ordered exclusively off the low-fat menu to see what had any flavor.

We found that some restaurants are still stuck in the 1970s when it comes to nutrition (Burger King and Kentucky Fried Chicken, for example, had few low-fat foods to choose from), but most of the places we visited had a decent selection of low-fat foods. And now they even have brochures at the counter trumpeting these items. It's important to note that a few of these selections get more than 30 percent of their calories from fat, the maximum percentage that many dietitians recommend for a healthy diet, but they were the leanest items we could find.

Here are our gut feelings on the foods we sampled. But remember, this is still fast food, so don't expect the Four Seasons.

Taco Bell

Taco Bell has reduced its light menu—it no longer offers its Taco Salad or Light Bean Burrito. But it's still worth going there just for the Light Chicken Burrito, which we sampled.

FAT STATS

The Health Angle

- Amount of weight the average American gains between ages 25 and 55: 30 pounds
- Amount of muscle that converts to fat during this time: 15 pounds
- Points blood cholesterol drops for every 5 pounds of weight lost: 7
- Percent of people able to stop taking blood pressure medication after losing just 10 pounds: 60
- Estimated yearly cost associated with obesity (including diabetes, cardiovascular disease, gallbladder disease, cancer and musculoskeletal disorders): $68.8 billion

- Light Chicken Burrito Supreme (410 calories, 21 percent of calories from fat). The tender chunks of spicy chicken, covered with tasty fat-free sour cream, pleased our tasters, especially when they added the hot sauce to give it a little extra bite. But one of these burritos probably won't fill you up. Consider teaming it with a Light Chicken Soft Taco.
- Light Chicken Soft Taco (180 calories, 25 percent of calories from fat). We found the shredded chicken to be moist and flavorful, although it was not very hot. But the fat-free sour cream tastes remarkably authentic, unlike the pasty stuff we have found at supermarkets.

Wendy's

You can find a lot of low-fat foods here, which is surprising since the owner, who does all those TV ads, isn't exactly slender.

FAT STATS

The Lowest-Fat Vending Machine Snacks

1. LifeSavers Gummi Savers: 0 gram
2. Twizzlers: 1.5 grams
3. Baked Rold Gold Pretzels: 2 grams
4. Cracker Jack: 3 grams
5. Snackwell's Reduced-Fat Chocolate Sandwich Cookies (4 pack): 4.5 grams
6. Starburst Fruit Chews: 5 grams

- Baked Potato with a Small Chili (500 calories, 11 percent of calories from fat). If you want a filling meal with a minimum of fat calories, this is your best bet. The spuds were about the size of a fist and nicely cooked. The chili was loaded with beans and meat and made a great topping for the potato. You won't need to use the butter and sour cream. Very satisfying.
- Grilled Chicken Sandwich (290 calories, 22 percent of calories from fat). The chicken was so dry and bland, we had to douse it with an extra glob of fat-free barbecue sauce. (You don't get the sauce with the meal, so ask for it at the counter.) Still hungry, we ordered a side salad (60 calories, 45 percent of calories from fat). It consisted of a single broccoli floret, one cucumber, one piece of cauliflower, a lonely wedge of tomato, carrots, shredded cheese and lots of iceberg lettuce. The reduced-fat Italian dressing helped.
- Grilled Chicken Salad (330 calories, 30 percent of calories from fat). This is the Hulk Hogan of fast-food salads, with about a half-pound of vegetables (tomato wedges, broccoli florets, cauliflower, cucumber slices and shredded carrots), a dozen cubes of barbecued white-meat chicken and shredded cheese on a bed of lettuce. (Taking off some

of the cheese will help bring the fat content down.) The only draw-back was the breadstick. It's a Smurf-size underbaked loaf with a gummy texture and a faint garlic/onion taste. If you're still hungry, grab a Wendy's Jr. Hamburger (270 calories, 30 percent of calories from fat) to go. It's fairly low in fat.

- The Super Bar. Here you'll find some low-fat foods mixed into a minefield of lard-laden toppings. You have your pick: fresh salads, pasta with sauce, tacos, macaroni and cheese, refried beans, Spanish rice, a collection of fatty and reduced-fat dressings, plus a pile of greasy garlic bread. Your best bet is to go Italian. Try the rotini (90 calories, 20 percent of calories from fat) with the spaghetti sauce. It isn't as tasty as the Alfredo sauce (30 calories, 40 percent of calories from fat), but it's fat-free. Neither sauce will remind you of your Aunt Rotunda's, but hey, this is Wendy's, after all. To round out the meal, top the pasta with some fresh broccoli or other vegetables for extra fiber and vitamins. Or cross cultures with a side of Spanish rice—a safe bet at only one gram of fat.

McDonald's

Now that they have those playgrounds out front to keep the kids occu-pied, you can actually eat in peace. But as for lean food that's tasty, the pickings are still slim.

- McGrilled Chicken Classic (250 calories, 11 percent of calories from fat) and fat-free barbecue sauce (50 calories). You can't tell that the small piece of chicken breast is grilled unless you turn it over and locate the tiny tread marks. (Perhaps this little guy met his fate when he was run over by a Hot Wheels truck.) The chicken tastes more boiled than grilled, but the barbecue sauce helps. Alone, the sand-wich wasn't enough food for a satisfying lunch.

Subway

These wildly successful sandwich shops are everywhere. Stop by, and you'll find a new light menu featuring a selection of six-inch subs, includ-ing turkey breast, roast beef and veggie, as well as a ham-and-turkey club. All weigh in at less than 300 calories, with five grams of fat. Unfortunately, there's less meat on these sandwiches than on Kate Moss's thighs. We counted just two paper-thin slices of deli meat in the turkey sandwich. You're better off getting the regular subs and asking for mustard or the house fat-free dressing instead of mayonnaise or oil. A turkey sub without cheese or mayo has just 180 calories and 15 percent of calories from fat.

Boston Market

Picture Thanksgiving dinner with plastic utensils and a soft-drink dispenser. It's hard not to like a joint that offers a year-round holiday feast, with turkey, chicken, meat loaf, stuffing, mashed potatoes, corn, steamed vegetables and cornbread.

- Turkey Breast Sandwich and Fruit Salad (500 calories, 14 percent of calories from fat). This may seem like a lot of calories, but the moist, thick slices of turkey on crusty, fresh French bread are worth it.
- Skinless Turkey Breast, Mashed Potatoes and Gravy, Steamed Vegetables and Cinnamon Apples (660 calories, 20 percent of calories from fat). This is the meal that comes closest to replicating a holiday dinner. All that's missing is Uncle Dave falling into the Christmas tree after drinking too much sherry. The mashed potatoes were creamy, and the turkey tasted surprisingly homemade—like Ma was back in the kitchen. The only drawback was the soggy and flavorless steamed vegetables. We skipped them and filled up on tasty apple slices in a cinnamon glaze.

Arby's

Currently only about one-third of Arby's restaurants nationwide carry a light menu, depending on local demand. So if you want it, ask.

The Arby's in our area doesn't carry the light menu, so we didn't get to sample this fare. But if your local Arby's does provide it, you shouldn't pass it up. The low-fat offerings include roast chicken, turkey and beef sandwiches, all on a multigrain bun with light mayonnaise, lettuce and tomato.

The roast beef sandwich has 296 calories and ten grams of fat (30 percent of calories), the turkey has 260 calories and seven grams of fat (24 percent of calories), and the chicken has 276 calories and six grams of fat (19 percent of calories). Arby's tasty barbecue and horseradish sauces have 15 calories per packet and no fat, so you can douse the sandwiches with the stuff. Arby's also offers plain baked potatoes, salads and soups.

Chick-fil-A

The name refers to chicken, so don't get any ideas. This restaurant offers a nice selection of pretty satisfying low-fat items.

- Chargrilled Chicken Sandwich (280 calories, 10 percent of calories from fat). Most of our tasters said this low-fat chicken sandwich was far superior to its crispier, fried counterpart, which packs three times the fat. Jazz up the sandwich with lettuce, tomato, pickle slices and an excellent fat-free Dijon honey dressing. The dressing, by the way, is a great flavor enhancer for just about everything on the menu; you can get it at the counter. The sandwich isn't all that big, so you'll want to get a side dish. But skip the tossed salad with light Italian dressing. It's typical of fast-food greenery—lots of lettuce and mediocre dressing. Instead, try the . . .
- Hearty Breast of Chicken Soup (110 calories, 8 percent of calories from fat). With big chunks of chicken, celery and carrots, it's like pot-pie without the crust. Like a lot of fast food, it's a tad salty.
- Grilled 'n' Lites (100 calories, 18 percent of calories from fat). This isn't a meal—it's barely an hors d'oeuvre: two moist but extremely small strips of skinless chicken in a foil wrapper. But it's great kid food. It's small, not messy and not fried, and there are no bones to choke on.
- Chargrilled Chicken Garden Salad (170 calories, 16 percent of calories from fat). You get a generous pile of tasty, lean, grilled chicken strips, but the stuff underneath is the typical iceberg lettuce and bland vegetables. Perk up the salad with the Dijon dressing. If you're a big eater, you'll need the soup, too.

Low-Fat French?
Mais Oui!

Timely tips on picking tasty,
low-fat dishes from even the
fanciest French menu.

The average American eats in restaurants more than 200 times a year. Most likely, that's 200 meals in which the nutritional content of the food remains a mystery.

While some cuisines, such as Japanese, are so naturally low in fat that it's hard to go wrong, just about every nationality offers a range of dishes, from exceptionally healthy to downright disastrous. Even French restaurants offer lean grilled fish and flavorful salads and vegetables along with their usual heart-stopping sauces and to-die-for (literally) desserts.

Menus often provide clues as to how food is prepared, so take time to peruse. Choose foods that are steamed, broiled, roasted or poached. The words *au gratin, marinated, crispy, fried, breaded, whipped, creamed* and *with gravy* all signal fatty foods.

Don't hesitate to ask how a food is prepared or to request that its preparation be altered to suit your low-fat needs. Many chefs are willing to hold the butter or use a bit of oil instead, broil instead of pan-fry, or put a sauce on the side or use less.

Check out the wide range of calories and fat in some typical meals from popular restaurants. You'll want to avoid the highest-fat foods on these menus. Instead, assemble a tasty low-fat meal with these best bets, compiled from the handy, purse-size *Restaurant Lovers' Fat Gram Counter* by Kalia Doner.

French without the Fat

Each region of France can be recognized by its distinctive culinary riches. In recent years, food from the warm and sunny south of France—grilled seafood or vegetables seasoned with garlic and spices and cooked or served with splashes of olive oil—has become popular in America.

More and more, French chefs are preparing nouvelle cuisine, including a special type called *cuisine minceur* ("cuisine of slimness"). To create these low-fat specialties that preserve the French touch, chefs use culinary techniques such as steaming or poaching seafood or poultry in vegetable juices and wine and serving side dishes of fresh vegetables, potatoes and grains.

When you're offered dessert in a French restaurant, skip the tempting pastries and request fresh fruit. While it may seem hard to ignore the pastry tray, your meal will end on a wonderful high note if you choose poached fruit (usually peaches or pears). It's cooked in a light wine sauce, which adds a delightful flavor with few calories.

High-Fat French

	CALORIES	FAT (G.)
Escargot (6 snails with butter sauce)	263	24
Coq au vin (¼ chicken)	706	55
Ratatouille (¼ cup)	192	14
Chocolate mousse (less than ½ cup)	348	23
Total	**1,509**	**116**

Low-Fat French

	CALORIES	FAT (G.)
Trout en papillote (5-oz. fillet with vegetables, steamed in a parchment-paper packet)	234	10
Potatoes lyonnaise (3 oz.)	155	9
Raspberry sorbet (½ cup)	80	0
Total	**469**	**19**

Choosy Chinese

Some menu items at Chinese restaurants are good choices because they emphasize rice and vegetables, with only small amounts of seafood or poultry. Bypass the appetizer dishes such as egg rolls and spring rolls— they're usually deep-fried and just brimming with fat. And whatever you do, avoid duck: Just 3.5 ounces of Peking duck has 30 grams of fat.

Stir-fried dishes generally get good low-fat ratings. They're usually cooked quickly in a lightly oiled, very hot wok, and the vegetables retain more vitamins than those cooked the traditional American way. Also, although chefs usually use peanut oil, which is high in monounsaturates, you should always ask that the chef use as little oil as possible. One favorite low-fat stir-fry is moo goo gai pan, a combination of mushrooms, bamboo shoots, water chestnuts and chicken, seafood or tofu served over rice.

High-Fat Chinese

	CALORIES	FAT (G.)
Dumplings with pork filling, fried (4)	252	16
Hot-and-sour soup (1½ cups)	233	12
Stir-fried shrimp with snow peas (5 or 6 medium shrimp)	355	29
White rice (½ cup)	176	<1
Total	**1,016**	**57**

Low-Fat Chinese

	CALORIES	FAT (G.)
Eggdrop soup (1½ cups)	77	4
Sweet-and-sour shrimp (5 large shrimp)	350	16
White rice (½ cup)	176	<1
Total	**603**	**20**

Mexican Lean Bean Cuisine

When chosen with care, Mexican food is inexpensive, delicious, high in complex carbohydrates and low in fat. Beans, rice, unfried corn tortillas,

High-Fat Mexican

	CALORIES	FAT (G.)
Guacamole (½ avocado)	218	20
Chips (12 to 14)	150	8
Enchiladas suizas (2 tortilla rolls)	678	47
Total	**1,046**	**75**

Low-Fat Mexican

	CALORIES	FAT (G.)
Black bean soup (1 cup)	215	7
Grilled swordfish with salsa (8 oz.)	395	9
Total	**610**	**16**

salsa, fish and salads are common staples. Vegetable-bean burritos, fresh fish marinated in lime sauce and beans with rice are low-fat specialties.

Some authentic Mexican recipes include distinctive vegetables with unique flavors. Jícama is a tropical fruit that looks similar to a rutabaga and tastes delicious. Occasionally, squash blossoms are served as a garnish. Whenever you have the opportunity, try tomatillos (similar to small, naturally green tomatoes), chayote (a pear-shaped squash) and nopal cactus. And of course, Mexico is famous for its delightful array of fresh peppers.

A good practice when selecting a new Mexican-style restaurant is to call ahead and ask if the chef uses lard, coconut oil or another oil in the refried beans. Many eateries have switched to small amounts of soybean oil or, ideally, add no fat at all.

Skip the sour cream, guacamole, red meat, pork and egg dishes as well as fried foods, and request to have no more than half the usual amount of cheese.

That's Italian—*And* Low-Fat

Delicious low-fat foods with a pleasing array of tastes make Italian restaurants a good choice for dining away from home. Pasta with marinara (tomato-based), vegetable, red clam or wine sauce is first-rate.

High-Fat Italian

	CALORIES	FAT (G.)
Baked stuffed clams (2)	162	8
Eggplant parmigiana (½ lb.)	410	29
Broccoli with garlic and olive oil	132	9
Focaccia with herbs (1 slice)	278	9
Total	**982**	**55**

Low-Fat Italian

	CALORIES	FAT (G.)
Minestrone soup (1 cup)	127	3
Pollo Cacciatore	330	12
Roasted pepper (1, no oil)	16	0
Steamed zucchini with pine nuts and balsamic vinegar (½ lb.)	64	5
Total	**599**	**27**

Shrimp al vino blanco (sautéed in white wine) gets high marks, too, for its low fat content.

If you see pollo cacciatore on the menu, it's another good option—boneless chicken breast served in a tomato and mushroom sauce. The list also includes nonmeat (vegetable) lasagna, but you need to ask for low-fat cheeses or less cheese. Or try cioppino—fisherman's stew with a variety of seafood and vegetables in a tomato-based stock—after making certain that the stock is low in fat.

Enjoy pizza? Hold the olives, and ask for extra vegetables but half or one-third the normal amount of cheese. Onions, green peppers and mushrooms are good low-fat toppings, but you'll also want to try fresh spinach, garlic, tomatoes, artichoke hearts, beans, seafood, skinless turkey or chicken breast and other ingredients for an inviting change of pace.

Fiber's Back—And It's a Fat-Fighting Superstar

Eating fiber-rich foods is a healthy way to whittle your waistline and clobber cholesterol.

A few years back, all we seemed to hear about were the health benefits of fiber. Several studies had found that a high-fiber diet seemed to lessen the risk of chronic illnesses such as cancer and heart disease. Fiber eventually faded into the background while other trends took the spotlight (low-fat, anyone?). But now fiber is back—and this time it's a weight-loss superstar. Experts are urging people who want to shed extra pounds (and stay healthy) to bring on the fiber—lots of it.

(continued on page 102)

The Eat-Less Laxative

Irregular as it may sound, dietitians at King's College in London say that bulk laxatives containing psyllium—a natural ingredient found in products like Perdiem and Metamucil—will not only loosen you up but also reduce your appetite.

When people took psyllium granules at breakfast time and just before lunch, they not only felt full longer, they ate less fat during the day.

Fiber slows the digestion of fats and sugar, so it helps to flatten out big swings in blood sugar, which can interfere with appetite regulation, researchers say. Psyllium and other water-soluble fibers also help to fight fat another way, by reducing cholesterol levels in your blood.

NEW IN THE MARKETPLACE

Munchable Skinny Chips

Remember good old potato chips? The kind that left oily stains on your paper plate? They were—and still are—off-limits to anyone serious about cutting fat.

But who cares? Some of the new low-fat and fat-free varieties are so tasty that we'd choose them any day over the greasy originals. And we'll never miss regular chips' ten grams of fat and 160 calories per measly serving (about 16 chips). The new versions offer much less in the way of fat and about one-third fewer calories (some brands have even fewer).

We did get to sample the hottest new low-fat chips on the block, those made with the fake fat olestra. A product line of these chips, called Max, by Frito-Lay, includes regular and barbecue chips, Ruf-

FOOD	PORTION	FAT (G.)	CALORIES
Doritos Max Nacho Cheesier Tortilla Chips	11	1	90
Ruffles Max Original Potato Chips	17	0	75
Lay's Max Original Potato Chips	20	0	75
Baked Lay's Low-Fat Original Potato Chips	12	1.5	110
Low-Fat Baked Tostitos	9	1	110

fles, Doritos and Tostitos tortilla chips. All boast one gram of fat per serving and 30 to 50 percent fewer calories than their regular versions. Popular Pringles potato chips will also soon have an olestra version. However, they do have to carry a label warning of potential gastrointestinal side effects and vitamin depletion. (See "Olestra: Procter's Big Gamble" on page 54.)

Keep in mind, too, that even low-fat chips don't offer much in the way of nutrients, that they're fairly salty, and that they still contain a fair number of calories. As usual, you're better off if you don't eat the whole bag!

We nibbled our way through the newest low-fat chips available nationally. Here are the results.

COMMENTS

The hands-down favorite of the olestra-containing chips. Crisp, fresh, flavorful. "Taste just like the real thing!" Even those of us who went back for thirds had no gastrointestinal problems.

These are also made with olestra. Ruffles fans said they liked the real thing better, but most of us liked these just fine. "These chips even *feel* greasy."

Another olestra chip, and good enough that we had to restrain ourselves after two handfuls. Crisp, light, flavorful, authentic-tasting.

The hands-down low-fat favorite for taste. Light, crisp and fresh. We also loved the barbecue and sour cream flavors.

Tender and flavorful, hold their own with salsa.

(continued)

Munchable Skinny Chips—Continued

Food	Portion	Fat (g.)	Calories
Gibble's Baked 95% Fat-Free Potato Crisps	25	1.5	110
Keebler Baked Munch 'Ems	28	4	130
Baked Not Fried White Corn Tortilla Chips	20	1	110
Fine Foods' Fat-Free Baked Potato Chips	20	0	100
Louise's Fat-Free Original Potato Chips	30	0	110

Why? For one thing, the only way to lose weight, besides exercising, is to cut calories, and foods that are high in fiber—whole grains, beans and lentils, fruits and vegetables—tend to be naturally low in calories. Furthermore, fiber can help satisfy hunger. "Because it doesn't get broken down by the digestive enzymes in our bodies, fiber goes into the intestines as is, giving us that 'full' feeling," says Connie Diekman, a spokesperson for the American Dietetic Association and a nutrition consultant in St. Louis.

In addition to helping us eat less, foods that are rich in fiber promote regularity. And there's also evidence that people who eat a diet that's high in fiber have lower rates of colon cancer, breast cancer, diabetes and heart disease.

What's the best way to reap fiber's benefits? Eat a variety of high-fiber foods—the less processed the better. Don't rely only on fiber supplements, which may not be as balanced and complete as naturally occurring fiber and which lack the nutrients found in plant foods. For example, many important vitamins, minerals and phytochemicals—the cancer-preventing substances researchers have just discovered—happen to be found

COMMENTS

A light, crackery chip sturdy enough to scoop up dip or salsa. "A very good substitute for the real thing."

A tangy, light cracker-chip with a neat geometric shape and a nice hot aftertaste. It's true that a serving contains 4 grams of fat, but you get 28 crackers per serving—a whole bowlful!

A nice compromise product, with a bit of fat and decent taste. Sturdy enough to shovel salsa.

Here again, proof that a little fat goes a long way toward taste. We panned the fat-free version but liked this brand's All-Natural, Low-Fat Baked Potato Chip, with 1.5 grams of fat in 20 chips.

Okay if you must avoid all fat, but you won't have to worry about eating a whole bag of these things.

in the same foods that contain lots of fiber.

To stay fit and trim, you should consume a total of 20 to 35 grams of fiber daily from a variety of sources, advises Karen Miller-Kovach of Weight Watchers International, which has launched its own "Fat and Fiber Plan." For many people, that means doubling up on fiber, at least. Most Americans get only 10 to 15 grams of fiber a day.

As a rule, try to eat fiber-rich foods at each meal and for snacks. Whenever possible, substitute a serving of whole grains, fruit or vegetables for the low-fiber foods you'd ordinarily reach for. Have whole-grain instead of white toast for breakfast, replace fat-free cookies with air-popped popcorn for an afternoon snack, or eat a piece of fruit or a fresh fruit salad instead of nonfat cake for dessert. And try these five easy ways to up your fiber.

- Add broccoli, carrots, peppers and asparagus to your pasta to get eight grams of fiber per serving.

- Use whole-grain bread to turn a turkey sandwich into a high-fiber lunch with seven grams of fiber.
- Fiber-up basic potato salad with kidney beans, corn, beets and carrots for a whopping 13 grams per serving.
- Have vegetarian bean soup and whole-wheat bread as a hearty, filling meal with ten grams of fiber.
- Toss your salad with carrots, peas, corn and chick-peas for half your day's fiber supply—16 grams!

Top Tips from Real Fat-Fighting Experts

Six veterans of the dieting front lines share their secrets for low-fat eating, year after year.

Doctors, nutritionists, diet consultants, personal trainers—which of these experts is best suited to lead you to victory in the Fat Wars?

All have plenty of advice to offer on how to reduce dietary fat and drop weight, it's true. But their training as health-care professionals never requires them to do the same themselves.

But that's not the case for the fat-fighting experts featured here, because they were down in the trenches once themselves. They speak from experience when they describe what worked for them when they decided to trim down and eat healthier. These are the stories of personal triumph in the fight against fat.

Christine Muehling: Internet Low-Fat Expert

"NOW THAT LOW-FAT COOKING AND EATING ARE MY WAY OF LIFE, I CAN SPLURGE EVERY ONCE IN A WHILE, AND I DON'T FEEL GUILTY—OR DEPRIVED."

At 36, Christine Muehling had just about everything she wanted. She was a happy newlywed, enjoying life to its fullest in ritzy Silver Spring, Maryland. But although she was far from obese, at 140 pounds and only five feet two inches tall, she felt unhealthy.

"It started bothering me when I couldn't bend over without losing my breath," she says. She had always been on the thin side, but, she says,

Before

After

Christine Muehling goes online to share the tactics she's used to cut fat from her diet and lose weight.

"Over the course of a few years, I had gone from a size two to a size ten, and when I realized that, it made me cry." She wanted to get her trim shape back. But when she dieted, she usually ended up gaining more weight because all she could think about was food.

Nevertheless, not knowing what else to do, Christine eventually dropped the excess weight using a strict diet—not one she'd now recommend—under her doctor's supervision. She had the willpower to lose 18 pounds in six weeks, but she soon realized that the diet, based on cabbage soup and salads, wouldn't do for the long haul.

"I wanted to live in the 'Real Food World'! I knew that perpetual dieting wasn't going to get me there," she says. "I finally realized that there were lots of low-fat foods I could enjoy, and I learned how to select them and to prepare them myself."

As part of that process, Christine became an expert label reader—checking fat grams and calories per serving before she put anything in her shopping cart. She has kept her fat intake down to a low 10 to 20 percent of calories. "I make a conscious choice about what I put in my mouth. I'm in control, not the food," she says.

Using her natural creativity, she has reworked favorite recipes into low-fat versions, opening up a whole new world of flavors. Fruits, vegetables and grains now take center stage on her plate, where red meat and rich cream sauces were once the main event. Dining is once again an adventure in the Real Food World, only lighter.

What started out as a weight-maintenance duty has become a passion for Christine. Not only has she maintained her new size four, she's become low-fat royalty of sorts as well. She has become so active responding to queries and comments on CompuServe's "Good Health" weight-loss forum (an online message center and exchange for people seeking information about weight management) that she jokingly proclaims herself the "low-fat/no-fat queen."

"I just love sharing fat-free food reviews and recipes online. It makes me feel good to help other people achieve the success I have, and to give them hope. The support I receive in turn helps keep me on track," says Christine. Besides, she adds, you can never have too many fat-reducing tips. Did you know, for instance, that Butter Buds work wonders as a replacement in butter-based sauces? And that evaporated skim milk or pureed nonfat cottage cheese can substitute for cream in most dishes?

Although she eats mostly vegetarian fare these days, Christine still allows herself a little indulgence every now and again as part of her Real Food World experience. A good cut of prime rib is her favorite food, so instead of denying her taste buds, she appeases them.

"I make sure to plan ahead for that steak, so I eat extremely low-fat before and after it," she says. Granted, the steak is only a fraction of the size it used to be, and it's accompanied by vegetables and nonfat condiments, with only a tiny spread of blue cheese, but it's a rarity that's enjoyed as something special. "Now that low-fat cooking and eating are my way of life, I can splurge every once in a while, and I don't feel guilty—or deprived."

Today, after keeping the 20 or so pounds off for well over a year, Christine can't imagine life without her healthier eating habits. She's obsessed not with her weight but with feeling healthy. In fact, she doesn't even own a scale!

"I can bend over without feeling pinched, and I feel so much better about myself," she says. "I think that's because I channeled my energy into something positive for myself and then shared it with others."

And who wouldn't feel good about that?

Joe Garrett: Healthy Heart Quest Left Him Leaner

"NOW THAT I KNOW HOW TO SPOT HIGH-FAT FOODS
AND KNOW WHAT THEY CAN DO TO ME, TWINKIES JUST
AREN'T AS APPEALING AS THEY USED TO BE."

Investment bankers know how to read numbers. Maybe that's why, when Joe Garrett of Berkeley, California, was told a few years ago that he had a cholesterol level of 235, he knew that he had a problem.

"My doctor sat me down and said, 'Look, your cholesterol is way too high, and I want you to do something about it,'" he explains. "I could tell from the look on her face that this was serious."

His new, leaner diet lets Joe Garrett enjoy an occasional steak or rich dessert but still keep his cholesterol within a healthy low range.

Joe, who was in his mid-forties, had seen his father deal with heart disease, but he hadn't really thought about how his own health might be in question. Long hours at work, where junk food was the fastest and easiest to eat, left little time for educating himself about heart disease, let alone preventing it.

"I knew nothing about nutrition, so I read a lot of books about heart health and grabbed whatever information I could on the topic. It was clear that diet was an important factor," he says. That meant high-fat foods like steaks and Twinkies were no longer guiltless pleasures.

He began concentrating on what he ate, opting for low-fat foods and oat bran, which he had read would help lower his cholesterol. To boost his efforts, Joe began working out three or four times a week, doing mostly cardiovascular exercise, and he took niacin supplements as well. "In six weeks, my cholesterol had dropped 40 percent. I was amazed," he says.

Although he wasn't aiming to lose weight, the lighter way of eating and the increase in exercise helped Joe shed 13 pounds, too. At 5 feet 11 inches, his old weight of 185 pounds didn't look or feel overweight to him, but at 172 pounds he realized that he had lost some flab, that his muscles had became visible, and that he looked much more fit than before.

Now 20 pounds slimmer than before, Joe has maintained both the lower cholesterol level and the trimmer physique for more than a year and a half. "It's not as hard as people think to keep the weight off when you acknowledge how it gets put on in the first place," he says. "I think an important aspect of long-term low-fat eating is not to get down on yourself if you slip up once in a while. You just have to get over it and get back on course again."

So Joe does allow himself not-so-heart-healthy things in moderation. He has a juicy steak once in a while, or a rich dessert, but he doesn't let that snowball into a daily occurrence. He dwells not on the foods he can't have but rather on the bounty of savory foods that he can have, such as whatever fruits and vegetables are in season.

"The easiest way for me to keep my diet in check is to read labels," he says. "Now that I know how to spot high-fat foods and know what they can do to me, Twinkies just aren't as appealing as they used to be."

At the same time, he doesn't let it bother him if he doesn't know exactly what's in every morsel of food he consumes. By not overeating and limiting his high-fat favorites, he has been able to keep his leaner eating style simple, his body fit and trim and his cholesterol well within the low-risk range.

Suzanne Cieutat: Tough Times Led to Shape-Up

"WHEN I LOST MY OLD JOB, I DECIDED I NEEDED TO LIVE HEALTHIER. I THOUGHT THAT I HAD BETTER DO SOMETHING GOOD FOR MYSELF OR I'D GO CRAZY."

The year 1993 isn't one that Suzanne Cieutat of Eugene, Oregon, remembers fondly. That was the year she was laid off from her job and found herself stuck at home. She was out of shape, 30 pounds overweight and understandably blue.

But 1994, the year of her 44th birthday, is a year she'll always cherish. That's because it marks the turnaround point in her life, starting with a healthier body. Why did Suzanne choose such a difficult time in her life

Hard times motivated Suzanne Cieutat to shape up, drop weight and reduce her cholesterol by 30 points.

Before   After

to get in shape? "When I lost my old job, I decided I needed to live healthier. I thought that I had better do something good for myself or I'd go crazy, so I started walking," she says. With that in mind, she turned a negative into a positive, plus some.

She began walking to gain energy. "I needed to be happy, and getting out there in the fresh air with my body moving really made me feel good," says Suzanne. Starting out with just short walks a few times a week, she gradually worked up to four miles a day, five days a week. "The physical activity was invaluable in reducing stress and maintaining my self-esteem during my employment search in a very competitive job market," says Suzanne. She had given up on trying to lose weight years before after twice losing, then devastatingly regaining, the excess pounds.

This time, without consciously trying to lose weight, she dropped ten pounds. Since this was a good start, Suzanne thought she'd see what would happen if she improved her eating habits. "I started cutting my fat intake to 20 percent of calories and gradually shifting to a primarily vegetarian diet," she explains.

By 1995, another 23 pounds had come off, she had gone down four dress sizes, her cholesterol had dropped from 200 to 170, and finally she was able to temporarily stop taking the blood pressure medications she had never liked. The bunions on her feet even got better. "I got a new job, too, and I'm sure the self-esteem I built from getting myself in shape was a factor," she says.

To keep herself at a trim 115 pounds, Suzanne makes sure she never says *diet*. "The word sounds so restricting; I like to keep my options open," she says. When she gets cravings for something to nibble on, pretzels and low-fat microwave popcorn satisfy her almost as well as chips, without all that unwanted fat. When it comes to sweets, she allows herself to indulge sparingly: a maximum of two cookies or a small piece of cake, the reduced-fat kind, of course. "At work, there are lots of rich sweets and junk food available, so I just don't take any, since I find it hard to stop munching once I start," she says. Instead she makes sure she has a supply of fruit available so that there is something on hand that she can eat without a second thought.

Her current exercise routine includes 50 minutes on a nonmotorized treadmill five times a week and a 40-minute outdoor walk at lunch four times a week. "I have a lifestyle that I can maintain, because I really enjoy it. If I eat too much on a rare occasion, well, I know that at least I'm exercising. If I miss a walk on a rare occasion, I know that at least I ate healthy that day. I have a safety net."

Don Mauer: From Cottage Cheese to Cottage Industry

"PEOPLE LIKE MY COLUMN, MY BOOKS AND MY LECTURES BECAUSE I'VE GOT 113 POUNDS WORTH OF 'BEEN-THERE' EXPERIENCE. HECK, I'M THERE RIGHT NOW."

People in the Chicago area may be familiar with Don Mauer's recipes and low-fat eating advice, which appear regularly in his *Daily Herald* column. Folks near Raleigh, North Carolina, where Don lives, may be familiar with some of the cooking seminars he gives. Healthy cooks may even be familiar with his *Lean and Lovin' It* cookbook. But what most people aren't familiar with is how this once-obese photo lab technician turned his quest for a healthier life into entrepreneurial prosperity.

In 1990, at age 42, Don was careening down disaster alley with his health. His five-foot-eight-inch body weighed 306 pounds, his cholesterol was at a dangerous all-time high of 260, he got out of breath easily, and he could hardly stand to look in a mirror. His doctor put him on a strict, hospital-supervised liquid diet, but he had been down that road before. "I must have lost 1,000 pounds, and put on 1,200 pounds, with all

The quest for low-fat living evolved into a new career for cookbook author Don Mauer.

Before   After

the yo-yo dieting I had done in the past," says Don. Remembering how lousy it felt to put the weight back on and realizing how expensive the hospital weight-loss program was, he swore, "If I lose this weight, I will keep it off for good this time.

"Most of my weight came off under the hospital's liquid diet, but their maintenance plan scared me to death," says Don, who also found his cholesterol dropped to under 200. "The doctors gave me an exchange diet plan that just made no sense to me."

Then, just as he was beginning to feel desperate, friends suggested that he get some books that list the calories and fat in foods. He did, but after poring through the books and trying some of the unexciting low-fat recipes, he knew he'd have to take matters into his own hands—or shall we say *pans*—in order to find a menu he could live with forever.

"I love to cook. It's one of my favorite things to do," he says. "I figured that if I know what's going into my meals, I can make sure I eat right." Soon gourmet low-fat recipes were flowing from his kitchen. His creations got rave reviews from friends and family, so he proposed to newspapers in his area that he write a column on healthy eating. The *Daily Herald* in Chicago picked up his column, and a new career was born. Today, cookbooks, lectures and even cable-TV cooking shows are all in a day's work for Don.

"People like my column, my books and my lectures because I've got 113 pounds worth of 'been-there' experience. Heck, I'm there right now," he says. Even though it has been five years since he lost the weight, Don keeps his healthy regimen going strong. Besides low-fat cooking, he credits regular walking, running and aerobics for his success. "I was always an obese kid, so exercise and sports were embarrassing things to do. But now I look forward to exercising and wish I had done it sooner," he says.

No stranger to temptation, Don keeps his thinking cap on when it comes to chocolate. "I like it so much that I had to come up with a chocolate cake recipe that is very low fat, just so I could get that flavor," he says. Another trouble spot is dining out. Don and his wife love to go out to eat, but these days they have learned how to get around the really rich foods that fill most menus. First they call and find out what days and times the restaurant is not busy, and they choose those days to go. Then Don asks the server to find out which dishes the chef can prepare with little butter or oil.

"Sometimes the waiter or waitress even recommends a healthy dish they normally eat there," he says. "More people than you think are trying to eat right." Don has even taken fat-free cheese to pizza parlors and asked the chef to use it instead of the regular stuff. "Most chefs, if they aren't busy, are very accommodating to nice customers who are watching what they eat," he says. "Sometimes I'm the only change of pace they get from their everyday jobs."

Don is careful not to make food a reward for losing weight. Instead, as he reached a weight-loss goal, he'd treat himself to a new article of clothing in his desired size. "I now have a closet full of beautiful sweaters and shirts I can wear, and each one reminds me of how good it felt the day I achieved another goal," he says. "And as I got too small for my old clothes, I didn't let them sit around in case I ever got heavy again. I filled a box with them, and the box went off to a church fund for underprivileged families."

Don also marked his weight-loss goals with purchases of new music. He now has a huge collection of jazz and classical CDs, and each time he plays one he's reminded of how far he has come.

"I tell anyone who asks me how they, too, can lose weight that it can only happen if you believe you can do it," says Don. "I think back to where I was several years ago, and I can hardly believe how well things turned out. And if I can do it, anybody can—maybe not the same way I did, but they can do it. I'm not saying it's easy, I'm just saying that it's really worth it."

Julie Hunt: From Pudgy to Powerhouse

"EVEN THOUGH I NOW WEIGHT TRAIN, I STILL USE MY
FOOD LOG TO HELP ME KEEP TRACK OF WHAT I'M EATING."

Julie Hunt was in the fourth grade when she began helping out at her father's corner variety store. Pizza, ice cream and lots of other fat-laden foods were all around her as she spent practically every day, from after school until after dinner, in the store. Julie, now in her late twenties, remembers how quickly she put on weight during that time. "I had to be there, food was all around me, it was free and in endless supply. What kid wouldn't eat a lot?" asks the Lewiston, Maine, nutritional supply sales agent.

By age 19, Julie weighed 230 pounds and was miserable. "I was tired of being the fat girl people made fun of all the time, tired of not being able to wear clothes like everybody else, of boys not noticing me," says Julie. "I know now there's more to life than that, but try convincing somebody that young of that."

Julie set out on her own to lose weight. She watched every fat gram and calorie, using her personal food log to record all the good and bad details of her eating habits. She gave up on her favorite foods, starting with hot dogs, when she saw how much fat those seemingly little things contributed to her diet. Her plan worked well enough to bring her weight down to 170 pounds in just under a year. But then she hit a snag.

Julie's weight hit a plateau despite her efforts to eat a healthy diet, so she turned to exercise in hopes of losing the rest. With some research, she learned that with just three 30-minute workouts a week, she might be able to boost her metabolism enough to achieve her goal of 130 pounds. "I was so ready to do something drastic that when I learned how little exercise I needed, I worked out five times a week just because I couldn't believe three times was enough," says Julie. She started out on a $40 secondhand stationary bike. "The first five minutes were always the hardest back then, but after that it got so much easier," she says. Before she knew it, the pounds were coming off again.

Julie became so enthralled with fitness that she began weight training at age 22. When she's not spending free time in the gym, she's helping judge body-building competitions, taking martial arts courses, roller skating and biking. But even with her high-intensity workouts, she keeps her eating habits healthy and low-fat.

When her low-fat eating plan stalled, Julie Hunt turned to exercise to help her reach her ideal weight.

Before   After

"Even though I now weight train, I still use my food log to help me keep track of what I'm eating," she says. While she's not fanatical about writing down every morsel of food that goes into her mouth, she does keep tabs on snacks and meals to make sure her fat count doesn't creep up too high on a regular basis. Julie now weighs 150 pounds, but at five feet seven inches, she's lean, tight muscle and still wears the same clothes she did at 130 pounds. She also feels better than she ever did before.

"When I tell people how big I used to be, they can't believe it. I hope all large girls out there can do what I did, because it's very empowering to take control of your life that way," she says.

Julie cautions others to be wary of quick-fix gimmicks that promise rapid weight loss without effort. "If you don't take a healthy approach, believe me, you'll either gain it all back eventually or you won't see any results," she says.

She also recommends that you forgive yourself for the slips you're bound to make and that you look to others for support. "Being around people who understand how important weight loss is to you, and who empathize with what you're going through, is really valuable," she says. "It can really keep you from feeling depressed and can help keep you motivated on your journey."

Craig Downey: Brotherly Bonding Leads to a Slimmer Sibling

"I was lucky my brother was there working out and eating better with me. We'd push each other to reach our goals, and we had an unspoken pact with each other to stick with it."

The wake-up call came to Craig Downey at age 20, when he was exhausted and sweating in an icy-cold fraternity basement after climbing just a few steps.

It was only his sophomore year in college, but he was fed up. The six-foot-two football player was unhappy being a formless blob under shoulder pads, valued more for his sheer mass than for his athletic talent. He was also unhappy with his weight off the field, to the point where he'd no longer get on a scale. During what should have been a carefree time in his life, Craig was disappointed at weighing 365 pounds. Things had to change.

"I was always a chubby kid, but good in sports, so people didn't bother me much about it. That made it easy to deny all the way into college," says Craig. "One day it just hit me: I'm really large now."

That same summer, Craig made his move toward a healthier life. He was home with his older brother, Aiden, who was looking to build up some muscles before he returned to school, and the two brothers got into shape together. They dined on low-fat turkey sandwiches, pasta and vegetables and gave up all junk foods and alcohol. They ate only fruit before noon, which eliminated all the high-fat breakfast foods like doughnuts and fried eggs. And they quit eating after 6:00 P.M., not an easy task for collegiate night owls.

"We tried to avoid as much fat as possible, but we didn't worry about calories," says Craig. They drank at least 64 ounces of water a day and accompanied each other to the gym and on runs every night. As the weeks flew by, Craig trimmed down and toned up to the tune of a 55-pound weight loss.

"I was lucky my brother was there working out and eating better with me. We'd push each other to reach our goals, and we had an unspoken pact with each other to stick with it," says Craig. Aiden was lucky, too, because he beefed up just as he hoped he would. The brothers also became closer and had a newfound respect for each other's accomplishments.

Buddying up with his brother helped Craig Downey stick with low-fat eating and shed 75 pounds.

Before   After

Back at school for his junior year, Craig's friends and teammates didn't recognize him. Even his face looked different without the excess fat. For football season, his lighter body (now 260 pounds) and increased strength brought Craig's play to new heights. He finally made first string. After the season, Craig took off another 20 pounds or so and has stayed that trim. "Even now, I try to always leave something on my plate and pass on second helpings if I'm not truly hungry anymore," he says. He still occasionally enjoys nachos with salsa and cheese, but mostly he snacks on low-fat pretzels or cereal. Low-fat foods have become his preference, not his penance. "I'm so used to eating healthy that I just automatically grab ground turkey instead of ground beef at the supermarket or make vegetarian chili instead of the regular kind," he says.

Today, Craig has replaced the pigskin with rollerblades, bicycles and golf clubs, and he and his wife walk or work out together as often as they can.

"I don't get bored or resentful, because my workouts are always changing," he says. His blood pressure and cholesterol are both low, thanks to his healthy lifestyle. Now in his late twenties, this healthy man is way ahead of most of his peers when it comes to preventing degenerative disease. "My father died of colon cancer when I was just a baby," he says. "So I know you can never be too young to reduce your risks through diet and exercise."

The Biology of a Pig-Out

What happens when you eat too much for your own good? A lot. Here's how your body deals with serious food overloads and how you can minimize the damage.

The proof is in the stuffing. If you're one of those rare souls who's trying to gain weight, your best bet is to stuff yourself with as much high-fat food as you can tolerate at a single sitting. That's because every time you eat a particle more fat than your body can use, it's immediately deposited into your fat cells. But if you're looking to *understand* weight gain, well, it's not quite so simple.

Normally, the body has a repertoire of physiological cues to help us cut short a pig-out. When we eat more than we're used to, receptors in the stomach send out a fullness signal. This feeling is actually illusory, though, because the stomach can continue expanding for a good while if you continue eating. As nutrients empty into the gut, hormones are released that signal the brain that we've had enough.

Just walking into a restaurant that serves gigantic portions can be an invitation to gorge yourself.

"These physiological cues may not necessarily keep you from eating more, because they're easily overridden by social cues," says Barbara Rolls, Ph.D., director of the Laboratory for Human Ingestive Behavior at Pennsylvania State University in University Park, who studies the behavioral and physiological influences of food intake.

One of the most powerful cues when it comes to overeating is social acceptability. We all have culturally bound ideas about how much we should eat, but when given permission from other people, we can eat

NEWS FLASH

Drink Up—And Chow Down

It's no news that immoderate drinking can make it hard to lose weight. But while it may seem obvious to place the blame on the high calorie content of alcoholic beverages, that's not the fat-fatal flaw that Canadian researchers discovered about those who like to tip back a few when they dine.

Twelve men took part in two sessions during which they were given either alcohol and a high-fat appetizer or no alcohol and a low-fat hors d'oeuvre. After eating their premeal treats, the men were free to choose how much they ate as an entrée.

When the men had alcohol and fatty foods first, they overate significantly more during the rest of the meal than when they had no alcohol and ate the low-fat equivalent.

"Since the total calories in both appetizers were the same, we believe the type of food, not the number of calories, influenced how much the men ate before they were full," says Angelo Tremblay, Ph.D., professor of physiology and nutrition at Laval University in St. Foy, Quebec.

"It may be that the low-fat appetizers helped satisfy hunger more quickly, taking the edge off appetite and signaling the men to stop eating sooner," Dr. Tremblay says. These appetizers contained mostly carbohydrates, which break down quickly in the body into glucose, or blood sugar, helping to produce a feeling of satiety. "Or maybe something about the combination of alcohol and fatty foods interferes with the body's normal signals to stop eating," he adds.

The next step is to find out what signals are at work in the body during these real-life situations, Dr. Tremblay says.

In the meantime, if you know that having a few beers makes you eat a whole pepperoni pizza, you'll want to avoid it or set strict limits on how much you'll drink when you're determined to cut calories, says Dr. Tremblay.

more. Think about Thanksgiving dinner or special birthdays.

Just walking into a restaurant that serves gigantic portions—or one that offers an all-you-can-eat buffet—can be an invitation to gorge yourself. In fact, a study at the University of Pennsylvania in Philadelphia found that restaurants with open buffets tend to cater to twice as many overweight customers as restaurants with table service. The attraction, it seems, is that a smorgasbord makes overeating more socially acceptable at the same time that it makes large amounts of appealing food available.

Even without tacit permission to overeat, dining with company tends to increase your food intake. Studies have shown that women are much more likely to overeat in a convivial group of women than when they're alone or with a date.

The pleasure of eating can also override the feeling of satiation, especially if the food is varied in flavor and texture. "When they're eating a single food, most people will stop short of overeating because they tire of the food. Eating several foods at once makes you more likely to overeat," Dr. Rolls explains. As anyone who has shared a variety of entrées at a Chinese restaurant can attest, sampling from here and there makes it much easier to finish off all the dishes.

How Your Body Handles Overeating

In the hours immediately after you eat a large meal, the body performs a rapid triage of the nutrients you've consumed, selecting which ones will be used immediately and which will be stored. Carbohydrates go first: They're immediately converted into glucose and burned to meet the body's energy requirements. If you eat more carbohydrates in one sitting than your body needs (a common occurrence), they're transformed into glycogen—a material that the body is able to store away in muscles and the liver, using it when it's needed for energy, explains Jean-Pierre Flatt, Ph.D., professor of biochemistry at the University of Massachusetts Medical School in Boston, who studies the factors that affect body weight.

Carbohydrates, then, are not immediately transformed into fat. For that to happen, you have to eat them in excess for several days, until the body slips into a kind of carbohydrate overload. Protein, meanwhile, is rapidly broken down into essential amino acids—the old "building blocks" needed for maintenance and repair of body tissues. Amino acids

What Happens to That 2,000-Calorie Dinner?

Here's how your body handles a major evening pig-out. Most of the carbohydrate and protein calories are burned as fuel or stored in the liver as glycogen, a form of sugar later used by the muscles as fuel.

Some 750 excess calories of dietary fat, however, will end up on your hips, waist or wherever as three additional ounces of body fat. Overeat enough times and you'll soon be carrying around a few extra pounds.

Nutrient	Total Calories	Calories Burned	Calories Stored	Form of Storage
Carbohydrate	700	550	150	Glycogen
Protein	300	200	100	Glycogen
Fat	1,000	250	750	Fat

pass from the digestive tract into the blood and are carried to tissues throughout the body.

The relationship between excess protein and carbs is a simple one: When you eat more protein than the body immediately needs, it is converted into carbohydrates. "Eating protein has about the same effect on weight as (eating) carbohydrates. Overeating protein at a single meal won't make you gain weight. But if you eat too much every day for a number of days, it will eventually be transformed into fat," says Xavier Pi-Sunyer, M.D., an obesity researcher at St. Luke's–Roosevelt Hospital Center in New York City.

Fat, of course, is the body's last choice for fuel. It is burned only when there aren't enough carbohydrates around to meet your energy requirements. This means that if you eat more calories at one sitting than you need, the fat is left there, a kind of nutritional wallflower. And there's the rub, because the body treats excess fat very differently than it does carbohydrates or proteins.

For instance, soon after a meal, fat is chopped up within the intestines into smaller and smaller components and made ready for delivery via the

(continued on page 124)

NEWS FLASH

The New Diet Pills: Why They Work

Have you ever wished for a magic pill to make you trim? Well, the new weight-loss pills that have the diet industry turned on its ear don't actually promise to melt pounds away, but they can help some overweight people curb the urge to overeat.

These drugs don't just help get the weight off, either. With long-term use, they help keep it off.

These medications help control the impulse to overeat by increasing the availability of certain brain chemicals—serotonin or norepinephrine. These send appetite-signal receptors in the brain a message of fullness and satisfaction: "I've had all I need. I can stop eating now."

Before you ask your doctor for a prescription, make sure you're a likely candidate for these drugs. They should be reserved for those who are at least 30 pounds overweight and have a long history of diet failures, says Steven Lamm, M.D., clinical assistant professor of medicine at New York University Medical Center in New York City and author of *Thinner at Last*. Occasionally, doctors prescribe them for people who are less than 30 pounds overweight but whose weight is contributing to serious medical problems such as diabetes or high blood pressure.

For people who fit the bill, the most commonly used drugs are fenfluramine (Pondimin) and phentermine (Ionamin), prescribed together and known as fen-phen. "Either drug would be effective, but together they help reduce each other's side effects," says Dr. Lamm. Fenfluramine is somewhat sedating, while phentermine acts as a stimulant.

As for side effects, two-thirds of people taking the fen-phen combination develop dry mouth, and fewer than 20 percent experience constipation, nausea, drowsiness, headaches, excitability or short-term memory loss.

Another form of fenfluramine, dexfenfluramine (Redux), has received the Food and Drug Administration's (FDA) stamp of approval.

Researchers hope that dexfenfluramine will be better tolerated and, if used with phentermine, may have fewer side effects than the fen-phen combination, says Richard L. Atkinson, M.D., professor of medicine and nutritional science at the University of Wisconsin in Madison.

A potential concern about dexfenfluramine is that several animal studies suggest possible nerve damage from continued use, which is one reason that a group of neuroscientists requested that the FDA withhold its approval until the safety question has been answered. Dr. Lamm and other supporters, however, say claims of nerve damage have not been substantiated, and damage probably would not occur at the dosages prescribed for humans.

The FDA has approved the use of fenfluramine and phentermine for up to 12 weeks for obesity. However, physicians across the United States have been impressed with the results of the combination of these two drugs and are using it for longer periods of time, says Dr. Lamm.

The FDA has approved the use of dexfenfluramine for up to one year as a treatment for obesity. Studies have yet to examine the possible side effects of using it for longer than a year, but this drug is similar enough to fenfluramine that it's unlikely that any new severe side effects will show up with its long-term use, says Dr. Atkinson.

Even while taking these drugs, you'll have to keep your fat intake at less than 30 percent of calories and exercise regularly. "They don't melt off fat. They just level the playing field so you can play the game like everybody else," says Dr. Lamm.

And unfortunately, if you stop taking the drugs, you'll have to work hard to maintain your weight loss. Many people find that the pounds pile back on, which is why many of the doctors who prescribe these drugs are recommending long-term use despite the FDA's recommendations, says Dr. Lamm.

bloodstream to cells throughout the body. Where *exactly* does it go? That depends on how much of it you've eaten and how active you are afterward. If the fat you've eaten is part of a meal that contains no more calories than your body needs, the fat is delivered to muscle and other cells that can burn it right away. If you eat a large load of fat, you still may be able to burn it over time if you are consistently very active—if you run marathons, say, or do cross-country skiing.

Muscles, it turns out, contain enzymes that promote fat-burning when the muscle is in use, explains Ronald M. Krauss, M.D., head of molecular and nuclear medicine at the Lawrence Berkeley National Laboratory at the University of California, Berkeley, and chairman of the Nutrition Committee for the American Heart Association. "If

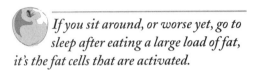

If you sit around, or worse yet, go to sleep after eating a large load of fat, it's the fat cells that are activated.

you sit around, or worse yet, go to sleep after eating a large load of fat," Dr. Krauss says, "it's the fat cells that are activated. It takes them only four to eight hours to absorb most of the fat you've taken in."

Although alcohol is fat-free, the body can transform it into fatty acids suitable for storage in fat tissues while also reducing the amount of total fat that is burned. Have a single margarita on top of a high-fat meal, and you've reduced your calorie-burning potential by 100 calories. Some buzz.

Morning-After Appetite?

Even if you go to bed feeling as if you never want to see another morsel of food, you may wake up with your usual appetite—or worse, you may be twice as hungry as usual.

"No one has ever done a formal study about how appetite is affected by eating a huge meal," says Dr. Rolls, "but over the years, I've informally surveyed people. About half say there's no effect; the other half find that their appetite is dramatically increased the next day. I can't explain why."

One reason that most of us have at least our usual appetite several hours after a huge meal is that between dinner and breakfast time, people in good health can effortlessly digest and metabolize even an exceedingly heavy meal—2,000 calories or more, with 1,000 of those from fat. That's as many calories as a woman should eat in an entire day if she wants to maintain a

FAT STATS

Who's Losing

- Over the past ten years, percentage increase in the number of overweight Americans: 28
- Number of American women who believe they are overweight: 48 million
- Number who actually are overweight: 32 million
- Number of Americans who are on a diet: 48 million
- Number of these who are women: 31 million
- Percentage of Americans who diet by cutting down on high-fat, high-calorie foods: 93
- Percentage of Americans who diet by counting calories: 39
- Percentage of people who have fasted for a day or more to lose weight: 24
- Percentage of people who have taken diet pills: 32

stable body weight, and way too much fat. So where does it all go?

"Overnight, your body uses nearly half of the calories you eat," Dr. Flatt explains. "You burn most of the carbohydrates and protein and store the rest as glycogen. But you only burn about a quarter of the fat, and by morning the rest of it— about 750 calories' worth— has already been stored away in your fat tissues. So you are pretty much back to ground zero."

 Repeat all-you-can-eat sessions regularly and weight gain will mount quickly.

Eating 750 more fat calories than you need translates into a gain of about a fifth of a pound of fat—a bit more than three ounces. That's not much, but if you had equipment that was sensitive enough, you could measure it. Repeat all-you-can-eat sessions regularly—the way many people do over the holiday season—and weight gain will mount quickly. You won't need sensitive equipment to see that.

Every time you overload on fat, fat tissues grow imperceptibly. As fat cells (adipocytes) absorb fat, they expand, and as adipocytes expand, so do the body's fat deposits. Researchers used to believe that adults had a fixed number of fat cells. But more recent studies have shown that chronic overeating can push new adipocytes to develop, which enlarges the pool of expandable fat cells.

Even knowing all of this, engaging in the occasional pig-out is hard to resist. And yet there is one more thing you can do to minimize the damage. "If you know you're going to be eating a very large meal, compensate in advance," advises Judith S. Stern, Sc.D., professor of nutrition and internal medicine at the University of California, Davis.

Dr. Stern suggests that you try "calorie banking," which consists of eating a lighter-than-usual dinner the night before, followed by a very small, low-fat breakfast and lunch on the day of the big meal. Finally, she says, "an hour or two before the meal, have a small snack, such as fat-free yogurt. Then you won't come to the table ravenous. You'll be less likely to really stuff yourself, and you'll enjoy the meal more."

The New Scoop
on Liquid Calories

Here's how to choose among coffees, soft drinks
and after-dinner drinks to save on calories and fat.

Determined to lose weight, you spend an agonizing hour on the stair-climber or stationary bike. Then, sweaty and thirsty, you reach for your favorite fruit drink. Big mistake. Unwittingly, you may have just swallowed more calories than you burned.

From flavored "water beverages" to coffee drinks and—here's a surprise—bottled iced teas, those seemingly harmless drinks can add up to a lot of calories by the end of the day. "Often people keep meticulous track of what they eat, but they don't record their fluid intake," says Felicia Busch, R.D., a spokesperson for the American Dietetic Association.

Particularly misunderstood are sparkling or flavored water beverages, such as Clearly Canadian and Sparkling Hawaiian Ice. They're often confused with no-cal carbonated mineral water. But there's a big difference. "Just because a drink is clear doesn't mean it's calorie-free," Busch notes. "Sparkling water may be one of the ingredients, but they also add corn syrup or some other sweetener and call it a sparkling water beverage."

An 11-ounce bottle of Clearly Canadian mountain blackberry drink, for example, contains 130 calories. That's almost equal to a 12-ounce can of Pepsi. On the other hand, says Busch, if the drink is just sparkling water, it will contain an essence of flavor but no calories.

Cappuccino Calories Count

Suppose you frequent one of the coffee bars that have sprung up everywhere. True, basic black coffee is virtually calorie-free. And a few drops of milk won't trip you up too badly. But cappuccinos, mochas and lattes, all brewed from espresso beans, are another story. The beans are not the culprits; it's what else goes into the drinks. Just what do you think makes those bitter beans so palatable? Fat, of course, from the whole milk, whipped cream and chocolate syrup that get added.

For example, a 16-ounce mocha from Starbucks contains 390 calories and 25 grams of fat. (A Quarter Pounder from McDonald's weighs in at 420 calories and 20 grams of fat.) Fortunately, Starbucks offers a skim milk option, and most coffee bars now serve drinks with low-fat milk—

Where the Calories Are

Soda is not the only beverage that's packed with calories. Here's how some popular drinks stack up against a 12-ounce can of Pepsi, which has no fat but 150 calories. (Some of these drinks are available in diet versions made with artificial sweeteners.)

BEVERAGE	SERVING (OZ.)	FAT (G.)	CALORIES
Arizona Iced Tea (lemon-flavored)	20	0	238
Clearly Canadian (mountain blackberry)	11	0	130
Crystal Geyser Mountain Spring Sparkler (peach)	10	0	111
Fruitopia (Fruit Integration)	16	0	240
Jamaican Gold iced cappuccino (mocha)	11	2.5	145
Maxwell House Cappio iced cappuccino	8	2.5	130
Minute Maid orange juice	16	0	230
Ocean Spray Cranapple	10	0	200
Snapple Iced Tea (lemon-flavored)	16	0	220
Sparkling Hawaiian Ice (Orange Sunset)	10	0	70

Bar Exam

Think you're doing your arteries (not to mention your potbelly) a favor by passing up the cheesecake in favor of a little Bailey's on the rocks? Think again. That tumbler of Irish Cream holds more than 200 calories and nearly nine grams of fat, about as much as that evil slice of cheesecake lurking on the dessert cart.

But how were you to know? Liquor manufacturers aren't required to put this information on their labels. So we did the analysis for you. Here are some of the leaner "dessert" drinks.

BEVERAGE	SERVING (OZS.)	FAT (G.)	CALORIES	% CALORIES FROM FAT
Amaretto di Saronno	2	0	190	0
Bailey's Original Irish Cream Light	2	3.8	152	22.5
Cockburn's Special Reserve Porto	3	0	159	0
Courvoisier V.S.O.P. Cognac	2	0	132	0
Kahlúa Coffee Liqueur	2	0	200	0
Romana Sambuca	2	0	258	0

but only if you ask for it. So ask for it. And espresso contains no calories or fat.

How Fruit Juice Adds Up

Even fruit juices packed with essential nutrients may deliver more calories than you bargained for. "Just think about how many oranges it takes to make a glass of orange juice," says nutritionist Chris Rosenbloom, R.D., Ph.D., professor of nutrition and dietetics at Georgia State University in Atlanta. "An orange has only about 60 calories, but if it takes five to make one of those large glasses (12 ounces or more) of juice, that can really add up." If you're trying to keep calories down, Dr. Rosenbloom suggests diluting juices with club soda or sparkling water.

Despite all of these pitfalls, drinking plenty of liquids is essential to good health. To stay properly hydrated, drink at least eight (eight-ounce) glasses of water or other liquids a day. Fruit juices and sparkling water beverages count toward this quota, but coffee should not. Although researchers debate coffee's fluid contribution, count your cup of coffee as half a glass of water. Java is a diuretic, which causes your body to excrete fluids. Don't count alcohol, either; it's another source of "hidden" calories. A 4-ounce glass of wine comes in at about 70 calories, and a 12-ounce beer has 145.

By all means, keep those liquids flowing. Just remember to think before you drink.

Minimize Fat
with Mini-Meals

**It's not just what you eat, it's when you eat
that counts. Here's how six mini-meals a day
can help keep the fat away.**

First came low-fat and high-fiber, still the top commandments for healthy eating. But evidence is piling up that there's an extra secret that people need to learn for an optimal diet. Many experts now believe that it's not simply what you eat, it's also how you eat that has an effect on your health and weight.

Enter the mini-meal philosophy. It's a way of eating in which you munch five or six mini-meals and snacks of filling foods—mainly high in fiber and low in fat—every day. That's in contrast to the usual three full meals daily. It's also a big shift from the all-too-common habit of skipping breakfast, skimping on lunch and then chowing down like Paul Bunyan at dinner and beyond. (Recognize yourself here?)

Researchers have known for some time that eating mini-meal-style can help reduce cholesterol. Now more studies indicate that the mini-meal philosophy may bring a whole slew of benefits for your heart, weight, blood sugar, brain, energy and tummy.

"Mini-meals may be one of the easiest healthy lifestyle changes people can make," says Murray Mittleman, M.D., Dr.P.H., director of cardiovascular epidemiology at the Institute for the Prevention of Cardiovascular Disease at Deaconess Hospital in Boston.

Nibbling for Better Health

The evidence suggests that the mini-meal philosophy may be able to help you improve your health in the following ways.

Our Take on Breakfast

- Percentage of people who regularly eat cereal for breakfast: 67
- Percentage who eat toast: 36
- Percentage who eat pancakes, sausages and waffles: 9
- Percentage of all soft drinks that are consumed at breakfast: 12
- Percentage of people most likely to skip breakfast on any given day: 9

It controls your weight. Here's one of the worst eating mistakes: You skip breakfast, except for coffee. Lunch is yogurt, salad and a diet cola. By dinner, you're famished, plus you feel entitled to a little reward. Whammo! Before bedtime you've finished off a whole pizza and half a box of glazed doughnuts. It's a caloric disaster.

What do weight-loss experts such as Dean Ornish, M.D., president of the Preventive Medicine Research Institute in Sausalito, California, suggest instead? Mini-meals. "It's far easier to manage appetite by eating small, frequent mini-meals so you never get too hungry," says Dr. Ornish. Studies show that most breakfast skippers later more than make up for the calories they miss in the morning. They tend to weigh more, too.

It helps avoid triggering a heart attack. When you eat a meal, your heart works harder to pump extra blood to your stomach and intestines. But how much harder it works depends on how many calories you've had, says Dr. Mittleman. "Very large meals can put your heart through a digestive stress test."

In one study, after a 240-calorie mini-meal of cornflakes and skim milk, women's hearts pumped an extra 84 quarts of blood during the next two hours. But after a 720-calorie meal with added sugar, bread and honey, their hearts pumped an extra 258 quarts of blood—enough to fill your car's gas tank about five times over! No wonder many doctors say that the number of heart attacks seems to increase in the 24 hours after big holiday meals like Thanksgiving dinner.

There's another possible heart attack trigger that you can minimize with mini-meals: blood clots, which are the immediate cause of almost all heart attacks and strokes. The bigger the meal, the more fat it's likely to have. And studies show that within hours of even a single high-fat meal, there's a hike in blood levels of substances that encourage clots to form.

It cuts cholesterol. Experiments with people eating six or more mini-meals a day, as compared with three square meals, have consistently found that nibblers' cholesterol levels are lower. According to David Jenkins, M.D., Ph.D., D.Sc., professor of nutritional sciences and medicine at the University of Toronto and director of the Clinical Nutrition and Risk Factor Modification Center at St. Michael's Hospital in Toronto, simply eating six mini-meals a day shaved cholesterol in one experiment by 8 percent, a potential 16 percent reduction in heart attack risk.

It optimizes energy and mental power. When more than four hours pass between meals, blood sugar—our energy fuel—drops low enough to let fatigue set in. And some studies show that both those who skip lunch and those who eat jumbo lunches do worse at mental challenges such as math problems.

It helps prevent insulin overload. Large meals force your pancreas to crank out lots of insulin. If you have Type II (non-insulin-dependent) diabetes, insulin is forced to higher levels in your blood after large meals. Many researchers, including Dr. Jenkins, suspect that these high insulin levels contribute to clogged arteries.

It prevents heartburn. The bigger the meal, the more likely that some of it may spurt from your stomach back into the esophagus. And when it's there, it causes discomfort. Eating smaller meals is the standard medical advice for heartburn sufferers.

Terrific Mini-Meal Tips

So how do you get started with mini-meals? For some people it comes naturally. Natural-born nibblers and those who are super-busy grab a bagel and milk for the drive to work, snack several times at their desks and nibble before and after their evening workouts. For others, getting the hang of mini-meals takes a little time. But it's easier than you think.

(continued on page 136)

Delectable Low-Fat Dips

Dips, as in "chips and dip," used to mean one thing—a sour-cream-and-onion concoction, made famous by Lipton, whose packaged soup mix made dip-making a snap.

Onion dip remains popular, but the fat-conscious among us now make it with low-fat or nonfat sour cream. And plenty of other skinny dips now compete with onion for a place on your party menu.

Even chips have been edged aside by healthier fare. Who'd have thought you could get your daily ration of fresh vegetables at a cocktail party? Crudités—plates of sliced, diced and fancied-up fresh

FOOD	PORTION	FAT (G.)	CALORIES
Breakstone Fat-Free Sour Cream with Mrs. Grass's 50% Less-Sodium Onion Dip	2 Tbsp.	0	29
Midland Harvest Fat-Free Taco Filling 'n' Dip	2 Tbsp.	0	50
Heluva Good Cheese Fat-Free Bacon Horseradish Dip	2 Tbsp.	0	25
Newman's Own Salsa	2 Tbsp.	0	10
King No-Fat French Onion Dip	2 Tbsp.	0	30
Land O' Lakes No-Fat French Onion Dip	2 Tbsp.	0	30

veggies—are a welcome change from the usual fatty fare.

Grab yourself a handful of baby carrots or red pepper strips and a few scoops of low-fat dip and you have yourself a more-than-decent appetizer. For seconds, try some of the low-fat or fat-free chips and crackers listed in "New in the Marketplace: Munchable Skinny Chips" on page 100.

Here's how we rated the newest low-fat and fat-free dips on the market. Look for them in supermarkets, health food stores or gourmet shops.

COMMENTS

Excellent. "Better than low-fat dips I've eaten" and "Full-bodied flavor, among the best."

Made with soy protein concentrate, this looks like a beefy filling Good texture and flavor, although you may want to add some hot salsa to liven it up.

Extremely good; sweet, creamy and bacony, with a nice horseradish bite.

Nice, hot, with good body, and unlike many bottled salsas, this one actually tastes fresh.

Only fair. Too sweet and thin.

Not too tasty—has a sweet chemical flavor.

Divide and conquer. The simplest way to plan six mini-meals is to divide your usual three meals a day into two segments each. For example, at breakfast have cereal, milk and orange juice; save a bagel or banana for your morning break. For lunch have a sandwich with turkey, romaine lettuce, tomato and mustard; save the pretzels or baked sweet potato for your afternoon break. For dinner you can have vegetable-bean soup and two small pumpernickel rolls; save the baked apple crisp with low-fat yogurt for an evening snack. Just don't add snacks on top of your usual diet, or you'll gain weight.

Go for high-fiber foods that are low in both fat and added sugar. Eat foods like fruit, veggies or whole-wheat bread. Avoid eating empty-calorie snacks like doughnuts.

Control portion size for any food except veggies. Snacks are too easy to overeat, warns Dr. Jenkins. If you're not careful, you may find yourself taking in more calories under the six-meal plan than under your usual three squares. Your best bets are foods that come in single-serving portions, such as yogurt in eight-ounce cups and pieces of fruit. For low-fat chips, unsalted pretzels and other loose snacks, make single servings using snack-size plastic bags.

Keep healthy snacks in your desk at work. Some ideas: instant lentil and couscous soup, instant oatmeal, dried apricots and flavored rice cakes. Use the lunchroom fridge (for things like nonfat yogurt and low-sodium tomato juice) and the microwave. Try air-popped popcorn sprayed with butter-flavored spray and sprinkled with herb seasoning.

Ensure nutritious mini-meals on the road. Keep a snack stash in your car, carry snacks in your purse at the mall, and stock your briefcase when you fly. Good portables are small boxes of raisins, mini-boxes of cereal, cans of low-sodium vegetable juice cocktail and whole-wheat hard pretzels.

Think of snacks as golden opportunities to eat foods that you often miss. For most of us, that's vegetables and fruit. Some ideas: broccoli florets with low-fat sour cream dip, a baked sweet potato drizzled with fat-free caramel sauce, tomato salsa with low-fat tortilla chips, frozen grapes or bananas, or shredded carrot salad with low-fat mayonnaise and raisins.

Remember that healthy snacks don't have to be time-consuming. Here are some good-for-you treats that are ready in minutes: cereal and milk, instant black bean soup in a cup, nonfat yogurt with Grape-Nuts cereal, wheat germ sprinkled on canned apricots, and a toasted whole-grain waffle with peach butter.

FAT STATS

Ten Foods Women Crave Most

1. Chocolate candy
2. Ice cream
3. Cookies, cake, pastry
4. Fresh fruit
5. Chinese food

6. Chips, popcorn
7. Seafood
8. Meat
9. Dark green vegetables
10. Other sweets

Designate a shelf in the fridge for kids' snacks. Children's small tummies and growing bodies actually require snacks. So keep one area in your refrigerator stocked with ready-to-eat, healthy treats. Try cubes of cantaloupe, orange sections, sticks of red sweet pepper and cucumber, mini-carrots, sugar snap peas, apples, nonfat pudding and low-fat string cheese.

Consider having a "family snack" instead of "family dinner." If everyone comes home ravenous at different times, it might make sense for each parent or older child to fix his own mini-meal (heating a serving of pasta casserole, for example). After everyone is home and settled, gather for dessert and family time.

In restaurants, order appetizers (ready-made mini-meals) instead of entrées. Most entrées could feed Godzilla, but in many restaurants, ordering only appetizers is perfectly okay. Another option is to eat no more than half of a full-size entrée and take the rest home.

The Too-Busy-to-Eat-Right Low-Fat Plan

True or false? Delicious low-fat food takes way too long to cook. False! And our tips prove it.

We admit it. Some foods, such as homemade bread, traditional brown rice and dried beans, do take their own sweet time. But there are quick and healthy versions of many dishes that you can make without spending the rest of your life in the kitchen.

Just what you've been looking for? You're not alone. Many people these days just don't have much time—or inclination, perhaps—to prepare elaborate meals. But fixing fast meals doesn't mean that you're stuck with the fat. In the time it takes to heat up a TV dinner or run to the nearest takeout window, you can prepare a healthy, tasty meal. Here's how.

Meals in Minutes: Low-Fat
Fast Food at Home

The key to quick low-fat cooking is to plan ahead. Having a well-stocked pantry, for instance, with the staples you need right at your fingertips, is one of the best ways to stay in control of your kitchen and your family's nutrition. It also gives you some interesting options if you want to whip something up.

Also, you need to plan what you'll be having for the week so that you can consolidate trips to the supermarket and avoid having to run out for forgotten items.

Even people who love puttering around the kitchen don't want to do that every day. Sometimes you'll want to get in and out of the kitchen as fast as possible yet still enjoy tasty, healthy food.

FAT STATS

How We Measure Up

- Percentage of people who strip naked before they weigh themselves: 20
- Percentage who simply kick off shoes: 20
- Percentage who get down to undies: 20
- Percentage of people who weigh themselves more than once a day: 5
- Percentage who weigh themselves daily: 8.1
- Percentage who weigh themselves twice a week: 10
- Percentage who weigh themselves twice a month: 36.5
- Percentage who never step on a scale: 10
- Percentage of people who, having to choose between a bathroom scale and a microwave, would give up the bathroom scale: 63
- Percentage of people who have lied about their weight: 33

When it's speed you desire, here are some time-saving tactics that you can use in your household.

Each weekend, invest ten minutes in meal planning. You'll receive an amazing time-saving payoff when you devote a few minutes each weekend to choosing the coming week's main meals.

By planning ahead, you streamline your shopping lists and help minimize the stressful "What should we eat tonight?" question that keeps cropping up when there's no plan.

You might even invest a few weekend minutes in precooking beans and other legumes. Or make some bread dough that you can freeze, then thaw, let rise and bake later in the week when you want a quick loaf of delicious homemade bread.

More Low-Fat Time-Savers

Streamline time in the kitchen with these additional quick tips.

- Buy packages of cleaned stir-fry vegetables to save prep time. You can even buy precut meat or poultry for stir-frying for an instant, good-for-you dinner.
- If you're barbecuing chicken, cook it halfway in your microwave first, until it starts to turn white on the outside but is still pink in the center. You'll cut your grilling time almost in half, and you'll be less likely to burn it on the grill.
- Buy an uncooked turkey breast and ask the butcher to slice it into $1/2$- to $3/4$-inch-thick fillet steaks for use in place of chicken breast fillets. Freeze with two pieces of wax paper between the slices so that you can remove them easily as needed.
- Clean and chop bunches of fresh vegetables at one time, then refrigerate them in resealable bags. For best results, punch a few holes in the bags or use the perforated kind made specifically for storing produce. Another good, easy option is to purchase vegetables—even salad greens—already cleaned and cut.

Delegate kitchen responsibilities. If you have children, dividing kitchen tasks saves time and brings family members closer together. As soon as the children are old enough, they can set and clear the table, wash dishes and even help prepare food. In many homes, these shared minutes are a simple, valuable daily ritual of connection.

Keep a step-saver list on hand. Whenever you start to run out of an ingredient, write it down immediately on an easy-access grocery list. Don't wait until you run out; that's how you end up making one-item raids on the grocery store. It makes life easier and saves trips to the supermarket when you write down everything that's on "low" before it's on "empty."

Add personal notes to recipes. Whenever you change a recipe, pencil the change in the margin. If you substitute an ingredient, adjust cooking time or change the seasonings to meet your family's preferences, jot down the change right away. Then, when you next prepare that meal, you won't have to wonder what you did the last time.

- Keep a few packages of frozen vegetables on hand. Vegetable combinations (without sauces) are a healthy, relatively inexpensive choice, and they work well as side dishes and in soups, stews and stir-fried dishes.
- Make good use of your microwave—not just to heat foods but also to prepare recipes and do basics such as cooking vegetables. Invest in a good microwave cookbook for cooking times and recipe ideas.
- You can buy low-fat cheese already grated, but it costs about twice as much as the brick form, and it often doesn't go as far volume-wise. It's easy to grate cheese in a food processor, but you can save time and effort by grating large quantities and freezing it for future use.
- Purchase chopped garlic in a jar instead of chopping your own.
- Keep a roll of masking tape and a permanent marker in your kitchen, and whenever you store foods (such as leftovers), make a label that will tell you what it is and when you stored it. You'll save yourself time and guesswork later.

Cut down on cooking time. Use your microwave to speed up defrosting and reheating foods. The microwave can be your best ally when you want to reduce preparation and cooking times. It's especially useful when there are items that cook slowly, such as casseroles, sauces, squash and some beans and other legumes.

A pressure cooker is another valuable kitchen tool to consider. There is no faster way to cook legumes. Two hours of simmering can be shortened to 30 minutes of pressure-steaming if you use a pressure cooker instead of a regular pot. And the time it takes to cook other dishes—brown rice, sauces, soups and chili, for example—can be reduced to one-third of the usual time if you use a pressure cooker. Despite the speed of cooking, there's no loss of flavor.

Get two meals from one recipe. Prepare a double recipe when cooking soups, chili, casseroles and other dishes that freeze well. After you've served

(continued on page 144)

NEW IN THE
MARKETPLACE

Low-Fat Salad Dressings

Where do you think most of the fat in a woman's diet comes from? French fries? Pastries? Chocolate? Would you believe salad dressing?

That's right. Those creamy, oily, bleu-cheese-laden toppings can turn the healthiest of foods into a diet disaster, contributing the largest portion of fat to the day's menu if you're a big salad eater, as are many women. One tablespoon of oil (of any kind) has 14 grams of fat. And the same amount of mayo weighs in at 12 grams of fat.

FOOD	PORTION	FAT (G.)	CALORIES
Seven Seas Fat-Free Raspberry Vinaigrette Dressing	2 Tbsp.	0	30
Ken's Fat-Free Sun-Dried Tomato Vinaigrette	2 Tbsp.	0	60
Good Seasons Fat-Free Honey French Dressing	⅛ envelope (makes 2 Tbsp.)	0	20
Wish-Bone Fat-Free Deluxe French Style Dressing	2 Tbsp.	0	30
Wish-Bone Fat-Free Creamy Roasted Garlic Dressing	2 Tbsp.	0	40
Kraft Free Honey Dijon Fat-Free Dressing	2 Tbsp.	0	50

But that doesn't mean that you have to eat your salads plain. Many reduced-fat and fat-free dressings today have excellent body and flavor and compare favorably with high-fat dressings.

Don't forget, too, that it's easy to make your own dressing using nonfat yogurt or sour cream. You can even add some shredded nonfat cheese or a bit of grated Parmesan for extra flavor.

We've rated the newest low-fat and fat-free salad dressings. Here are the results.

COMMENTS

Zesty and flavorful, good with a fruit-and-greens combination salad such as spinach and orange.

Nice blend of tangy and sweet, with enough body to really stick to greens. "Would be good for bean salads." We also like Ken's other low-fat flavors, especially the Low-Fat Creamy Parmesan and Caeser Dressing.

You add vinegar and water to this packaged dressing. Very good flavor.

Tastes like regular French dressing. "Much better than any other fat-free French I've tried."

A must-try for garlic-lovers. Roasting cuts garlic's bite and gives it a sweet, full-bodied flavor. A good dip for raw vegetables.

A nice balance of sweet and tangy, with real bits of ground mustard seed. Also good as a dip.

the meal and the food has cooled down, put the leftovers—enough for another whole meal—in containers with tight-fitting lids and place them in the freezer. *Voilà*—an entire "frozen dinner" that's ready to go.

On days when you're running late and don't have time to cook, thaw and bake (or microwave) the frozen food, add a quick salad and some bread, and dinner is ready. These low-fat meals taste far better—and are far less expensive—than any frozen meal-in-a-box from the supermarket.

Freeze your favorite loaves. Keep one or two loaves of your favorite whole-grain bread and a package or two of rolls in the freezer for quick defrosting. They can round out a meal in minutes.

Soak ahead for legume recipes. Many of the most healthful and delicious recipes for beans and other legumes require some quick and simple advance preparation, such as overnight soaking. This is where planning ahead will help. If the beans have already been soaked, they don't take long to cook.

In a pinch, canned beans are a good last-minute substitute. Their one drawback is that they're high in salt. But there's a simple way to reduce the sodium in canned beans: Drain them and rinse in a colander.

Enjoy more salad greens—with less work washing them. Do you love salads but find yourself skipping them because of the time it takes to clean the fixings?

When you bring home fresh greens from the market, wash enough for several meals. Then, because dry greens stay fresh longer than wet ones, remove all the water with a salad spinner. Gently wrap the greens in a clean cotton kitchen towel, place them in a plastic produce bag and refrigerate until needed. This way, you have only one cleanup, and the washed-and-dried salad fixings stay fresh for three to four days.

Hoard the makings of quick sauces and soups. When you're stocking up on canned nonfat chicken or vegetable broth, always buy more than you need so that you have an ever-ready supply on the shelf. The cans take only an instant to open, and either kind of broth adds flavor to many dishes.

Standbys to Swear By

Back in the days of high-fat living, many moms had their standbys for each day of the week. Meat loaf on Monday. Chicken on Tuesday.

Spaghetti and meatballs on Wednesday, and so on. Not much variety, but these reliable, familiar recipes were easy to prepare.

Well, the fat focus has changed, and with it the nature of the meals. But there's still a lot to be said for reliable standbys that you can count on. What follows are substitutes for the old high-fat main courses, side dishes and even desserts. To keep these standbys from getting stale, add new spices to keep the tastes interesting. They're fast, easy and delicious—and very low in fat.

Pizza and Pita-za Specials

Many grocery stores now carry whole-wheat pita breads and traditional and whole-grain Italian focaccia flatbreads. They're especially easy to store in your freezer since they lie flat and take up little space. With these you can whip up a homemade pizza any time, with less fat than a to-go meal from your neighborhood pizzeria.

In fact, making lean pizza takes less time than a pizza delivery. To make a pita-bread pizza, for example, set the oven at 350° and bake the pita until it's slightly crisp. Add tomato sauce, chopped vegetables and seasonings and then bake briefly until the add-ons are heated through. You'll add tasty variations such as low-fat cheese, but basically, that's all there is to it.

Premier Pasta—With Variations

Pasta is a popular fast dinner. But to keep it from turning into the same old thing, try mixing and matching pastas, sauces and toppings. Keep different pasta varieties on hand: traditional and whole-grain spaghetti, linguine, rotini and wagon wheels for the kids.

A simple tomato sauce, whether store-bought or homemade, is easy to modify and spark up with new flavors. Add leftovers—cooked chicken or seafood, tofu or a soy-based ground beef substitute (see "New in the Marketplace: Burgers, Hot Dogs and Cold Cuts" on page 38), cooked beans, vegetables, fresh herbs, onions and garlic. And with a bit of skim milk or evaporated skim milk you can transform a traditional tomato sauce into a creamy red sauce.

Memorable Almost-Instant Pilaf

A pilaf has simple ingredients, all low-fat and nutritious, so you can create an Eastern-style, exotically flavored meal in record time.

Sauté some onions and garlic, then add a quick-cooking grain like instant brown rice or pearled barley, defatted chicken or vegetable broth and a few pinches of herbs. Simmer until the grains are cooked, then sprinkle with finely grated orange or lemon rind.

Oriental Expressions

For another great fast-meal option, cook or reheat some brown rice, add Chinese or soba (buckwheat) noodles and top with quickly sautéed vegetables and, if you like, some chicken, seafood, tofu or legumes and some low-sodium soy or teriyaki sauce.

Appealing Rapid-Bake Poultry

You can broil skinless chicken or turkey breasts in just a few minutes, and almost instantly you have the foundation of a fast low-fat meal.

And the side dishes for this meal don't take much longer. It takes five minutes to make couscous (a delicious grain dish) and about the same amount of time to steam vegetables. Serve with a tossed salad made with low-fat or nonfat dressing and some whole-grain bread, and you have a very complete meal in under half an hour.

Believe-It-or-Not Beanwiches

Heat up homemade or canned refried (but fat-free) beans and spread a layer inside a whole-wheat pita bread. Top your beanwich with nonfat sour cream, salsa, tomatoes, lettuce or sprouts, a little low-fat Cheddar cheese, green chili peppers and diced onions. It's a great-tasting low-fat sandwich that takes about ten minutes to make.

Quick-Mex in Minutes

For a variation on beanwiches, use whole-wheat tortillas or low-fat soft or hard taco shells. Make them with the same fillings as the beanwiches, or try a soy-based ground beef substitute mixed with taco seasoning.

Low-Fat Burgers

If you have ground turkey breast or a quick low-fat "veggie burger" mix on hand, you're ready to cook a quick meal any time. Keep some whole-grain buns in the freezer and thaw them in the toaster oven or microwave while you're getting the condiments ready. Add tomatoes, lettuce or sprouts, onions and pickles; you can choose other favorite ingredients to

NEWS FLASH

Dieting Commercials Spur Snacking

Whatever you do, don't expect diet commercials to inspire you to forgo food. In one study, 86 women who were usually restrained eaters (read: dieters) drank a milk shake, then watched a sad movie that included either no commercials, neutral commercials or ones featuring successful dieters. All of the women were supposed to test bowls of peanuts and M&M's during the flick. Women seeing the diet commercials ate nearly twice as much as the other women.

Researchers suspect that the skinnies in the ads reminded the women that they had broken their diets, which disinhibited them from eating. So to stick to your plan, keep the remote handy.

go on top. To create a homemade low-fat burger meal like this takes about 15 minutes.

High-Speed, Low-Fat Antipasto

Keep your refrigerator and pantry stocked with cans of white beans, black beans, water-packed tuna, pimentos, baby corn, artichoke hearts (packed in water, not oil), pickled red beets and other quick side dishes and garnishes. All of these fast-to-the-table items are low in fat. If you drain and rinse the canned items that come in brine, they'll be light on the sodium.

Arrange a decorative selection of your favorites on a large plate lined with fresh green leaf lettuce. Sprinkle with lemon juice or balsamic vinegar and fresh herbs.

Prime-Time Fruit Purees

Keep peeled and sliced fruit in plastic bags in your freezer. Any time you're ready for dessert, put a fruit mixture in the food processor, puree

(continued on page 150)

NEW IN THE
MARKETPLACE

Slimmed-Down Cookies

Thanks to the low-fat or fat-free cookies on the market, there's no reason that even a dedicated fat fighter can't have a glass of skim milk and some cookies now and then—or even every afternoon!

To be labeled as fat-free, a cookie must contain less than ½ gram of fat per serving. Low-fat cookies must contain no more than 3 grams of fat per serving. The standard serving size is 28 grams (one ounce), but some cookies have larger or smaller servings, so check labels. Your cookie may not be such a low-fat bargain after all.

Some regular cookies, such as ginger snaps or Fig Newtons, are

FOOD	PORTION	FAT (G.)	CALORIES
Baking on the Lite Side Apricot Linzer Cookies	1	0	55
Keebler Reduced-Fat Pecan Sandies	1	3	70
Pepperidge Farm Reduced-Fat Soft-Baked Oatmeal Raisin Cookies	1	3	110
Pepperidge Farm Reduced-Fat Vanilla Creme Chantilly	1	2	70
Entenmann's Fat-Free Oatmeal Raisin Cookies	2	0	80
Delicious Fat-Free Apple Cinnamon Fruit-Topped Cookies	1	0	50
Snackwell's Fat-Free Raspberry Cereal Bars	1	0	120

just as lean as their trimmed-down cousins, and they're often cheaper. But most cookies, both commercial and homemade, have lots of fat. So if you're a big cookie fan, choosing low-fat or fat-free versions can really help you cut down on fat.

Just remember that even low-fat cookies can be high in calories, so don't eat the whole bag!

We nibbled our way through the newest contenders in the skinny-cookie market. Here are our favorites, along with their vital statistics.

COMMENTS

A double layer of moist, sweet cake with tart fruit filling. "Tastes like a Christmas cookie!" Their Raspberry Linzer also is a top seller.

Has the same crumbly, nutty texture as the high-fat original. An "excellent dunker."

"Tastes homemade." This large cookie has a bit of a crunch that makes it perfect for dunking.

A nice combination of soft cream filling and crunchy cookie. Tastes rich and buttery, with a hint of lemon.

Chewy, moist and tasty. "A keeper!" said one taster.

A bit too sweet and soft for some of us, but the fragrant apple topping and no-fat feature won votes of approval.

We liked the sweet raspberry filling but found the cookie-covering bland.

it until smooth and serve immediately. Some of the best candidates for this instant puree are peaches, kiwi, raspberries, blackberries, blueberries and strawberries, but just about any fruit works well.

Fast Fish

Fresh fish fillets cook so quickly that they're done before you know it. Just be sure to choose uniformly thin fillets, which cook the fastest. Put the fish in to broil, then check after three minutes and baste evenly with your favorite juice (orange or lemon juice or spicy vegetable-tomato cocktail) or nonfat marinade.

Flavor-Packed Instant Couscous

This side dish packs great taste, goes with everything and is simple to prepare.

First sauté some chopped onions and minced garlic in a little olive or canola oil. Stir in some couscous (bulgur), chicken or vegetable broth and a little seasoning such as parsley, basil or curry powder. Cover, remove from the heat and let stand for ten minutes. Fluff with a fork and serve. For variety, add some diced tomatoes, water chestnuts or sliced roasted red peppers.

Short-Order Shortcuts for Time-Pressed Cooks

Every cook develops quick tricks that make recipes simpler and faster to prepare. These shortcuts are important, because once you start using them, you'll find that it's just as easy to prepare fresh fruits, vegetables and garnishes as it is to use prepared foods or prepackaged items. Here are shortcuts that shave minutes off preparation time.

Peel Garlic in Seconds

Place individual cloves on a cutting board. Smash them with the flat side of a broad knife such as a chef's knife. The peels should slip right off. Then press them through a good-quality garlic press.

Cook Yams in Minutes

To slice 50 minutes off the cooking time of nutrient-packed yams or sweet potatoes, first cut the unpeeled tubers into big cubes. Boil the cubes for about ten minutes, or until tender. Drain and serve.

For variety, cut yams or sweet potatoes into $1/2$-inch-thick slabs and coat them with low-sodium soy sauce mixed with a few drops of olive or canola oil. Grill until crisp and golden brown.

There's a microwave option, too: Pierce the sweet potatoes several times with a fork and microwave until tender. One potato takes about 4 to 5 minutes. With four potatoes in the microwave, the cooking time is more likely to be 10 to 12 minutes.

Have Your Squash in Ten

Your microwave stands ready to make tender, tasty squash in under ten minutes. Cut the squash in half and pierce the skin with a fork. Spaghetti squash takes eight minutes to cook in the microwave. Butternut or acorn squash, when cut in half this way, cooks to perfection in ten minutes.

Find a Rice Substitute

Brown rice needs to be boiled a full 45 minutes before it's ready. If you haven't the time for that, and you don't have any precooked brown rice stored in the refrigerator, try one of these other quick-cooking grains, which are ready to eat in 5 to 12 minutes.

- Bulgur wheat: 7 minutes
- Quick-cooking barley: 12 minutes
- Couscous: 5 minutes
- Quick-cooking brown rice: 10 minutes

PART TWO

Big Gains in
Weight Loss

And the Winners Are . . .

Meet some people who surprised the experts by discovering how to keep the pounds off.

We've all heard it a million times: Diets don't work. Consider the facts, experts tell us. Of those who start a commercial program like Weight Watchers, as many as 70 percent never complete it. Of those who sign up for medically supervised liquid-formula diets, half drop out. And the topper is, 90 percent of dieters who lose weight regain all or part of it within five years.

There's just one problem with those statistics, says James O. Hill, Ph.D., associate director of the Center for Human Nutrition at the University of Colorado Health Sciences Center in Denver. They're way too gloomy. That 90 percent failure rate, for example, is based almost entirely on studies of just the sort of people you'd expect to fail—namely, chronically obese women and men who turn to university research programs as a final, desperate step. People who successfully lose weight on their own, he says, don't get counted.

Don't get Dr. Hill wrong, though. He's quick to acknowledge that it is frustratingly difficult for some people to lose weight and keep the pounds off. But he also believes that there are many others out there who have figured out one important lesson: Successful weight loss isn't a matter of losing pounds and then going back to old eating and exercise habits; it's a lifelong commitment.

"It's not that, gee, these people have figured out what to do," Dr. Hill says. "Nearly everyone knows what's required: Take in fewer calories than you burn. It's that they've figured out *how* to do it."

Dr. Hill has more than theory on his side. Several years ago, he and Rena Wing, Ph.D., a psychologist at the University of Pittsburgh, put out a nationwide call for "successful losers," people who had lost 30 pounds or more and kept them off for at least a year. Despite limited publicity—a southern

One woman was so proud of her weight loss that she included a revealing photo that she had taken for her husband for Valentine's Day.

California newspaper ran a small item about the project that was later picked up by a few other papers around the country—the response has been startling. "The typical reaction has been, 'I'm so glad someone finally asked,'" says Dr. Hill. One woman was so proud of her weight loss that she included a revealing photo she had taken for her husband for Valentine's Day.

The Real Losers

The ongoing project, billed as the National Weight Control Registry, promises to reshape the dieting landscape. "There are two beliefs out there," says Dr. Wing. "One is that almost nobody succeeds at weight loss. The other is that for the few people who do, success requires such an extreme sacrifice that they basically do nothing but count calories and exercise all day. We see no reason to believe that either is true."

Already Dr. Hill and Dr. Wing have collected detailed histories of 831 people, ages 19 to 81, and have analyzed the first 500. Fully a third of the people lost between 30 and 44 pounds; more than half lost 60 pounds or more. "Some people lost weight very fast and kept it all off," says Dr. Wing. "Others lost a lot and regained half, but kept the other half off. And then there were those who lost some, regained a little, then lost some more, but constantly headed in a downward direction."

With more names coming in all the time, they believe they've uncovered only the tip of an iceberg of success stories. Indeed, other researchers are turning up similar findings. A few years ago, John Foreyt, Ph.D., professor of psychology and director of the Behavioral Medicine Research Center at Baylor College of Medicine in Houston, pored over the dozen or so existing studies on diet successes—only a handful had more than 100 subjects—and compiled a list of factors that best predict a person's chances of winning the weight-loss game. Dietitian Anne Fletcher, R.D., scrutinized the same studies for her book *Thin for Life: Ten Keys to Success from People Who Have Lost Weight and Kept It Off*, then went one step further and recruited successful dieters through fliers, newspaper notices and commercial weight-loss programs. Fletcher eventually surveyed 160 masters, as she calls them, including a former showgirl and a chocolate scientist.

Beating the Odds

The stories that emerge from both the registry and the other studies defy conventional wisdom. It's commonly believed, for instance, that permanent weight loss is out of reach for people who were fat as children, who are middle-aged or who have repeatedly gained and lost pounds over the years. Yet many of the people Dr. Hill and Dr. Wing have quizzed beat those very odds. One man, for instance, whose entire family was overweight and who had been fat since childhood, lost 107 pounds and has kept them off for 20 years. His younger sister was inspired to lose 60 pounds, a loss she has maintained for 5 years. Another woman, who weighed 400 pounds at age 40, got down to 120, which she's maintained for 4 years. Similarly, 70 percent of Fletcher's masters had been fat as kids or teens, a third lost their weight after age 40, and nearly 80 percent had tried at least three or four diets before getting it right.

Dr. Hill and Dr. Wing are quick to point out that what they're learning can be as helpful to someone trying to lose 15 pounds as it is to someone aiming for more ambitious goals. The lessons are the same, they say.

Eventually, Dr. Hill and Dr. Wing hope to sketch a composite picture of a successful dieter and answer specific questions that have baffled researchers for years. Are special fat-free products helpful to dieters? Are people who are successful at weight loss more obsessed with their weight than others? Do their lives change dramatically for the better?

 Nearly 80 percent had tried at least three or four diets before getting it right.

But the question at the heart of all of these investigations is this: What happened in these people's lives that enabled them to overcome their weight problems once and for all?

Do It for Yourself

Most of us are motivated to lose weight by a snide comment from a spouse or co-worker, an upcoming wedding or some other external event. The problem with that, according to Dr. Foreyt, is that such events keep us motivated for only about six weeks. After that, you have to constantly build in rewards to keep yourself going.

(continued on page 160)

Should You Lose Weight?

Everyone acknowledges that too much body fat is hazardous. But no one, it seems, can agree on how much is too much. The government's 1990 weight charts, for example, gave very broad ranges of healthy weights and set different standards for those over age 35, implying that it's okay to gain weight with age. Then, in 1993, the Nurses' Health Study released the startling findings that unless a woman is practically bone thin, she risks an early death. A five-foot-five-inch woman who weighs 180 pounds, the researchers warned, has four times the risk of dying of heart disease as a woman who weighs a mere 114 pounds. Finally, in 1994, the government published *its* latest guidelines (see below), which fall somewhere between those extremes.

Given the confusion, how are you supposed to know whether you're overweight? Here are some suggestions.

- First, use the government's new weight chart as a rough guide. The weights apply to all ages and offer a fairly broad range of healthy weights for any given height. (The upper end of the range is about 10 to 15 pounds lighter than in the previous charts.) The further you are above the range, the higher your risk of diabetes, high blood pressure and heart disease.

HEIGHT (WITHOUT SHOES)	WEIGHT (LB.) (WITHOUT CLOTHES)
4'10"	91–119
4'11"	94–124
5'0"	97–128
5'1"	101–132
5'2"	104–137
5'3"	107–141
5'4"	111–146
5'5"	114–150
5'6"	118–155
5'7"	121–160
5'8"	125–164

- If you're overweight according to the chart but otherwise healthy, do two things. First check to see where your fat is located. Fat around your abdomen and chest is riskier than fat around your hips and thighs—and much easier to get off. From a health perspective, a man with a beer belly has more reason to lose a few pounds than, say, a woman with big thighs.

  Second, take a hard look at your health habits. If you're very active and you eat a low-fat diet, you're probably at the best weight for your height. By contrast, a person whose weight falls within the healthy range but who's sedentary and eats a high-fat diet probably weighs too much.

- If you already have a weight-related condition, it's definitely worth trying to lose some pounds. If the condition is life-threatening, doctors may recommend drastic measures to get the weight off, including fasting or even surgery.

- No matter what your situation, you should exercise for 30 to 40 minutes every day, eat a low-fat diet with lots of fruits and vegetables, go easy on calories and try not to put on any more pounds. If you do those things, says experts, you'll be healthier and live longer, regardless of your weight.

HEIGHT (WITHOUT SHOES)	WEIGHT (LB.) (WITHOUT CLOTHES)
5'9"	129–169
5'10"	132–174
5'11"	136–179
6'0"	140–184
6'1"	144–189
6'2"	148–195
6'3"	152–200
6'4"	156–205
6'5"	160–211
6'6"	164–216

Unless you're losing weight for yourself, your weight loss efforts may be doomed, says Fletcher. When she asked yo-yo dieters what motivated them to finally keep off the weight after all their previous attempts, she found that they'd undergone a change in attitude. Some described it as a "click" inside the brain or a "light bulb going on." A few cited an actual turning point in their lives. One 475-pound man lost 250 pounds after he nearly drowned in a boating accident because his weight obstructed rescuers. Others decided to lose after learning that they had a weight-related medical condition, such as high blood pressure or heart disease.

Biology isn't destiny. One man was inspired to slim down because he was 50 pounds heavier than his identical twin, who'd always been more active.

This time, she found, they knew what was needed and decided that trimming down was worth the changes they would have to make, whether starting an exercise program, getting marriage counseling or quitting a job that required them to be around food all the time. "They know there's no magic answer," says Fletcher. "They accept that it's going to be work and that nobody can do it for them."

Set Realistic Goals

Another reason that many people find it hard to maintain weight loss is that they set their hearts on losing, say, 40 pounds, and when they find out that it requires too great a sacrifice, they give up, blaming themselves or their genes.

Heredity does play an important part in shaping our shapes. Genes, for example, can make the body inefficient at burning fat or make metabolism sluggish. Studies on identical twins confirm that when one twin is overweight, the other usually is, too—an association that occurs far less often in fraternal twins, who don't inherit the exact same genes.

Still, biology isn't destiny. Even among identical twins, weights can be far apart. Fletcher cites the case of one man who was inspired to slim down because he was 50 pounds heavier than his identical twin, who'd always been more active.

"Genes set the lower and upper limits of your weight," says Dr. Hill, "but it's lifestyle that moves you up or down within that range." Not surprisingly, a lifestyle that consists of sitting in front of the television eating cheeseburgers is more likely to push a person to the right of the range, into the fat zone, than to the left.

When trying to set a realistic weight goal, adds Fletcher, ask yourself these questions: What is the least that you've weighed as an adult, for at least a year? What is the largest clothing size you'd be happy with? (Should you settle for a size 14, say, instead of a 10?) What weight were you able to maintain during previous diets without feeling constantly hungry? Many of the dieters she surveyed found that their original weight goal was too low to maintain comfortably; those who succeeded were willing to settle for a more realistic target.

Losing just 5 to 10 percent of your current weight, surveys show, brings major physical and psychological benefits. "You might not become the skinny person of your dreams," says Dr. Foreyt, "but even a small loss can make you feel better about yourself."

Don't Deprive Yourself

When she first began her research, Fletcher wasn't much interested in how dieters lost weight. Instead, she wanted to find out how their eating habits changed afterward. But in talking to many dieters, she quickly learned that the issues couldn't be separated. The more extreme the original diet, they told her, the harder the transition to a maintenance diet.

The more extreme the original diet, the harder the transition to a maintenance diet.

Still, one common thread showed up among all those who succeeded. No matter how weird or wacky their diet started out, they eventually adopted a sensible eating plan that they were content to stay on for the rest of their lives. How did they do it? For one thing, they made sure not to deny themselves their favorite foods.

Other studies back up that finding. Health educator Susan Kayman, R.D., Dr.P.H., studied 74 women who were enrolled in Kaiser Permanente Medical Offices in Fremont, California, who'd lost a lot of weight. She discovered two behaviors that distinguished those who maintained a significant weight loss from those who didn't. The successful dieters weren't as rigid about what they ate, and they didn't feel deprived. Instead, they compromised on portions.

"One woman would take a half-gallon of ice cream, cut it into cubes and wrap each cube individually so that she wouldn't devour the entire carton at one sitting," says Kayman. While that may strike some as a bit obsessive, it illustrates how successful dieters find ways to make their diets work for them. Kayman speculates that because they don't label any foods as forbidden, they're able to indulge without triggering feelings of guilt. Dieters with an all-or-nothing mentality inevitably give up when they stray even a little.

> *Successful dieters don't label any foods as forbidden, so they're able to indulge without triggering feelings of guilt.*

The actual indulgence may matter less than the sense of control it imparts, says Fletcher. She describes one woman who joined Weight Watchers at a time when the program was more restrictive. The only way she could tolerate staying on the program was to "cheat" by eating three chocolate chips every day. The tiny extravagance paid off: She lost 57 pounds, and she has kept them off for 20 years.

Cut the Fat

When Fletcher asked successful dieters to name the three most important factors in keeping weight down, the number one diet-related response was "watch my fat intake."

No wonder. Gram for gram, fat has more than twice the calories of carbohydrates. That's not all. Researchers have found that certain individuals are inherently bad at burning fat. That means their bodies go to extraordinary lengths to store fat in fat cells rather than burn it for energy. To lose weight, then, these people may have to restrict the fat in their diets to as little as 15 percent of calories—much lower than the currently recommended 30 percent. That works out to 34 grams of fat a day on a 2,000-calorie diet, or roughly 49 fewer grams than the average American gets each day.

Dr. Hill believes that it's important to watch fat intake, even if you're not a poor fat burner. That's because as fat stores shrink, the rate of fat oxidation—how much fat the body burns for energy—drops. The result, says Dr. Hill: "If you eat the same proportion of fat in the diet as you did before you lost weight, you'll be more likely to store that fat in fat cells."

Rest assured, though, that cutting the fat doesn't have to mean leading a spartan life. One man from the registry who lost more than 100 pounds likes to toss enormous salads with his own "Thousand Island" dressing, made from fat-free yogurt, ketchup and pickle relish. Others created their own low-fat versions of muffins, potato salad, pizza, lasagna, enchiladas and even pasta-shrimp primavera. Many successful dieters made finding tasty low-fat foods into an enjoyable hobby. As one put it: "Once low-fat was a permanent way of life for me, the search for great low-fat or nonfat chocolate treats began."

Get Moving

It's telling that a whopping 96 percent of people listed on the registry exercise regularly. Moving around, after all, keeps energy levels up, fends off stress and contributes to a general sense of physical and emotional well-being. What's more, by burning extra calories, exercise helps to compensate for the metabolic drop that usually comes with weight loss.

It's telling that a whopping 96 percent of people listed on the National Weight Control Registry exercise regularly.

When Dr. Foreyt reviewed the existing weight studies, he found several additional factors that predicted success. Among them were getting continued emotional support and maintaining normal eating habits, such as sitting down to three meals a day. But topping the list was physical activity. "Ninety percent of people who lost weight and kept it off were regular exercisers," he says.

That doesn't mean that you have to take up marathon running or step aerobics to stay trim. A surprising 98 percent of registry enrollees who exercise simply walk. Exercising 45 minutes a day is ideal, says Dr. Hill. For most people, that's enough to ensure permanent weight loss. But he advises people not to worry about how long or how far they go. "Just make it a routine," he says.

Track Your Progress

New habits can take years to become second nature. It's no wonder, then, that many successful dieters find it helpful to weigh or measure their food

NEWS FLASH

The Latest on Leptin

If chunkiness runs in your family, you may be following the new "fat gene" research with keen interest. Wouldn't it be great if genetic engineering allowed you to retool your body into a slimmer model?

Although they still have a long way to go, researchers are hopeful that overweight people will be able to benefit from this revolutionary research before too long. Here's what's happening.

Researchers now know that inside each human fat cell, an "Ob" (for obesity) gene produces a unique appetite-dampening hormone called leptin. When your body has gotten all the food it needs to keep going, fat cells release leptin into the bloodstream. From there, it travels to the brain, where it signals brain cells that you've had enough. Your hunger satisfied, you stop eating.

"That's how two-thirds of Americans stay trim so easily," says Jose F. Caro, M.D., chairman of the Department of Medicine at Jefferson Medical College of Thomas Jefferson University in Philadelphia. "They stop eating because they get the body signal that makes them feel full."

and to chart their daily exercise. One reason is that most people fool themselves when it comes to calories. In one study, ten people who said they'd been unable to lose weight no matter what they did estimated that they ate only 1,028 calories a day and spent 1,022 in exercise, but lab measurements showed that they ate closer to 2,081 calories and worked off only 771.

Self-monitoring—counting calories each day or keeping an exercise diary—was one of Dr. Foreyt's predictors for success. Successful dieters, he found, tracked themselves not only while losing weight but for some time afterward. One woman who thinned down more than 12 years ago,

The picture is different for overweight people. They produce lots of leptin—much more than trimmer people—but that leptin apparently never gets the opportunity to signal the brain to tell the hand to put down the fork, Dr. Caro says. In fact, some research indicates that leptin receptor sites (similar to docking platforms) on brain cells may be malfunctioning in obese people, short-circuiting the "I've-had-enough" signal.

"The next step is to find out how to correct this problem," says Dr. Caro. "If the factory that is producing the leptin is working, how can we get the brain to read the body's own signal?"

New research will determine whether adding more leptin to the body has weight-loss benefits.

And Dr. Caro is optimistic that researchers will soon figure out how to activate leptin receptors in the brain. Once that happens, it shouldn't be long before there is a treatment that makes it a lot easier to stick with those dietary resolutions. Much easier than picking your parents.

for example, stopped counting calories only in the last 6 years.

Once they've reached their goal, many successful dieters keep tabs on their weight, either by stepping on the scale or by noting the tightness of their belt or a favorite pair of jeans. Fletcher found that successful dieters typically set a weight "buffer zone" for themselves. If they gained more than three to five pounds, they got it off right away. "I was surprised at how many would weigh themselves daily or weekly," she says. "Some people might say, 'Oh, they're just slaves to the scale,' but actually it was more of a routine morning activity, like brushing their teeth."

Get Organized

The biggest obstacle to permanent weight loss may not be lack of willpower but lack of time. "Someone who always eats fast food is going to have to shop, plan and cook if they want to lose weight," says Kayman.

The solution for many dieters isn't a lecture on calories but rather a lesson in problem-solving. Dr. Foreyt has found that people who are good at organization and problem-solving have an easier time keeping weight off. They're able to find time to exercise, and they know how to cope with stress without resorting to bingeing on comfort foods like doughnuts or chocolate cake. They also know how to identify and manage risky situations. "These are people who bring fruit plates to parties," Dr. Foreyt says.

Even those people who are not naturally inclined to tackle problems head-on can learn the skills. Kayman took a small group of would-be dieters and randomly assigned half to attend seminars, where they heard basic nutrition advice. The other half, who got the same advice in the form of handouts, spent the seminar time looking at their problems and learning how to incorporate healthy behaviors into their lives. "We focused on issues such as finding time in a workday to fit in a walk," says Kayman. "We didn't jump to conclusions, like telling someone to walk at lunchtime. Instead we'd ask, 'Why is she working so hard? Maybe she needs to talk to the boss about her hours.' After a year, 65 percent of the problem-solvers had maintained their weight loss or were continuing to lose, compared to 25 percent of those who got only diet tips.

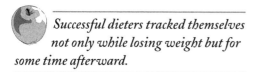

Successful dieters tracked themselves not only while losing weight but for some time afterward.

All of this helps to explain why some people reach their weight goals only in middle age. "They have more control over their lives," says Daniel Kirschenbaum, Ph.D., a psychologist and director of the Center for Behavioral Medicine in Chicago. "They're more settled; they don't have children around to care for."

Plan for the Long Haul

Dieters go through predictable stages of emotion, according to Dr. Kirschenbaum. He calls the first stage the honeymoon because it's filled with optimism but usually fades within a few months to a year. Next comes the frustration stage, when dieters realize that they have to work harder than people of normal weight to lose weight and keep it off. "There's annoyance and anger and a 'Why me?' effect that can last for many months or even years," says Dr. Kirschenbaum. "The average American doesn't exercise even two times a week, and we're asking overweight people—who often feel more awkward and may have more knee and back problems—to exercise almost every day and do it forever," he says. "That's asking a lot." During this time, he adds, weight-loss efforts are easily derailed by any kind of crisis—a death in the family, a job loss or even minor surgery.

Only in the third stage—called tentative acceptance—do dieters come to terms with their lot and achieve a peaceful sense of resolve. "They stop thinking, 'It's not fair that I have to eat less than my wife, who weighs half of what I do' or 'It's not fair that I have to exercise every day,' " says Dr. Kirschenbaum. "They no longer consider their effort a sacrifice. It feels more natural, more healthy." Once you go from understanding what it takes to actually living it, he says, there's no turning back.

Escape Your Shape

Whether you're top-heavy, bottom-heavy, straight as a stick or curvaceous, here's how to make the most of what you have.

Is your workout bad for your body? It could be. If what you really want is to change your shape, just any old exercise won't do.

Spending 60 minutes on a stair-climber will definitely work up a sweat, but it may actually be counterproductive, depending on your body type and your goals.

First you have to figure out what that type is. Then you can choose a fitness routine designed to make the most of what you have. And that's where our Escape Your Shape workout comes in.

Basically, body type refers to your proportions, whether you're "top-heavy" or (everybody's favorite) "hippy." There are the old ectomorph (sticklike), mesomorph (curvaceous) and endomorph (roly-poly) molds, which do a fine job of describing most people but never tell you what can be done about it. The same is true for the traditional apple or pear distinction, which consigns you forever to one fruit or the other.

Enter the Cone, Spoon, Hourglass and Ruler. These new body types come from Edward Jackowski, CEO of Exude Fitness in New York City. You may or may not instantly recognize yourself as a common household object, but we all tend toward one or another of these forms. Of course, genetics do predispose you toward a certain type—if your mother looks like Vendela, you're less likely to end up with arms that flap like the American flag in a Fourth of July breeze. But that doesn't mean that you're helpless, either.

These new body types aren't about slapping another label on your forehead. Instead they're designed to help focus your fitness routine. It's simple: Depending on your body type, you will strength-train to build on

FAT STATS

How We (Don't) Exercise

- Annual sales of sporting equipment: $1.6 billion
- Annual total spent on video rentals and cable TV: $26.6 billion
- Percentage of Americans who have exercised during the last two weeks: 18
- Percentage reporting irregular or no leisure-time physical activity: 58
- Minutes per day the average person spends watching TV: 154
- Minutes spent exercising: 15
- Most common type of exercise: stationary bicycle
- Least favorite type of exercise: stationary bicycle
- Amount of time a 132-pound woman would have to run to burn a pound of fat: 5 hours and 48 minutes

what's small and choose cardiovascular activities that burn fat for what's big. In other words, that stair-climber might be great for a small-on-the-bottom cone but would be deadly for a spoon (leg building is the *last* thing she needs).

Start by taking the typecasting survey on page 170, then find the workout that corresponds to your type. In no time you'll begin to see your body balance out. Better yet, you will see the power of exercise—and your power to make the most of the body you have.

For the Cone

The Plan

Cardio: Choose activities that work the legs and burn major calories to help reduce fat deposits in your upper back and bust.

Toning: Shape your lower-body muscles to balance a full upper body.

NEWS FLASH

Typecasting

Remember, it's all about proportion, so it's possible to be an overweight Ruler or an underweight Hourglass. To determine where you fit in, check off the one pair of statements to which you can answer emphatically, "That's me!" Then read on for your workout.

_____A. "Busty" definitely applies. I have a hard time trimming my upper body.

_____B. When I look in a mirror, I see hips, thighs and buttocks. Fat goes straight to my hips—and stays there.

_____C. I have a definite figure. When I'm in or out of shape, both my upper and lower body are equally in or out of shape.

_____D. Gumby has more curves than I do. When I lose weight, I shed mass evenly.

If you checked A, you're a Cone, which means you carry most of your weight in your upper body.

If you checked B, you're a Spoon, a body type that widens below the waist and may bulk up in that same area with certain types of exercise.

If you checked C, you fall into the Hourglass category. You're lucky in that you're well-proportioned. However, you may tend to gain weight as easily as you lose it.

If you checked D, you're a Ruler. Unless you're seriously overweight, you have the advantage of enjoying almost any type of exercise without worrying about bulking up in the wrong places.

A.   B.   C.   D.

Best Bets for Cardio

Every chance you get: Bike, run hills and steps or take fitness or step classes.

Sometimes: Jump rope or run flats.

Rarely: Swim, row or lift heavy weights for the upper body.

The Top Three Cone Toners

What you need: A 9- to 15-pound Body Bar ($30 to $40; call the STEP Company at 1-800-SAY-STEP) or a barbell without plates, and 2- to 3-pound ankle weights.

SQUATS
WORK THE QUADRICEPS.

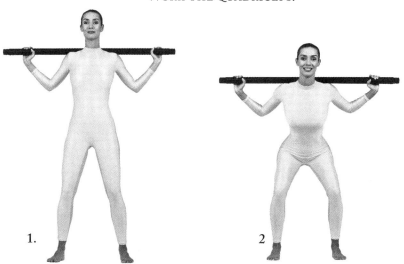

1. 2

1. Place a bar across your shoulders and take a wide stance with your knees slightly bent. **2.** Keeping your head and chest up, bend your knees and lower your hips as if you were sitting on a chair. Sink as low as you comfortably can or until your thighs are nearly parallel to the floor. Make sure your weight is back—your knees should not stray beyond your toes. Press through your heels and straighten to the starting position. You'll feel it in your thighs. Do two or three sets of up to 20 reps or until you feel fatigued.

KNEE-UPS
TONE THE QUADS ON THE STANDING LEG AND THE HIPS AND OUTER THIGHS ON THE OTHER LEG.

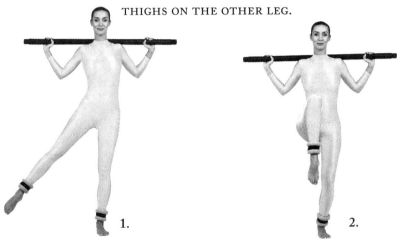

1. With the ankle weights on, stand with your feet shoulder-width apart and the bar resting behind your neck. Begin by shifting your weight to your left leg. Lift your right leg straight out to the side with the knee pointing forward.   **2.** Bending your left knee slightly, bring your right knee up to the center of your body, at waist height. Slowly return to the starting position, lightly tapping your toe on the ground for balance before raising your knee. Do up to 20 reps at a steady pace before switching legs. You'll know how many you can take when you begin to feel the burn.

VERTICAL SCISSORS
STRENGTHEN THE INNER THIGHS.

1. With the ankle weights on, lie on your back. Lift your legs to form a comfortable V over your hips. Keep your feet pointed or flexed, whichever feels best.   **2.** Open your legs as wide as you comfortably can. Then draw your legs together in the starting V. Repeat, slowly, 15 to 20 times, making sure that your lower back stays on the floor.

For the Spoon

The Plan

Cardio: Megadoses of constant motion. It's toughest to reduce fat deposits in the hips and thighs, the area that's most resistant to change. So think distance, distance, distance (which means intensity should be on the moderate side).

Toning: Focus on your upper body and abs to balance out your bigger bottom half.

Best Bets for Cardio

Every chance you get: Row, kayak or swim; use an upper-body ergometer and take superlong, fast-paced walks or hike flat terrain; go on long bike rides in low gears; dance; do aerobics. Take classes that include resistance exercises using weights or bands or do circuit training with machines.

Sometimes: Play singles tennis or full-court basketball, take martial arts classes or do in-line or ice skating on flat terrain.

Rarely: Stair-climb, take step classes, work at high tension on a stationary bike, ride a mountain bike or skate up hills or use heavy weights for your lower body.

The Top Three Spoon Toners

What you need: A bench, a 9- to 15-pound Body Bar or a barbell, and dumbbells.

DUMBBELL FLIES
WORK ON THE PECTORALS (THE CHEST MUSCLES).

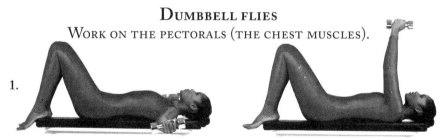

1.

1. Lie on your back on a bench with your knees bent so your feet are flat on the bench. Hold your abs in so that your lower back doesn't arch. Start with dumbbells in your hands, with your arms out at your sides so they're parallel to the floor and your palms are facing up. (Just be sure not to lock your elbows.) **2.** Keeping your arms slightly bent, contract your chest muscles to bring the weights toward each other over your chest. Pause, then lower. Choose a weight that lets you handle two or three sets of up to 12 reps.

BARBELL ROWS
TONE THE BACK, SHOULDERS AND ARMS.

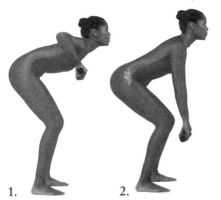

1. Begin in a football player's stance, crouching with your feet wide apart, your back straight and nearly parallel to the floor and your head up. With a shoulder-width grip and straight arms, hold a bar so it's directly beneath your shoulders. Keep your abs tight to support your lower back and don't let your chest collapse. **2.** Bend your arms to raise the bar toward your chest. Don't scrunch up your shoulders, and keep your elbows wide. Lower slowly and repeat. Do two sets of 8 to 12 reps. (If you have lower-back problems, do this same move with a dumbbell, using one arm at a time, so that you can support yourself with your other arm and kneel on a bench.)

PUSH-OUTS
WORK THE SHOULDERS, BICEPS AND FOREARMS.

1. Stand with your knees slightly flexed and your feet about shoulder-width apart. Hold a bar, overhand, in front of your thighs with your hands on either side of your legs. **2.** Keeping your arms and wrists straight, lift the bar to shoulder level. **3.** Bend your elbows to bring the bar in toward your chest. Make sure that your arms and elbows stay lifted. Reverse the move to lower the bar. You can lean forward slightly to avoid arching your back. Do two or three sets of 8 to 10 reps.

For the Hourglass

The Plan

Cardio: Stay active to control easy weight gain. Just be sure to mix sports and fitness activities that use both the upper and lower body. Better yet, opt for total-body workouts.

Toning/balance: Work your upper and lower body evenly. Stick with moderate weights, because muscle tends to come quickly.

Best Bet for Cardio

Every chance you get: Swim or play volleyball, cross-country ski or snowboard, take combination fitness classes that include upper-body toning.

Sometimes: Kayak; play basketball; take martial arts, boxing or yoga classes; rock climb; walk, bike and run—as long as you give your upper body equal time.

Rarely: Obsess over one sport or activity or use superheavy weights.

The Top Three Hourglass Toners

What you need: Just you!

REVERSE PLANKS
FOR THE ARMS, BACK AND HIPS.

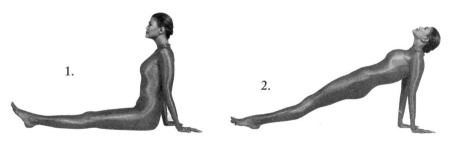

1. Sit on the floor with your legs straight and place your hands behind your hips so that your fingers are pointing backward.   **2.** Keeping your elbows straight, squeeze your shoulder blades together and slowly lift your hips. As your hips rise, look up at the ceiling and concentrate on elongating your body. Hold for several deep breaths, feeling your chest open and your body stretch. Return to the sitting position and repeat as many times as you can in good form.

FAT STATS

The Good Side

Number of pounds of skin removed from a Los Angeles man who lost more than half his 800-pound body weight: 25 (the skin was donated for transplants and research).

NEW DOWNWARD DOGS
WORK THE UPPER BODY, SHOULDERS, ARMS, BACK AND HIPS.

1.

2.

3.

1. Kneel on all fours.   **2.** Straighten your knees and lift your hips until your body forms an upside-down V, with your head down between your arms.   **3.** Lift your right leg toward the ceiling with your knee straight and your toes pointed. Hold for several deep breaths and feel the long line through the right side of your body from fingertips to toes. Then lower your right leg back into the downward dog and repeat on the left side. Repeat twice on each side, or more if you're up to it.

V SITUPS
FOR THE ABS AND THIGHS.

1. Lie on your back with your legs in the air, with your knees bent and pulled in toward your chest. Extend your arms overhead so your palms face upward. **2.** Reach your arms forward past your knees and at the same time straighten your legs to point your toes toward the ceiling. Tighten your abs to keep your shoulders as far off the floor as possible. Pause and then slowly lower yourself back to the starting position. Repeat as many times as you can in good form, which means without straining your neck.

For the Ruler

The Plan

Cardio: Anything goes, although to add definition, it's best to go for intensity rather than duration and play sports that require power.

Toning: Get strong. Focus on your back, shoulders and chest to add shapeliness. Strengthen your upper back and stretch your chest muscles to improve poor posture.

Best Bets for Cardio

Every chance you get: Box, swim, row, circuit-train or take calisthenics classes.

Sometimes: Hike, bike and skate hills or take yoga classes.

Rarely: Slouch.

The Top Three Ruler Toners

What you need: A 9- to 15-pound Body Bar or a barbell.

BARBELL KICKBACKS
WORK THE TRICEPS, ARMS AND SHOULDERS.

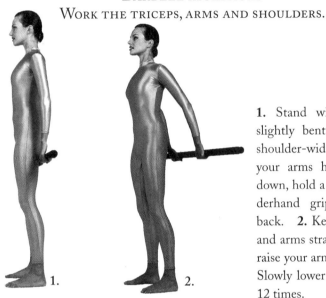

1. Stand with your knees slightly bent and your feet shoulder-width apart. With your arms hanging straight down, hold a bar with an underhand grip behind your back. **2.** Keeping your back and arms straight, exhale and raise your arms to lift the bar. Slowly lower and repeat 8 to 12 times.

REVERSE LUNGES
WORK THE BUTT AND THIGHS.

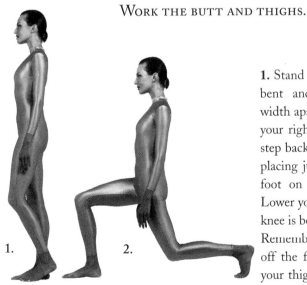

1. Stand with your knees slightly bent and your feet shoulder-width apart. Shift your weight to your right leg. **2.** Take a giant step backward with your left leg, placing just the ball of your left foot on the floor behind you. Lower your body until your right knee is bent at a 90-degree angle. Remember to keep your left heel off the floor. It's okay to touch your thigh for balance, but don't arch your back. Slowly return to the starting position. Repeat 10 to 15 times, then switch legs. Don't push yourself beyond mild fatigue on this one or you could be sore and sorry tomorrow.

SHOULDER ROTATIONS
HIT THE SHOULDERS AND UPPER BACK AND HELP IMPROVE POSTURE.

1. Stand with your knees slightly bent and your abs tight. Hold the bar in front of you with your hands shoulder-width apart and your palms facing your thighs. **2.** Raise the bar to the tops of your shoulders just below your neck, so your elbows are bent and your palms are facing forward.   **3.** Lift the bar slowly over your head and behind your neck. Reverse the move, pausing at your shoulders, then lower the bar to your thighs. Do two sets of 8 to 12 reps.

The 30-Minute
Fat-Burning Workout

You can do this supercharged circuit indoors or outdoors and shift your weight-loss program into high gear.

Trainers call it hitting the wall. Science types have a 75-cent phrase: general adaptation syndrome. Both mean the same thing: Your workout doesn't work. Your body doesn't change. Your fat lingers. Sound familiar?

The solution is to let yourself in for a shock. Here's a maximum fat-burning circuit that will jolt your system into responding to exercise.

This is how it works. "When you first started working out, you probably noticed significant changes in your shape, experienced at least some weight loss and felt tired after exercise," says Mike Caton, an exercise physiologist and fitness director at the Cooper Fitness Center in Dallas. "But after a few months, your body learned to respond to your demands." It's just like what happens when you first wear a new pair of shoes: You get a blister, it heals, the spot becomes a callus and you stop feeling pain. Essentially, your body becomes callused to the stress of the same workout month after month.

And that's where this maximum fat-burning workout comes in. Instead of the typical half weight-training, half aerobic session, this fast-paced circuit offers basic strength moves punctuated by two-minute bursts of cardiovascular revving. "The way you force your body to respond is with a dramatic change," says Caton. "This in turn speeds up your metabolism." Your body needs more energy, so it burns more calories. You zap more fat.

Do this 30-minute circuit three times a week for about a month, and

NEWS FLASH

Another Reason That Exercise Works

Exercise *and* diet? That demanding duo may seem like a double penalty for dieters, but in fact, it could be a tag-team for success. A study has found that working out somehow makes it easier to bypass the Ben and Jerry's and reach for the broccoli instead. In other words, regular exercise may actually enhance your ability to stick to a diet of healthy, low-fat foods.

In the study by researchers at the University of Chicago, 30 women went on a 12-week weight-reduction diet. Even while participating in the program, most had difficulty sticking to the diet. But 13 women who did a three-times-a-week 45-minute aerobic workout were much less likely to overeat than women who did not exercise. The bonus? Those who worked out lost an average of two pounds more.

What magic in exercise helped the dieters avoid overeating? Researchers speculate that its well-known mood-boosting effects made it easier to stick with the diet plan. In fact, the exercisers expressed less anxiety and depression than the diet-only group.

"And the feeling of self-control that comes with exercising may have extended to eating habits," says study leader Dale A. Schoeller, Ph.D., associate professor of medicine at the university.

Then again, it could have been that exercisers had less time to spend staring at the fridge, or perhaps they could more easily envision themselves someday turning heads at the health club.

we promise that you'll break through the wall. After you return to your regular routine, shake it up with the circuit every three or four months, or any time you feel the need for another big burst.

Ready, Set...

Set up your circuit in advance. Choose a weight with which you can complete 12 to 15 reps; the last 2 or 3 should be challenging. You can do the circuit in a gym with dumbbells, a stair-climber, a treadmill and a stationary bike. Or be creative and set up a circuit in your backyard, with weights, your own bike and a staircase nearby.

Remember, the key to this workout is to keep moving. That said, don't go overboard. Our time clock is only a guide. Good form and controlled movements are always more important than speed. Always start with a five-minute warm-up and then finish with a five-minute cooldown and stretch.

Go!

DUMBBELL SQUATS
WORK THE QUADS AND GLUTES.

1. Hold the end of a dumbbell in both hands and let your arms hang straight down. Standing with your feet shoulder-width apart, bend your knees until the top of the dumbbell is about even with your knees. Keep your weight distributed equally over both feet, with your heels on the floor. **2.** Contract your quads and glutes as you slowly straighten up. Concentrate on keeping the natural arch in your lower back; don't let your back or shoulders round forward. Do two sets of 12 to 15 reps.

Burst! Hop on a bike—either a stationary bike or your own manual machine—downshift or adjust the resistance so it's fairly easy to pedal, and start pumping. (Don't have a bike? Jump rope instead.) You want to be working hard but with consistent effort. Ride for two minutes and rest for one minute.

STAIR-STEP CALF RAISES
WORK THE CALVES.

1. With a dumbbell in each hand, stand with your feet a few inches apart on the edge of a step. The balls of your feet should be on the step, with your heels hanging over. Keep your knees straight but not locked, and maintaining the natural arch in your back, slowly raise up as high on your toes as you can. **2.** Slowly descend, but only until your heels are a few inches below the step. If you feel pain, you've gone too far. Do two sets of 12 to 15 reps.

Burst! Hit the bike again, only this time crank up the resistance or use a high gear so that you have to work hard to push the pedals. If that means standing to give yourself some leverage, do it. Rest for one minute.

DUMBBELL FLIES
WORK THE SHOULDERS.

1. Sit in a chair and hold a dumbbell in each hand. Start with your arms overhead with your elbows bent, as if you were hugging a tree trunk, and your palms facing down. **2.** Open your arms, pulling down and out, stopping at the point where your elbows are in line with your shoulders and your upper arms are parallel to the floor. Don't go any lower; that would put too much strain on your shoulders. Do two sets of 12 to 15 reps.

Burst! If you're outside, find an athletic field with bleachers or a steep hill. If you're indoors, use a staircase. In a gym, use the stair-climbing machine. Run at a medium pace for two minutes. Don't feel as if you have to run up for the duration; down is good, too, because it forces you to use your muscles in a way they're not used to working. Work for two minutes, then rest for one.

STANDING ONE-ARM DUMBBELL ROWS
WORK THE BACK.

1. Take a wide stance. Bend your knees and bend slightly forward from the waist. For balance, place your left hand on your left thigh just above your knee. Hold a dumbbell in your right hand and let your arm hang straight down from your shoulder **2.** Keeping your chin up, bend your elbow, raising the weight until your upper arm is roughly even with your back. Slowly lower the weight. Do a set, then switch sides and repeat. Do two sets of 12 to 15 reps on each side.

Burst! Use the same bleachers, hill, staircase or stair-climber, only this time, sprint. If after one minute you reach the point where it's a challenge to raise your legs up to reach the next step, you're working hard enough. Hang in there—you've still got a minute to go. Rest for one minute.

DUMBBELL CURLS
WORK THE BICEPS.

1. Stand with your feet shoulder-width apart and your knees slightly bent. Hold a dumbbell in each hand, palms up. **2.** Tucking your elbows in toward your waist, bend them until the weights are nearly at shoulder height. Your arms should angle slightly out—in other words, don't bring them straight up—because this is the way our arms bend when we let them hang naturally. Remember to keep your palms up throughout the move to get the most concentrated muscular contraction. Do two sets of 12 to 15 reps.

Burst! Do a striding run. Don't jog, but try to take exaggerated strides, bounding with larger steps than you would take on a distance run. Go for two minutes either on a treadmill or outside. Rest for one minute.

DUMBBELL KICKBACKS
FOR THE TRICEPS.

1. Hold a dumbbell in your left hand. Stand in the same position as for the standing one-arm dumbbell rows, with your knees bent and your right hand on your thigh for balance.   **2.** Keeping your upper arm tucked close to your body, slowly straighten your elbow to push the weight straight back. Stop when your arm is parallel to your side. Do a set, switch and repeat. Do two sets of 12 to 15 reps on each side.

Burst! Take another run, but this time think fast. In other words, fly as fast as you can for two minutes. Focus on using your legs to propel you forward.

The 24-Hour Workout

How many calories does a busy mother burn in the course of an average day? Our intrepid writer wore a monitor to find out.

Editor's note: Author Teryl Zarnow is a columnist for the *Orange County Register* and a (now) very active mother of three.

The first time I see myself in a bathing suit each summer, I regret not joining a gym. But realistically, I'm too busy lifting groceries to spend time lifting weights. And as for working out on exercise machines, why climb pretend steps to nowhere when I climb the real stairs in my house at least 25 times a day?

Okay, so maybe I don't qualify as bikini material. But deep down inside, I've never believed that those news stories about couch potatoes apply to me. People courting serious heart trouble wear their stomachs on their thighs, and the only time they leave the sofa is when they walk to the refrigerator for a high-fat snack.

I'm considerably more active than that. Although I haven't been exercising regularly, I've been running my household and running after three school-age children, and that has kept me on the move. So when I was offered the opportunity to be outfitted with a monitor to see how many calories I use dashing about in a normal day, I didn't expect to be totally embarrassed.

I wasn't. Not *totally* embarrassed, anyway. I found out that I don't need to rearrange my life in order to exercise—but I also found out that I need to work much harder than I originally thought.

Watching Calories—Literally

My assignment was to wear a waistband monitor, a device known as CAL-TRAC, which is made by Muscle Dynamics Fitness Network in Torrance, California. Slightly larger than a beeper, this unobtrusive little box provides a constant digital display of how many calories the body uses in the course of the day.

First I had to enter some personal data—my gender (female), my age (43) and my height and weight (five feet two inches, 118 pounds)—to calculate how many calories my body burns just because I'm alive, a measurement known as my basal metabolic rate (see "Metabolism: How Calories Burn" on page 188). I was surprised to find out that just by having a functioning heart, lungs and other organs, I use up 1,312 calories per day. Not bad, I thought.

> *I was surprised to find out that, just by having a functioning heart, lungs and other organs, I use up 1,312 calories per day.*

Then I set my monitor to calculate how many more calories I burned in the course of my daily activities. This was the disappointing part.

Monday was dismal. Because it was rainy, I spent most of the day in the house working behind my desk, and I drove everywhere else. The most walking I did was from the stove to the table when serving dinner. That evening, I discovered that I'd used up a measly 230 calories, making my daily total 1,542 calories burned—a lot fewer, no doubt, than the number of calories I consumed. I promised myself tomorrow would be better.

Tuesday was an improvement. I followed my more normal routine of walking my children two blocks home from school, grocery shopping and vacuuming the entire house. For good measure, I threw in a brisk 15-minute walk that I don't always take.

Uh-oh—Still a Slug

At the end of the day, I had burned 562 calories through activity. I felt pretty satisfied with that—until I talked to exercise physiologist Jim Herkimer, assistant professor of movement and exercise science at Chapman University in Orange, California, who had agreed to serve as my consultant during the course of this experiment.

Metabolism: How Calories Burn

The number of calories you burn is not affected only by your activity level. In fact, it's largely determined by your metabolism, the rate at which your body expends energy. If you have a fast metabolism, it's easier to stay thin. If yours is slow, you're more likely to gain weight.

But as important as metabolism is, exactly how it works remains a mystery. Here are some things that researchers do know.

- Believe it or not, you burn 60 percent of all your daily calorie intake while you sleep, according to Rudolph Leibel, M.D., co-head of the Laboratory of Human Behavior and Metabolism at Rockefeller University in New York City. "Your body requires a large amount of energy to maintain all your systems while you're at rest—heart, respiration, cell functions," Dr. Leibel says. This is what's known as your basal metabolic rate.
- Your metabolism is probably inherited. Researchers think that metabolism has a "set point" that determines how quickly a body burns calories. This set point is probably genetically determined, although early development and eating patterns may also play a role.
- The less muscle you have, the slower your metabolism. A 20-year-old woman eats the same amount as a 40-year-old. The 20-year-old maintains her weight; the 40-year-old gains weight. Why? The younger woman has more lean body mass—muscle—as opposed to fat. And it's muscle that burns calories. After age 40, most women

My heart sank as Herkimer told me that this level of activity—burning a total of 1,874 calories through activity and metabolic rate combined—makes me an average, sedentary American. In other words, I was a potato looking for a couch.

Herkimer suggested some improvements that I could make. He told me to do a little bit extra, more often. Instead of automatically hopping into the car, he suggested that I walk to as many places as possible. I also should get into the habit of taking the stairs instead of the escalator and playing outside with the kids instead of reading inside. You don't need a high-intensity workout to stay healthy, he assured me, just lots of activity.

have lost ten pounds of muscle mass, largely due to the aging process, and that makes it more difficult to burn calories.

- To speed up your metabolism, you have to develop more muscle, says Georgia Kostas, director of the Cooper Clinic in Dallas. And to gain muscle, you have to exercise. But aerobic exercise using the legs (walking, jogging, biking) is not enough. You also need to do muscle-building exercises such as weight lifting, swimming, tennis and other activities.
- Yo-yo dieting doesn't affect your metabolism. After all of the conflicting studies in recent years, the bottom line on yo-yo dieting is this: While it may be psychologically frustrating, yo-yo dieting does not result in a slower metabolism, nor does it harm your heart.
- Medication usually does not slow down your metabolism. Certain medications, such as antidepressants, may cause you to gain weight, but it's not because they slow down your metabolism. Rather, the medication increases your appetite, causing you to take in more calories.
- Metabolic problems may someday be treated with drugs. According to Dr. Leibel, as more research points to the biological nature of metabolism (rather than its being something we can deliberately control), metabolism problems may someday be treated with medication, just as high blood pressure and high cholesterol are today.

I liked the way that sounded; I've always found it hard to stay motivated when it comes to rigorous workouts. I can discard an exercise plan faster than I can a candy-bar wrapper. But Herkimer made exercising more seem more manageable than I had ever thought. I vowed that the next day I'd make it a point to keep moving.

On Wednesday, I seized every opportunity to stay active. I walked with my friend and her meandering dog for 50 minutes, practiced soccer drills for 45 minutes, did 20 minutes of aerobics to a Richard Simmons tape, walked the long way to pick up the kids and played some driveway basketball. My efforts added up: By the end of the day, I had burned 695

NEWS FLASH

Mister Sandman, Bring Me Ice Cream

Busy, busy, busy? Too busy to go to bed? Then you should know that not getting a good night's sleep can do more to hurt your appearance than just contributing to bags under your eyes. Research shows that it can also pile on pounds.

"People deprived of sleep get carbohydrate cravings. Then they indulge in things they shouldn't be eating," says David Rye, M.D., Ph.D., medical director of the Sleep Disorders Center at Emory University Medical School in Atlanta. "Weight gain is a common complaint from people who are having serious trouble sleeping."

And when you're weary, you might not exercise your body or your willpower as much as you would if you were rested—which means big trouble if you're watching your weight, Dr. Rye says.

Sleep deprivation may be brought on by poor-quality sleep, often caused by sleep apnea, a common condition of impaired breathing during sleep, Dr. Rye says. From patients with this condition, he says, "I regularly hear the lament, 'I'm the heaviest I've ever been.'"

In these cases, getting to bed early does no good, says Dr. Rye, because poor-quality sleep leaves you feeling wiped out no matter how long you're in bed.

Sometimes being overweight causes sleep apnea because extra fat accumulates in the neck and throat, obstructing breathing. Trimming down should correct this problem, says Dr. Rye.

In other cases, changes in sleeping positions, medications or surgery resolve sleep apnea troubles.

If you think you have sleep apnea, ask a bedtime companion to listen for snoring that is interrupted by periods of silence followed by gasps for air or snorting. If you sleep alone, check yourself with a voice-activated tape recorder. Those sounds are sleep apnea tip-offs, says Dr. Rye. Then visit your doctor or a sleep disorders clinic.

calories through activity—making my total number of calories burned 2,007. I was thrilled that I'd been able to crack 2,000.

Unfortunately, Herkimer was not exactly in awe. The best he could say was that on Wednesday I was moderately active. For comparison, he told me that a 250-pound defensive tackle, during fall training in college football, burns 6,000 to 7,000 calories per day. "Burning 2,000 calories per day is not enough if you eat pizza at lunch and Häagen-Dazs ice cream at dinner," he said. "But it's great if you're having cereal and nonfat milk for breakfast and fruit for snacks." (I had to confess that although I try to stick to a healthy diet, neither pizza nor ice cream is a complete stranger to me.) To provide a margin for error, Herkimer told me to try to burn another 200 calories (30 minutes of activity) per day. Now I was embarrassed. I thought I had reached my goal, and he told me I had achieved my starting point.

Going for the Burn

By now I felt a bit more frantic. What did I need to do to make sure I was getting enough exercise? Was it really possible to burn enough calories without spending large portions of my life at a gym?

Herkimer insisted it was. He told me that to reap the health benefits associated with exercise, I needed to burn about an extra 1,500 to 2,000 calories a week beyond what I'd been burning so far. I could do that, he assured me, by increasing the intensity of my activity. If I walked briskly to my car, for instance, I could burn twice as many calories as I did if I strolled.

And so began my obsession with moving quickly—and with watching my monitor. For the remainder of

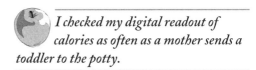

I checked my digital readout of calories as often as a mother sends a toddler to the potty.

the week, I checked my digital readout of calories as often as a mother sends a toddler to the potty. (That is, constantly.) The more I moved, the more I liked what I saw. I discovered that by leaving the house ten minutes early for a brisk walk before picking up the kids, I could buy myself an extra 50 calories daily. If I was ready early enough to also walk them to school (and then to take a brisk walk on the way back), I could get up to 100.

Some activities turned out to be an unexpected calorie-burning bonanza. One afternoon, I raced through four stores in 90 minutes buying supplies for my seven-year-old's birthday party—and I burned up 100 calories without even realizing it. The party itself, from baking the cupcakes through playing Duck, Duck, Goose to vacuuming up the crumbs, burned 239 calories. (And the kids had a great time to boot.)

The trick, I realized, was to keep my body in drive and avoid parking. The faster I moved, the better the results. For instance, I discovered that a brisk 45-minute walk could burn 250 calories, but if I walked at an even brisker stride—and swung my arms as I went—I got that up to 400.

By Saturday, I had this calorie-burning business down pat. I began my day by walking (very briskly, of course) for three-quarters of an hour. I practically flew up and down the stairs when I was doing laundry. When I went to the shopping center, I parked at the farthest corner of the lot and returned to the car after going to the drugstore, then back again to buy groceries. I spent lots of time outside, racing after the kids. That day, I broke 900 in physical activity.

As I collapsed into bed that evening, I realized that I couldn't keep up that pace all week long. But I felt confident that I could manage to burn at least 2,000 extra calories on most weekends and maybe another 1,500 during the week. That's even about what Herkimer told me to aim for. Hey, I thought, maybe I could even manage to burn enough calories to start losing weight.

Now my experiment is over, and I feel slightly humbled. My week with CALTRAC taught me that if you don't play sports, don't go to a gym regularly or don't have an extremely active job, you don't automatically exercise enough. But it also showed me that making a special effort isn't as difficult as I'd thought.

Even though my assignment is finished, I still strap my little calorie-counter monitor to my belt from time to time. It's a good way to remind myself to try to fit fitness into my everyday routines. No, I don't always burn as many calories as I'd like. But the fact is, I'm burning a lot more these days than when I began.

Walk It Off

The no-gain, no-pain plan for permanent
fat-busting results.

It's easy to lose things. Throw a pair of socks in the wash, and only one comes out of the dryer. Leave your keys on the dining room table for five minutes, and they become invisible. It's easy to lose unwanted pounds, too. People lose weight all the time. You've probably lost weight on several separate occasions in the past simply by eating a little (or a lot) less. But once the diet was done, you no doubt discovered the sad truth: Unlike your missing keys or socks, pounds return automatically. In fact, if you just sit there and do nothing, they will fly back like a flock of pudgy homing pigeons.

Luckily, the secret to giving those lost pounds the permanent slip is surprisingly simple. You've gotta walk. The latest research not only shows that the land of thinness is reachable by putting one foot in front of the other, it also suggests how many steps away it is.

Of course, the research also shows that the journey is one that needs to be made regularly. You'll have to walk today, tomorrow, next year—and ten years from now. In other words, walking must become a permanent part of your life. And, as with anything in life, you can make it easy on yourself or you can make it downright impossible to maintain.

Let's go for easy.

How Much, How Often, How Hard?

Research conducted over the past several years has consistently shown that walking is an excellent way to maintain weight loss. One study, conducted at William Beaumont Hospital in Birmingham, Michigan, has given us an idea of just how much walking may be involved.

In the study, 45 obese people were put on a very-low-calorie diet and experienced an average weight loss of approximately 61 pounds. Two years later, the members of the group were not only reweighed but also questioned as to their daily exercise habits. As you might imagine, the people who were in the low-activity group (burning less than 850 calories a week in exercise) gained back much of the weight—72 percent of what they had lost two years earlier.

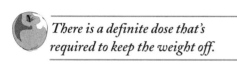
There is a definite dose that's required to keep the weight off.

Surprisingly, the moderate-activity group (burning a more respectable 850 to 1,575 calories per week) fared even worse, regaining 75 percent of the weight. But here's the kicker: The high-activity group, burning more than 1,575 calories, gained back only 24 percent of what they had originally lost. And for those burning more than 2,000 calories, the gain was a mere 13 percent.

"The majority of the people we studied achieved these results by walking," says Charles Lucas, M.D., chief of the Division of Preventive and Nutritional Medicine at the hospital. "But the real story is the difference between the amount of weight regained by the moderate-activity group and the high-activity group. It suggests that there is a definite dose that's required to keep the weight off."

And the dose starts at around 1,575 calories burned a week. Let's call it 1,600 for good measure. It may be that if you can walk off 1,600 calories a week, you have a good chance of buying clothes today and still fitting into them ten years from now.

But 1,600 is just a number. How does it translate into time spent hoofing it? A person weighing 130 pounds burns about 320 calories by walking four miles in an hour. Walking at that pace five times a week adds up a grand total of 1,600 calories burned. So you have your target. An hour a day, five times a week, at four miles per hour. Or to make it simple, 20 miles per week.

Before Getting Started

An hour a day? Five times a week? For the rest of your life? Who has that kind of time to spend meandering around the local park system? "Well, just ask yourself this," says James O. Hill, Ph.D., associate director of the Center for Human Nutrition at the University of Colorado Health Sciences Center in Denver. "If you could make an extra $5,000 a week in only five hours, would you do it? You bet you would. So you do have the time; it's just a matter of seeing exercise as being every bit as valuable as that $5,000."

You can't start an exercise program that you intend to make permanent without first doing a little thinking. And as Dr. Hill aptly points out, one of the things you need to think about is how to make exercise seem like something that you just can't do without. But there are plenty of other things to consider as well. So before putting on your walking shoes, consider the following factors.

Give it value. Sure, the real reason you're going to start walking is that you don't want to have to re-lose the same 20 pounds over and over again.
But exercise provides many other goodies as well. It can help lower your blood pressure and cholesterol levels. It can also reduce your risk of heart attack and stroke. "And all the benefits are not strictly physiological," adds Dr. Hill. "Exercise can help you sleep better and feel more relaxed and even keep your moods on a more even keel."

 If you want to give yourself a real reason to exercise, just go visit your doctor for a full examination.

Another way to give it value is to realize what happens to you if you don't exercise. "You can't believe how valuable exercise starts looking to some of our sedentary patients after we check them out and show them how high a body-fat content they have or how poorly they do on a treadmill test," says Tedd Mitchell, M.D., medical director of the Cooper Wellness Program at the Cooper Aerobics Center in Dallas. "If you want to give yourself a real reason to exercise, just go visit your doctor for a full examination."

Make it irresistible. Unfortunately, all the information in the world, both positive and negative, is not going to keep you exercising throughout your life if you hate what you're doing. "In other words, you've got to choose an activity that you really love to do," says Rod Dishman, Ph.D., professor in the Department of Exercise Science at the University of Georgia in Athens. "Weight maintenance is a long-term goal that, on a daily basis, is not strong enough to get you out of bed. But if you have fun doing what you're doing and it makes you feel good . . . and you miss it

Tips for Overweight Walkers

Being heavy may make things a little harder, but it needn't stop you from walking—or from enjoying it! Here's what you need to know.

- Walk on as soft a surface as possible. Choose cushioned high school tracks or wood-chip-covered fitness trails rather than asphalt or concrete surfaces.
- Make a habit of stretching your calves and hamstrings immediately after walking.
- Look for durability and cushioning in a walking shoe. Don't settle for a bottom-of-the-line casual walking shoe; it won't have enough support for a heavier walker. Better choices include the Avia 382, the New Balance 800 and the Nike Air Healthwalker Plus. All have polyurethane midsoles and are well-designed for stability, which is beneficial to overweight walkers.

when you don't do it . . . that's what keeps you going back for more."

We suggest walking for a couple of reasons. First, it's accessible to just about everyone. Maybe that's the biggest reason it's the most popular physical activity in the country. (Millions of people could be wrong, but are you going to argue with them?) "And second, people who have been overweight in the past have been putting extra stress on their joints," says Dr. Mitchell. "Walking is a low-impact activity that goes easy on those joints."

But—and this is a big but—if, say, mountain climbing rather than walking happens to be your thing, and you have daily access to a mountain, then far be it from anyone to stand between you and the Matterhorn. Love what you do and you boost your chances of succeeding.

Give yourself a history lesson. If you're like most people, you've already had a past affair with exercise that for some reason or another ended in divorce. Why? Did you dislike the exercise you chose? Were there scheduling problems? Didn't you get enough support from friends and family? Figure it out, because those who do not learn from history are doomed to repeat it.

Consider your environment. "When people talk about getting support for their exercise program, they mostly mean support from family and friends," says William McCarthy, Ph.D., director of science at the Pritikin Longevity Center in Santa Monica, California. "But your environment can also provide support, or a lack of it."

People living in California log a much higher average number of hours expended in physical activity than do those living in Minnesota. Why? Maybe because snow is something that many Californians see only on television—not lying two feet deep on their sidewalks. "Likewise, you'll probably find less exercise in metropolitan areas than in the suburbs, partly because of a safety factor," says Dr. McCarthy.

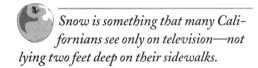

Snow is something that many Californians see only on television—not lying two feet deep on their sidewalks.

The bottom line: Your environment can make or break your exercise plans. "But your environment is not an insurmountable obstacle if you plan ahead," says Dr. McCarthy. "We encourage people who come to the Pritikin Center from Northern climes to get a treadmill. That way when bad weather hits, they're covered. Likewise, mall-walking is another good suggestion: It's safe and warm."

Get a backup. It's hailing golf balls. They're drilling for oil on your favorite walking path. Your cat just had kittens in your right shoe. In other words, you don't feel like walking today. "We always encourage people to have an alternative activity that they enjoy," says Dr. McCarthy. "That way, minor injury, boredom or unforeseen circumstances don't break the routine." Have sore feet? Go for a swim and keep your excuses to yourself.

Make it a great big deal. Tell your family, your friends and the people you work with that a new exercise program is about to be born. This is an important step for a couple of reasons. "The reason a lot of commercial and university weight-loss programs work is that the participants know they are going to be weighed and watched," says Dr. Hill. "It's called accountability. You want to make sure someone you know asks questions every so often to keep you honest."

Second, people won't know how important your exercise time is to you unless you tell them. "Let them know when you intend to walk and how serious you are about it," says Dr. Mitchell. "That way they'll know not to schedule other activities for you."

The Weighty Issue of Thyroid Trouble

It's true that lots of people gain weight and slow down as they get older. But both of these symptoms can also be signs of a sluggish thyroid gland, and it may be well worth your time to have yours checked, especially if you also have such symptoms as fatigue, memory loss, unusually dry, coarse skin, constipation, lost pleasure or interest in usual activities, sensitivity to cold or hair loss (in women).

If you suspect that your weight gain is due to a thyroid problem, you'll want to ask your doctor specifically for a new test that makes it easier than ever to detect early thyroid problems, called a sensitive or ultrasensitive thyroid-stimulating hormone (TSH) test, says Stanley Feld, M.D., chief executive physician of Endocrine Associates of Dallas and past president of the American Association of Clinical Endocrinologists in Jacksonville, Florida.

This is a new way to measure the levels of hormones in your blood and detect the early stages of thyroid problems. High or low levels of TSH detect thyroid disease, which can then be easily treated.

Since women are five to eight times more likely than men to have hypothyroidism—low thyroid function—new guidelines from the

Finally, keep it simple. One of the big mistakes that beginners make is being overly optimistic concerning their motivation. Are you really going to get into the car after dinner and drive over to that lovely park on the other side of town, take an hour walk and then drive home—every night? Probably not. "The more steps you have to take to exercise, the less chance that you will actually do it," says Dr. Mitchell. "A walk around your neighborhood may not be as scenic as a hike in the hills, but it's a lot easier to do regularly."

American Association of Clinical Endocrinologists recommend that all middle-aged and older women have a TSH test done annually to determine if they have thyroid disease. You might ask for it during annual exams or gynecological checkups, says Dr. Feld. Men and younger women need this test only if their symptoms warrant it.

Hypothyroidism affects some six million to seven million people in the United States and up to 20 percent of women age 70 or older, according to the American Association of Clinical Endocrinologists. "But because symptoms can be vague, doctors fail to diagnose half of all cases," says Dr. Feld. Left undetected, severe cases of hypothyroidism can contribute to heart problems and depression.

Drugs can bring your thyroid hormone levels back to normal in two to three weeks. Be forewarned, though. While treatment may provide some initial weight loss as your metabolism returns to normal, it can't take off all of the accumulated pounds from years of living with an underactive thyroid. But once you start to feel peppier again, you may find a weight-loss program easier to tackle, says Dr. Feld.

Going from 0 to 20 Miles

All right. You've decided to walk. You've figured out what went wrong in the past. You have alternative exercise plans for any possible emergency short of an interplanetary alien invasion, and you've announced your intentions to the world. It's time to pump some pavement to the tune of one hour a day, five times a week, four miles per session. And that's what you'll do right from the start no matter how much it hurts, right?

Wrong.

You're going to be doing this for the rest of your life. What's the rush? "It's been found that people who start out exercising moderately are twice as likely to still be exercising at the end of a year as people who start out at high intensity," says Dr. McCarthy. "And we only suggest starting out at even a moderate level if it feels comfortable. The best way to make the best beginning is a step approach. Do what feels good and build from there. That way you won't scare yourself off the program." Sensible advice. Here are a few more tips not only to get you going but to keep you going as well.

The best way to make the best beginning is a step approach. Do what feels good and build from there.

Take it by the numbers. "In any exercise program, you want to first establish frequency, then duration and then intensity," says Dr. Mitchell. "In other words, the first thing you should do is try to walk five times a week, even if it's only for five minutes at a time."

Trying for five small workouts makes sense for a number of reasons. "First of all, we are creatures of habit," says Dr. Mitchell. "You want to get yourself used to the idea of walking five days a week, incorporate it into your schedule and make it feel natural before taking on a more challenging workout."

Second, a five-day-a-week schedule may actually be easier to maintain. "It's true," says Dr. Dishman. "If you ask people to exercise five or six days a week, you get better adherence over the long term than if you have them do three or four days. A possible explanation is that an every-other-day program isn't constant enough to become habit, but five or six days is."

Once you're walking five days a week, make each walk longer until you're doing an hour at a time. "Then, and only then, do you start building the intensity and going for that four miles per hour," says Dr. Mitchell. "Again, the golden rule is to do what feels comfortable so that you'll want to do it again and again."

Keep the schedule firm. Five days of walking means two days off. But those two days should not be considered "get out of jail free" cards to be used whenever you please. "Any time you have to make a decision as to what days to exercise and what days not to, you are setting yourself up for problems," says Dr. Mitchell. "Keep the decisions to a minimum by creating a schedule that stays the same from week to week. Personally, I feel that walking every day, Monday through Friday, and taking the weekend

Different Strokes

The cardinal rule for long-term exercise adherence is that you have to love what you do. If walking doesn't quite float your boat, however, there's a whole host of other ways you can burn 320 calories per day. (Burning 320 calories five days a week meets the 1,600-calories-per-week requirement.) And many of these activities can do it for you even faster than walking does.

Activity	Minutes to Burn 320 Calories*
Aerobic dance, vigorous	41
Badminton, leisurely	57
Basketball	40
Bicycling, level (6 mph)	92
Bicycling, level (12 mph)	43
Cross-country skiing (4 mph)	38
Handball	38
Hiking, with pack (3 mph)	55
Ice skating (9 mph)	59
Jumping rope (70 jumps/minute)	34
Racquetball	31
Rowing machine, moderate	46
Running (10 min./mile)	34
Running (12 min./mile)	41
Snowshoeing, soft snow	33
Stationary cycling (10 mph)	51
Step aerobics (7" step)	36
Swimming, crawl (slow)	43
Tennis, recreational	50

*Based on a 130-pound person

off makes the most sense. You work during the week, you walk during the week."

Pamper yourself initially. "The first four to eight weeks is the critical time period that determines whether you quit or keep going," says Dr. Mitchell. "Conversely, it's also the period when exercise isn't quite delivering the rewards that it will be down the road. You may feel tired. You may feel a little sore. It's less than motivating, so you'll want to pamper yourself a bit."

Give yourself a little extra time to psych up before your walk and a little extra time to rest afterward. Get a calendar specifically for walking and give yourself a gold star on each day you do it. Lay out your exercise clothes within easy reach at the beginning of the week so that there's no scrounging to do it at the last minute. "I even have patients who reward themselves with a weekend trip with their spouses if they make it to eight weeks," says Dr. Mitchell. The key is to do whatever it takes to get through that first eight weeks. "After that, it not only starts to become habit, but you also start feeling some of the benefits that walking can provide," he says.

Don't fret about your progress. "The more time you spend worrying about whether or not you're walking fast enough or burning enough calories, the less time you spend enjoying the walk," says Dr. Hill. "Just get out there and do it. As your fitness level rises, you'll naturally find yourself walking farther, walking faster and burning more calories." Remember the cardinal rule: If you don't have fun, you won't do it.

You have a particularly bad day and suddenly a drink, a La-Z-Boy and a remote control look a lot more attractive than a pair of walking shoes.

Do it in the morning. "Statistically speaking, we find that people who work out in the morning are more likely to have better long-term adherence than those who wait until evening," says Dr. Mitchell. "Primarily, it may be because morning schedules are a little easier to control than evening ones, where a late meeting at work, an unexpected trip with your child to the doctor or any number of other unforeseen problems can put walking on the back burner."

But motivation plays a part as well. "You have a particularly bad day and suddenly a drink, a La-Z-Boy and a remote control look a lot more attractive than a pair of walking shoes," says Dr. Mitchell. "Now, that's not to say that there aren't some people who might do better walking at night, but, to be honest, it takes a lot more discipline."

Hang out with the active. Studies made of people who quit smoking show that the ones most successful at the one-year mark tend to socialize with nonsmokers. "I would guess the same to be true of people pursuing physical activity," says Dr. McCarthy. "We do have some clues that exercisers tend to hang around other exercisers, but nothing conclusive."

Dr. McCarthy is quick to point out, however, that at the Pritikin Longevity Center, so many people on staff exercise that it almost creates a cultural norm, which acts as an encouraging social pressure to exercise. And deep down, you know you'll be much more likely to exercise if your friends run marathons rather than sit around watching sitcom marathons on cable television.

Do a little if you can't do a lot. There will be days when, for one reason or another, an hour-long walk seems as likely as a Beatles reunion. In cases like this, the best thing you can do for yourself is to try for at least ten minutes. "Yes, you're not doing the exercise as it should be done, but you are at least holding the place in your schedule and not breaking continuity," says Dr. McCarthy. "Place holding, however, should not become an excuse to do less on a regular basis. But when an hour just isn't possible, it can keep you from stopping completely."

Get yourself two pairs of walking shoes. The one thing you'll want to avoid is having to take a few days off due to sore feet, since there's always the chance that those few days will stretch into weeks, months and years. "To avoid that, you need to realize that no pair of shoes is a perfect fit," says Dr. McCarthy. "Each pair stresses different parts of the foot. But if you alternate between two different pairs of shoes, then what's being stressed today gets a rest tomorrow."

Make other lifestyle changes. Since you're beginning a new walking program, now's the time to make a few other changes as well. Cut down on the alcohol and caffeine and lower your fat intake. "Not only can these changes help to make you feel better faster, but they also become supportive of each other," says Dr. McCarthy. "The more changes you make to your life, the harder it is to go back to your old habits—and that includes going back to being sedentary." Think of it as a little constructive bridge burning.

Stairway to Weight-Loss Heaven

How stair-climbers can add clout to your weight-loss efforts.

Hear ye, hear ye! Step right up to see the eighth wonder of the weight-loss world. The marvelous, the magnificent, the one and only Stairway to Weight-Loss Heaven!" Inside the big tent, shiny stair-climber machines are lined up as far as the eye can see, all occupied by novice "steppees" stepping away in high gear.

Okay, this is just a health writer's afternoon reverie, but that gadget being hawked by the overstimulated salesman is no snake oil. Stair-climbers are bona fide fat burners that can boost your buns right off that weight-loss plateau they've been resting on.

A mile of stair climbing burns 40 to 60 percent more calories than a mile of brisk walking. But how do you use that knowledge to your best advantage when waging the battle of the bulge? Not by dropping your walking routine, heading for the health club and replacing your daily half-hour walk with the same time on a stair-climber. That route to weight-loss heaven could easily lead you to a stair-stepper hell of sore shins, sore buns and burnout.

We still recommend walking as the exercise of choice for weight loss. Consistency counts, and walking is the easiest way to be consistent because of that "any time, anywhere" factor. It's also pleasant, relaxing and stress-reducing to walk outside in a natural setting, advantages that you're unlikely to enjoy on a stair-climber. So stick with the great outdoors when you can. And use the stair-climber judiciously to boost your total calorie burn. The idea is to add stair-climbing to your current exercise schedule. Because stair-climbing can be a very strenuous activity, we suggest that you add it to your workout only after you've been walking briskly and regularly (three to five days a week for at least a half-hour each day) for about a month. That should give you sufficient stamina and conditioning to begin working at the intensity a stair-climber requires—without giving up after the first three minutes. Stair-climbing gives you slightly different muscular training and a higher-intensity cardiovascular workout.

The Vertical Advantage

Why use a stair machine instead of walking faster? Well, you *could* walk faster. Walking at a 12-minute-per-mile pace burns over 500 calories an hour, compared with about 400 calories an hour for a 15-minute-per-mile pace. Speedwalking and racewalking are fun. But they take a fair amount of training, technique, coordination and mental effort to accomplish.

You could add a little jogging to your walks, but you'd be tripling the impact on your feet and joints. Stair-climbing is very low impact, like walking, because your feet never leave the pedals.

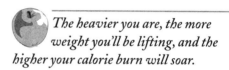 *The heavier you are, the more weight you'll be lifting, and the higher your calorie burn will soar.*

On a stair-climber, just by virtue of the vertical lifting of your body weight, your heart rate accelerates rapidly. And the heavier you are, the more weight you'll be lifting, and the higher your heart rate and calorie burn will soar. You don't have to learn how to do it or concentrate hard—it just happens.

Stepping Right

The stair-climber is one of the most popular exercise machines at health clubs, YMCAs and spas around the country. Assuming that you'll be using a club machine to introduce yourself to stepping, make sure you schedule your visits at times when you won't have to fight for one. (Many clubs give trial memberships for low fees or even for free.) Watching other people work out may feel exhausting, but the calorie burn for spectators is just a hair above that for sleeping.

Your first time on, have an instructor explain how to use all the special features. You may be able to choose a preformulated program or create your own. You can often set your time and intensity and vary the terrain

---

Knee Pain? Proceed with Caution

If yours are among the millions of wounded knees in the world, you don't have to avoid stair-steppers. Cedric Bryant, Ph.D., director of sportsmedicine for the StairMaster company, suggests using a stair-stepper cautiously. "Go through as full a range of motion as you can without pain," he says. "If you feel pain, back off immediately. Stay with shorter steps, and as you strengthen the muscles that support and protect your knee, you can deepen the steps you take."

Stair-climbers have been used by physicians to rehabilitate knees after reconstructive surgery. The biomechanics are very similar to climbing real stairs except that you don't expose your joints to high amounts of stress. Since you're always "going up," you eliminate the most stressful phase of the activity and avoid the excessive body-weight pressure of going down the steps on those all-too-easily-injured joints.

---

automatically. As exercise physiologist Doug Garfield, Ed.D., founder and CEO of Motioneering, Inc. in Napierville, Illinois, says, you're not climbing steps, you're creating your own stairway!

At first, just get used to all the variety of the machine. Jump on for five-minute stints to acclimate your muscles and your mind to how the machine works. Find out what is most comfortable for you in terms of pace and depth of step. Just make sure you never allow the pedals to come all the way up or to hit bottom, as that can jar your joints.

Cedric Bryant, Ph.D., director of sportsmedicine for the StairMaster company, suggests that you practice stepping up rather than trying to push the pedals down. It's a subtle distinction, but there is a difference.

"We supported a study at Stanford University and found that people who try to push down are more likely to experience numbness or tingling in their feet from too much pressure on the nerve," says Dr. Bryant. "It's like lying on one arm too long and having it fall asleep—uncomfortable but not dangerous, and completely avoidable."

Allow your foot to go through the normal range of motion. Don't stay up on your tippy-toes as you pump the steps. Think about your walking form. Use a heel-to-toe roll and allow plenty of ankle movement. Stand tall, with your head erect. Don't lean on the console or the arm rails. For every ten pounds of body weight that you support by leaning on the handrails, you burn 7 percent fewer calories. And don't read, which may put undue tension on your neck, back or shoulders. "Your shoulders and hips should stay pretty level," says *Prevention* adviser Wayne Westcott, Ph.D., strength-training consultant for the YMCA of the USA. "Otherwise you may stress the lower back, hips and knees."

> *For every ten pounds of body weight that you support by leaning on the handrails, you burn 7 percent fewer calories.*

As you get acclimated, you may even be able to swing your arms naturally at your sides.

Getting the Max

For optimal weight loss, work out at a pace that allows you to talk but one in which carrying on a conversation would be a little difficult. Long, slow workouts are good fat burners for beginners, but they don't have the corner on the market when it comes to shedding pounds. As you become more fit, higher-intensity workouts can burn calories faster (and total calories burned is what's important for dropping weight).

If you can maintain the pace, you'll burn more calories. And sometimes just a change of activity seems to shock the body into moving toward your weight-loss goal.

At first you may become breathless quite quickly on the stair-climber, but after three or four sessions, you'll be able to find a reasonable adjustment among depth of step, speed and heart rate. Work up gradually to 30-minute sessions, adding two or three per week to your walking workout. You should be able to judge by the way you feel that you're working harder than you do during your normal walking workout. If it seems too easy, step up the pace or deepen your steps. But be careful not to take too long or deep a step, which may lead to injury. The depth of the step you take should allow you to maintain good posture as you're exercising. If your hips and shoulders are moving up and down, your step is too deep.

Short, quick steps don't involve enough muscle mass to give you maximum calorie burn, but they are great for warming up and cooling down. As you work up to longer workouts, use short steps for your warm-up, progress to deeper steps for the high-intensity core of your workout and then cool down with five minutes of shorter steps at the end. Go for high intensity, Dr. Westcott suggests, because the fun factor of a stair-stepper is not very high, and you may get bored very quickly compared with walking. So you may as well burn lots of calories while you're in the stepping mood.

The Science of Intervals

Most stair-climbers allow you to set a course that varies the intensity of your workout, although you can set the high and low parameters. Intervals (short bursts of intense activity followed by a longer rest period) are great for weight loss.

Here's how it works. Instead of maintaining a steady, moderately fast pace, you fluctuate between going very fast and recovering at a slower pace. Studies have shown that most people are able to burn more calories this way because their average speed tends to be a little bit higher than what they could sustain continuously at a moderately difficult pace. And because they get a chance to rest and recover, they don't feel they've worked that much harder.

Step Wear

Your walking shoes should be fine for stair-climbing, as long as they fit well to begin with. And that would mean plenty of room around your toes and a snug-enough heel to avoid slipping. Your feet are doing a lot of the work here, and your feet and toes may temporarily swell as you work out, so give them room by buying shoes with an adequately roomy toe box.

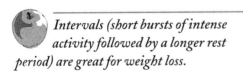
Intervals (short bursts of intense activity followed by a longer rest period) are great for weight loss.

Dress in layers. You may need a sweatshirt as you start out in what seems like a frigid gym, but you'll be peeling off those layers lickety-split as your body heats up during the workout. Strip down to a T-shirt or leotard once you get cookin'. You won't have the benefit of a breeze as you would if you were walking outside. And keep a water bottle handy. You're going to work up a sweat, and you could dehydrate fairly quickly. While it's true that the

FAT STATS

Celebrity Size-Up

- Range in size of the 900 dresses Oprah Winfrey sold at a benefit for a community outreach program: 8 to 22
- Number of miles Oprah runs each day: 5 to 10
- Number of minutes Oprah spends on a StairMaster: 45
- Number of sit-ups Oprah does each day: 350
- Percentage of fans who believe Oprah will not regain weight this time around: 66

stair-stepper works the muscles of the lower body more than walking does, don't worry about bulging muscles. "You'll get some more toning in that area," says Dr. Bryant, "but most people get more endurance rather than gains in muscle strength."

To ward off shinsplints (and if you're a regular walker), this exercise can help: Take a five-pound weight, tie a shoestring through the center hole or to both ends if it's a dumbbell, and hang it over your shoe. Sit on a high desk or bench, and using your foot only, raise and lower the weight by bringing your toes up toward your shin. Do this three days a week, and it will help keep your ankles strong to withstand the increase in activity, prevent shinsplints and avoid stress fractures in that area. Follow any stair-climber workout with leg stretches.

The New No-Willpower Exercise Plan

Here's how to plan your exercise routine so there's no room for excuses.

The truth is, people who stay faithful to their exercise plans don't actually have willpower. They don't need it. What they have is a habit. A routine. Exercise for them is like brushing their teeth. They don't spend a single brain cell making decisions about it. They just get up and do it.

And they feel great about it.

"It's been said that if you could put the benefits of exercise in a pill, it would be the single most prescribed medication in the world," says Kerry Courneya, Ph.D., assistant professor at the University of Calgary in Alberta, Canada, and author of numerous studies on what makes people stick to an exercise routine. No small part of those benefits is the effect of exercise on weight loss. Studies show that when people have lost weight and acquired an exercise habit, they're more likely to stay trim than people who try to keep the pounds off through dietary changes alone.

Turning an exercise routine—and all its benefits—into a permanent resident in your life is a matter of housecleaning your priorities, setting up a schedule and toning up your motivation (until you're hooked, that is). Here's the plan.

Step One: Make Exercise a Priority

Take a look at the agenda that's behind tomorrow's agenda. That is, take a look at the priorities that are driving your calendar. Put exercise on that priority list—high on that list, next to working and bill paying and watching Dan Rather. "If exercise is my third priority and it's your fifteenth, you're not going to find the time to exercise, and I am," says Dr. Courneya.

Where people run into trouble is in making something like "getting fit" a priority but then not making the tasks required to get there a priority, too. "I often say that if you want to get to the top of the stairs, you must negotiate the steps," says time-management consultant Virginia Bass, who teaches people to organize their lives through Day Timers, Inc. "If you continue to put a lower priority on the task or activities required to reach your goal (exercising in the evenings, for instance) than on the goal itself (improving health, for example), then you're not going to make it."

Step Two: Find the Time

Waiting for exercise to fit into your life "when I have the time" is like waiting to win the lottery when you haven't bought a ticket. You have to find the time. Try this: For about a week, write down where you've spent your time, as if minutes are checks that you're entering in your checkbook register. This gives you a picture of how you're spending your time, says Bass.

Chances are, there are points that can be nipped and tucked to free a bit of time every day. Maybe you're on the telephone with a neighbor when you could be walking around the neighborhood together. Maybe your CNN addiction could be sated from the seat of a stationary bike.

If reshuffling this time inventory still hasn't yielded a full 30 minutes for exercise, wipe your schedule clean, reach for your priority list and highlight those activities of highest importance (including exercise) on your daily calendar. Then let the rest of your life flow around those immovable time commitments.

Step Three: Assign a Time

To make exercise a habit, it needs to be on the agenda in a specific time slot, not on that "to do" list that you turn to "when I have a minute." Where on that list? Any time that you'll do it. Some people prefer a walk and a bath as a nightcap. Others find that noontime workouts free them from finding a sitter for the kids.

When it comes to making exercise a habit, however, science is on the side of the early birds. People who work out in the mornings are much more likely to stick to their programs than people who leave it until

Superglue: Tricks That Make a Program Stick

You can do almost anything for a week (except hold your breath). It's during the second week of an exercise program—and maybe on into the sixth—that you find yourself looking for some extra strategies that will bond you and your new routine like superglue. Here are some tricks to help.

Have your stuff handy. Nothing can derail your intentions faster than sneakers that are still soggy from the weekend hike or Walkman batteries that make Frank Sinatra sound like Lurch from *The Addams Family*. Flatten those paper-tiger obstacles by keeping your gear ready to roll and, above all, handy. If you have to trip over your walking shoes on your way out the door, you're one step closer to leaving with them on.

Hitch exercise to an essential. Attaching exercise to something you absolutely have to do every day (until exercise itself becomes that thing) will boost your chances of doing it. Some exercisers leave the house without showering so they have to go to the gym on their way to work. Others leave an essential piece of equipment like eyeliner or concealer in their gym lockers so they either go there or go without.

Be engaging. Sign up your friends, your spouse and anyone else you trust to keep you pointed in the right direction. Most people need something or someone to obligate them to exercise for the first month or two of a new program, says Tedd Mitchell, M.D., medical director of the Cooper Wellness Program at the Cooper Aerobics Center in Dallas. For instance, if you've chosen to begin your workday at 8:30

later—when spur-of-the-moment meetings or family responsibilities can knock the best intentions off balance.

Don't be so quick to roll your eyes and groan that you're not a morning person. Neither are most of the people who exercise at or before the crack of dawn. They're just people who have gotten up and gone exercising; they're not necessarily out there humming "Oh, What a Beautiful Morning." Some morning walkers have found that it's not that much more difficult to get up 30 minutes before the alarm usually goes off. Says one convert who never thought she'd exercise in the morning: "Getting up is

A.M. instead of 8:00, "have your secretary hold you accountable for your decision," he says. "In other words, you come in at 8:00 and he or she might say, 'You're not supposed to be here yet—have you done your walk?'"

Find a role model. Oprah is not a role model. Sure, she's lost weight and she exercises. But can she get the kids from baton lessons to baseball practice, put the finishing touches on tomorrow's report, cook dinner and still walk for an hour a day during the workweek? Find someone like yourself, with your kind of obligations and obstacles, who works out like clockwork. She's the one who proves that it can be done.

Acknowledge the cost of doing business. Back when you made that pros-and-cons-of-exercise list, there undoubtedly was a "con" or two. Don't ignore what's there. The person who doesn't give a nod to the fact that exercise may cause some muscle stiffness might pack it in when exercise has that effect.

Eat from the company-only china. Or do whatever else feels like a reward. After you exercise for a while, the glow that you feel after a walk in the park is a reward in spades. But in the first few months of a program, you might need to give yourself a blue ribbon now and then. It doesn't have to be extravagant, says psychologist James O. Prochaska, Ph.D., of the University of Rhode Island in Kingston. Just remember to reward the behavior, not the outcome. That is, reward yourself for walking five times this week, not for losing a pound.

difficult whether I do it at 6:00 A.M. or at 7:00 A.M. So I just get up early and do it."

Your morning schedule might not even need much revising to include exercise. "I tell people to let their secretaries know that Monday through Friday, they're not going to be seeing people until 8:30 A.M. instead of 8:00. You get up at the same time, but you have your workout done by the time you get to work," says Tedd Mitchell, M.D., medical director of the Cooper Wellness Program at the Cooper Aerobics Center in Dallas.

No matter what time of the day you don your walking shoes, keep it

Don't Sweat the Skips

Inevitably, real-world obstacles will occasionally come between you and the gym (or your park path). Don't sweat it. "Once you've committed to exercising daily for the next 75 years, missing a day here or a week there isn't catastrophic," says Kerry Courneya, Ph.D., assistant professor at the University of Calgary in Alberta, Canada. View the "skip" as just that—a temporary skip—and go on from there. "People can get back on track quite readily," says James O. Prochaska, Ph.D., of the University of Rhode Island in Kingston.

consistent. "One way to make something a habit is to have the same environment, the same situation every time you exercise," says Dr. Courneya.

"I tell people to consider exercise as part of the workday, just as you consider getting up and getting dressed to be part of the workday," says Dr. Mitchell. That process of donning the workout gear at a designated time is far more important than how long or how hard you work out, he says. Once the consistency is ingrained in your routine, you can pay more attention to the quality of your workout.

Step Four: Do It

Now that you know where you're going to put the exercise in your day, figure out what kind of workout you're going to do in that slot. Let hedonism be your guide. Why do something that's no fun? (Isn't that why you quit last time?) Use your creativity to boost the fitness potential of activities, such as walking the dog, that you might not even consider "exercise."

Then be reasonable about how much exercise you're really going to be able to do five days a week, every week, all year long.

Start by promising yourself 30 minutes of exercise per session (20, if you're new to exercise). Wimpy? Nope. Realistic is more like it. When you have a breakfast meeting every day and special dinners and meetings all week, you'll find a 30-minute workout manageable and a 90-minute one nearly impossible.

The point isn't to do "lite" exercise. It's to shift your thinking from "this is what I'm going to have to do to get in shape" to "this is a habit I have." If you've been sedentary for a while, even 20 minutes of exercise every day is going to have you feeling great in no time.

In the first few weeks, however, don't underschedule yourself. A 30-minute workout means 30 minutes of moving around. Not 5 minutes for finding your shoes, 1 for tying them and 15 for looking for your shades, applying sunscreen and pulling yourself together afterward. So be realistic; schedule an hour if that's what you really need to accomplish a 30-minute workout. Eventually, you'll get more efficient at preparation and re-entry, and you'll have more time to exercise.

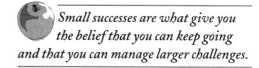

Small successes are what give you the belief that you can keep going and that you can manage larger challenges.

The key is setting yourself up to be successful at your new program. Success breeds success, reminds Ronna Kabatznick, Ph.D., psychological and motivational consultant to *Weight Watchers Magazine.* Small successes are what give you the belief that you can keep going and that you can manage larger challenges, she says.

How Long till It's a Habit?

There's no magic number for how long it takes habits to take hold. But there are strong hints that it can happen as quickly as six to eight weeks. "I always tell people that after the first few months, my job becomes very easy—I don't have to tell people to exercise anymore," says Dr. Mitchell. "Once they feel the benefits of it, they'll establish it as a lifestyle."

You'll soon see that a routine is anything but routine. It's simply a matter of following a format that makes you feel good, about making promises to yourself and keeping them.

"Making a change isn't really about deprivation," says Dr. Kabatznick. "Sure, there are impulses you're not going to follow. But you're making a decision on your own behalf that will improve your life."

It's a sign that you're keeping commitments to yourself that you know are smart. That you're on your way to having exercise become automatic. That you're getting stronger and making things happen. It takes a little effort every now and then. But why wouldn't you want to work to your full potential?

Never Overeat Again!

How to short-circuit your appetite's autopilot and regain control of your intake valve.

Ssshhh! Don't tell anyone: Dean Ornish real-l-l-ly likes chocolate!

Yes, the world-famous doctor who's the leading exponent of ultra-low-fat eating eats chocolate regularly. "Yes, I like chocolate," he admits. "I'm healthy, my cholesterol is 130, I don't have heart disease, and I've been eating a low-fat vegetarian diet since I was 19. A little chocolate isn't going to hurt me."

The mega-important term here? *A little!* When Dr. Ornish says "a little," he really means just a little! And here's his secret: He indulges in food in a very focused way—a way that maximizes pleasure and minimizes quantity.

How One Bite Can Satisfy

For Dr. Ornish—who is director of the Preventive Medicine Research Institute in Sausalito, California—the taste treat that thrills him most deeply is a dark, bittersweet chocolate candy with a bit of caramel in the center. "One piece is bite-size," he notes, "only the calorie equivalent of maybe a teaspoon of premium ice cream."

But Dr. Ornish makes the eating of just one bite of chocolate a great big party for one. "I'm not talking to anyone, and I'm not on the phone or reading. First I look at it. Then I close my eyes and smell it. I bite in slowly. I notice all the different flavors, the textures, the way it feels going down my throat. I notice that the flavors occur at different times, almost like a symphony, in different parts of my mouth and throat. Then there are different aftertastes."

The whole encounter takes several minutes. "I do it two or three times a week," says Dr. Ornish. "And usually I find that one piece is all I want. It's enough. The experience lingers."

Eating with Your Mind

There's a reason that we're revealing Dr. Ornish's deep, dark-chocolate secret. He's one of the experts from a wide variety of fields who have told us that paying close attention to what you are eating can help prevent overeating, whether you're indulging in a treat or sitting down for a whole meal.

Thomas Wadden, Ph.D., director of the Weight and Eating Disorders Program at the University of Pennsylvania School of Medicine in Philadelphia, puts it this way: "If you pay more attention to your food, you may enjoy it more. And the payoff is, you may be satisfied by eating less."

The Raisin Meditation

A little farther up the East Coast, at the University of Massachusetts Medical Center Stress Reduction Clinic in Worcester, they've reached a similar conclusion.

There psychologists teach patients who come in with a variety of medical problems how to increase their awareness of themselves, their surroundings and the present moment. This way of thinking—which the doctors call mindfulness—helps the patients to turn down the stressful thoughts that exacerbate medical problems, including overeating.

The very first lesson that's taught to everyone who comes to the clinic is "The Raisin Meditation." Interestingly, it's very similar to the way Dr. Ornish eats chocolate.

"Each patient is given two raisins. Then we take about five minutes to eat just one of them," explains clinic director and founder Jon Kabat-Zinn, Ph.D. "First we examine the raisin. We feel its texture and notice its colors. We imagine the grapes growing on the vine in the fields, the sun pouring on them, the rain falling, the people picking them. We smell the raisin. Then, with awareness of what the arms, lips and teeth are doing, we slowly put the raisin into our mouths. We chew slowly, experiencing the taste with full attention. After swallowing, we even imagine our bodies being one raisin heavier. Then patients eat the next raisin the same way."

Those two little raisins carry a powerful lesson, says clinic psychologist

Elizabeth Wheeler, Ph.D., especially for the people who come for the clinic's eight-week compulsive-overeaters program. "The overeaters invariably say they've never eaten anything that slowly!" notes Dr. Wheeler, who leads the program. "They're really surprised by how much they enjoy it, how much they taste it, how different it is from the usual eating experience."

A Mindful-Eating Exercise

"Many people who have food problems eat on automatic pilot," she adds. "A lot of times the only way they know that they've eaten is because the food that they had on their plates is gone. That's not satisfying."

To short-circuit automatic-pilot eating, Dr. Wheeler's patients learn a powerful awareness exercise that they're instructed to use before, during and after meals. To put this quick but powerful mindful-eating technique to work for you and your taste buds, see "Four Minutes to Stop Overeating" on page 221.

Mindfulness makes a big difference, says Dr. Wheeler. "A lot of people start to say, 'I don't need to eat as much, because I'm enjoying my food more.' Some patients start losing weight immediately—sometimes even people who didn't come to the clinic for overeating." Follow-up studies of patients suggest that a program built around mindfulness works. "Our patients significantly reduce symptoms of compulsive eating," says Dr. Wheeler. "They're less likely to eat when they're not hungry and less likely to eat beyond the point of fullness."

Diet Secrets of a Professional Eater

Eating beyond the point of fullness isn't a problem for Gail Vance Civille, which is a little surprising, given her job description. As president of Sensory Spectrum in Chatham, New Jersey, she's paid by food manufacturers to evaluate their products. In other words, she often spends her entire day looking at food, thinking about food and, of course, tasting food.

No one would be surprised to learn that Civille has a weight problem—except that she doesn't have a weight problem! At "well over 50," she's slender and healthy.

"Part of it is that I just don't find myself overeating very often," says Civille. "I think the reason is that I get a lot of satisfaction from each eating experience. For me, each mouthful becomes an event!"

FAT STATS

What's in That Spare Tire

An average man carries stored fat calories equivalent to 1,650 pancakes.

Food for Thought

While Dr. Ornish comes to his chocolate with the goal of maximizing sensual pleasure, and the Massachusetts patients aim at total awareness of food, Civille sits down at the table with the intention of thinking about food as well as savoring it.

There's a parallel, she explains, between the way she eats and the way her son, a film student, watches movies. "When my son watches a film, he puts a lot more effort into it than I do—I just let the film pour into my eyes. You can tell my son gets intense satisfaction from movies because he's analyzing them while he watches. Well, that's the way I am with my food. I'm thinking about it while I eat."

Civille believes that if we think more about the things that we're eating, we'll appreciate food more—and eat less. Anyone, she says, can make the most of his food in the same way that she does.

"Whenever you eat, ask yourself, 'What am I perceiving? What texture? What flavors? Are they what I expected from this food?' " she says.

While the main point here is maximizing satisfaction, says Civille, occasionally you'll learn—by concentrating—that you don't like a food as much as you thought you did. "You might not even want to finish it."

Kitchen Classroom

If you were trained by Civille as a taster, the first place she'd send you to learn about flavor and aroma is the spice shelf in your own kitchen. "I tell my trainees, 'Go home, open your spices and start smelling them.' That's how you start to learn some more about flavor and aroma.

"For just one example, we should all learn the difference among cinnamon, cloves, coriander, ginger, cardamom and nutmeg—but most of us don't have a clue what the difference is! If you make an effort, though, you can learn. Then, when you taste a food, you can analyze what spices or herbs you're detecting."

Step One: Give Yourself a Limit

There's clearly a lot to be said for paying attention to your food, says Dr. Wadden. "Still, for most people with a weight problem, there's one essential step that must come before mindfulness can be effective. That step is portion control. You should set a limit for yourself ahead of time."

The right limit, of course, depends on your individual energy needs. But to some extent, you can let common sense be your guide. For example, if it's chocolate you adore, check the calories and the fat content. Limit yourself to something reasonable—for a deluxe bon-bon, that might be one piece. (If you've been advised by your doctor to avoid all saturated fats, you might select a treat such as one fat-free chocolate sorbet bar or one single-serving cup of fat-free chocolate-cherry yogurt.)

For your dream macaroni and cheese recipe, it might be a half-cup. At a cocktail party, it might be three hors d'oeuvres—your favorites from whatever's offered. If you're setting limits for a whole meal, aim for about the same quantity of food that you'd find in a reduced-calorie frozen dinner.

Step Two: Maximize Satisfaction

Once you've set your portion size, go for it—squeeze every drop of pleasure you can from that food by eating it mindfully. By the way, even if your treat is low in calories—a ripe mango, say, or a bowl of home-cooked vegetable stew—by eating mindfully, you'll make the pleasure of any food more intense.

Here are more tips to maximize satisfaction. The goal? Eating less without deprivation!

Eliminate distractions. "I used to eat while I was watching CNN or talking to someone," recalls Dr. Ornish. "I'd be paying attention to that

Four Minutes to Stop Overeating

By setting aside a few minutes before, during and after your meal for awareness exercises, you can reduce the likelihood of overeating. These exercises are based on those developed by Jon Kabat-Zinn, Ph.D., founder and director of the University of Massachusetts Medical Center Stress Reduction Clinic in Worcester, and clinic psychologist Elizabeth Wheeler, Ph.D., and taught to overeaters at the clinic. "They help people maintain some level of calmness, control and choice," says Dr. Wheeler. "And they help take the whole eating process off automatic pilot."

1. Two minutes before the meal: Sit in your chair quietly. Take five or six long, deep breaths. Let yourself feel relaxed.

2. One minute before the meal: Turn your attention to the coming meal. This is like saying grace, but it needn't be religious. If you're with other people, you might like to hold hands around the table. Think about how your food is the product of sunlight, rain and earth, and of other people's labor. Think about the work required to prepare and cook it. And appreciate the fact that it's going into your body to nourish you.

3. Midway through the meal: Take another minute. Stop eating and take five deep breaths. Sit quietly for just a moment. You might even realize that you're not hungry anymore!

4. Ten minutes after you've finished eating: Take one more minute to do another series of five deep breaths. Focus on the physical sensations that the food might be causing in your body. Hopefully, most are pleasant. "But if a food makes you feel not so good afterward, you may decide to eat less of it in the future," says Dr. Wheeler. So you've still learned something useful!

instead of to what I was eating, so I could go through a whole meal and not even taste the food. Then I'd look down and the whole plate would be empty and I'd wonder, 'Who ate this?' When I began to focus on what I was eating," he adds, "I enjoyed the food much more and I was able to become aware when I had had enough."

FAT STATS

The Price of a Pound

- Average cost per year to participate in a commercial weight-loss clinic, such as Jenny Craig: $608
- Average cost of a one-year membership at a health club: $504
- Number of people in diet programs who lose weight for the long term (at least seven years): 1 in 250
- Price per pound lost on the following diet programs in the Boston area (based on a 200-pound person, enrolled in a 12-week program, losing 24 pounds on a meal plan or 48 pounds on a liquid diet):

Liquid Diets

1. Medifast: $5.45
2. Health Management Resources: $6.82
3. Optifast: $8.64

Meal Plans

1. Weight Watchers: $0.91
2. Diet Centers: $3.64
3. Nutri/System: $7.50
4. Jenny Craig: $9.32

- Average cost of liposuction per pound: $5,000
- Percentage of patients who experience fat "regrowth" after liposuction: 29

Shut your eyes. It's the ultimate way to shut out distractions, says Civille. "I often do this when I'm eating. My children are always embarrassed; they would prefer I not look like I'm having a seance with my food." But it's worth it, she adds. "When you close your eyes, you turn off the other distractions. You can just enjoy the food and become intimate with it."

Involve your nose. Civille says she always takes a deep whiff of her food before eating. "I try not to be too grotesque and put my nose in my plate," she says. "But by taking a moment to savor the smell of your food, you enhance the experience."

What's more, you may be fooling your brain into thinking you've eaten more than you did, says neurologist Alan Hirsch, M.D., director of the Smell and Taste Treatment and Research Foundation in Chicago. "The brain interprets the amount of food you've smelled as food you've eaten," he says. "By sniffing your food before you eat it, you get more of the aromatic molecules, called volatiles, up into your nose. They are carried to the olfactory bulb behind the bridge of the nose, where a lot of flavor perception takes place," says Dr. Hirsch. "That may diminish appetite, so you eat less."

Slurp. Obviously, this isn't intended for public consumption. But at a table for one, in the privacy of your own home, you might want to try getting eccentric. Think of it as a cross-cultural experience. In Japan, it's weird not to slurp your noodles. There, slurping signifies enjoyment—and that belief is based in biological fact, says Dr. Hirsch. "Bringing air into the food aerates more of the volatiles, so more flavor reaches your olfactory bulb, " he explains.

Chew a lot. Chewing your food for a long while has the same effect as slurping: It transports the volatiles up the nose, to maximize flavor and reduce appetite, says Dr. Hirsch.

Warm it up. Warm foods have more flavor, again because more of the volatiles are released. Civille says that this is why she usually warms up her leftovers. "If you eat the ravioli out of the fridge, you won't be getting as much of a 'flavor hit' as if you warm it up. When it's cold, you might end up eating more, looking in vain for the flavor experience."

Watch your appetite wane. Cultivate an awareness of the changes in your appetite during a meal. Specifically, as you eat, you not only become less hungry, of course, but food also doesn't taste as good to you as it did at first, notes Dr. Hirsch. "The first bite of steak always tastes the best," he says. "By the end, you've saturated your olfactory receptor sites, and you could be eating horse meat." If you're no longer hungry, and you're not savoring it—that's a really good time to stop.

Dieting: When Your Friends Want You to Fail

Yes, you can say no. Put yourself first instead of trying to please everyone. All it takes is practice.

Eve offered Adam an apple, and look at the grief that caused. If only well-meaning friends stuck to fruit. But more often it's chocolate cake and french fries that they tempt us with.

How do you circumvent those who invite you to stray from healthy eating? Try these tactics to counter food-pushers without alienating them.

Understand that your saboteur may be motivated by envy, love or fear of losing you. "It feels uncomfortable to them when you start to change. But if you hold your ground, they'll adjust," says Susan Head, Ph.D., research director at the Duke University Diet and Fitness Center in Durham, North Carolina.

Express your needs. At a family meeting, reveal how others can help or hinder you, advises Laurie Meyer, R.D., of Milwaukee, a spokesperson for the American Dietetic Association. Lay down rules, such as banning candy from the house.

If your husband resists eating low-fat food, compromise. Get him to agree that if he wants something that isn't on your menu, he fixes it himself or eats it elsewhere. Let him hide his own stash of fattening snacks. Serve pasta topped with low-fat marinara sauce. Use ground turkey in his favorite meat loaf recipe. Sneak low-fat sour cream into his mashed potatoes. "He doesn't even have to know he's eating low-fat cuisine," says Meyer.

Don't feel obligated to eat the sweets you're offered. Thank the giver, then remind him or her of your healthy intentions. Mixed signals lead to mixed results. "Don't say no with words and yes with your eyes," suggests

Perks from Paring Fat

Change your centerpiece and change your outlook. That is, when you fill up from the fruit bowl instead of the candy dish, don't be surprised if you find yourself empty of tiredness and blue moods.

In one study, when 555 women zapped their dietary fat in half for a year, they ended up feeling more vigorous, less anxious and less depressed than they did when eating high-fat foods. They learned to chop fat through small group meetings with a nutritionist.

The findings were a bit of a relief to the researchers.

"We had been checking for any ill behavioral effects associated with a reduced-fat diet," says study leader Deborah J. Bowen, Ph.D., associate professor at the Fred Hutchinson Cancer Research Center and the University of Washington, both in Seattle. "So we were relieved to find that, coupled with group support and education, a low-fat diet had a positive effect on mood."

In fact, "the people in the support group said they had a really good time," Dr. Bowen adds. That, along with the fact that the "groupies" lost an average of nine pounds, would be enough to brighten anyone's outlook. Chopping the fat in half took their diets down to a reasonable 20 percent of calories from fat—an amount that's doable for most women.

Meyer. She warns against establishing negative patterns: "And whatever you do, don't eat the gift box of chocolates, because if you do, you'll get chocolates again."

Mentally practice your responses so you'll never be caught off guard. Some options: "Gee, I've already eaten." "Thanks. It looks wonderful, but I'm full." "I just had a large lunch." "No thanks. My doctor insists that I lose weight (or watch my cholesterol)."

If you take a client or friend to lunch or dinner, order first and order healthy. Suggest a restaurant with low-fat fare, says Meyer. If the circumstances are casual, you can also ask that half your meal be put aside in a "doggie bag" before it's served.

Tell those who equate food with love that you'd prefer spending time chatting with them instead of eating. Then make sure you do that. Ask questions about what they're doing, listen to what they say and share your own thoughts.

Do unto others as you'd have done unto you. Bring only healthy treats to friendly gatherings.

Finally, be prepared. "The more approaches and flexibility you have, the more likely that you'll be able to deal with temptation on an ongoing basis," Meyer says. "There are always going to be holidays and birthdays and friends who want to get together to entertain with rich food. They're a part of life—for your entire life."

The Ups and Downs of Yo-Yo Dieting

The latest news on weight cycling is that yo-yo dieting isn't as dangerous as we thought.

Let's say that a certain talk show host has had a weight problem. And let's agree that this popular talk show host has, over time, become almost as well-known for his girth as for breaking new ground in broadcasting. But for all his faults, Rush Limbaugh is not a yo-yo dieter.

The question arises: Should he, like his more famous cohort Oprah, make his weight problem public? Should he risk trying to lose, say, 40 pounds, even if he's the type of person who'll gain it back in a hurry? Maybe so. There is new evidence that says that the evils often associated with yo-yo dieting have been overstated. A number of major studies by doctors and researchers have settled some of the more compelling questions about weight cycling—often defined as repeatedly losing and then regaining at least 10 to 20 pounds.

Anyone who has had a problem with weight and conquered it only temporarily knows the refrain: Every time you lose weight only to put it back on, you make it harder to lose the same weight the next time. That's false, we can now say. At least that's what a painstaking review of 43 studies spanning nearly 30 years found. Susan Z. Yanovski, M.D., and her colleagues at the National Institutes of Health (NIH) in Bethesda, Maryland, reported that the act of weight cycling doesn't make it tougher to drop 25 pounds the next time you try. In other words, yo-yo dieting apparently doesn't cause you to gain more weight on fewer calories.

Yo-Yo Dieting Is Bad for Your Head

Even if losing and regaining weight doesn't seem to have adverse physical effects, it can still do a number on your head, says John Foreyt, Ph.D., professor of psychology and director of the Behavioral Medicine Research Center at Baylor College of Medicine in Houston. In a study, Dr. Foreyt found that people whose weight fluctuates are less healthy psychologically than those whose weight stays stable. "Yo-yo dieters feel bad about themselves, so their self-esteem suffers and their depression worsens," he says.

In the study, nearly 500 men and women attempting to maintain weight loss were monitored for weight gain and loss within one year. To check for stress, abnormal eating behavior and weight perception, the study participants completed a series of questionnaires.

The results showed that the weight maintainers had a greater sense of well-being, felt less stressed and had better control of their eating. The weight fluctuators, regardless of their weight, felt a sense of failure and frustration.

"The key to healthy weight maintenance is changing your lifestyle, not constant dieting," Dr. Foreyt says. "By gradually adopting low-fat eating and exercise habits, you'll feel better physically and mentally."

Yo-Yo Dieting Doesn't Damage Health

Nor, it appears, is weight cycling dangerous to your health. "There is no convincing evidence that weight cycling in humans has adverse effects," the NIH team concluded. This may be good news for millions, since at any given moment 40 percent of women and 25 percent of men in the United States are dieting.

After a few experiences with weight cycling, overweight people might do well to drop just a little bit of weight instead of trying to get thin again.

Still, many diet experts believe that these reports are asking the wrong questions. Even if the act of yo-yo dieting isn't dangerous, isn't the act of

NEWS FLASH

Weight Maintenance:
The 15 Percent Disadvantage

Most dieters will agree—losing weight is the easy part. It's maintaining that weight loss, big or small, over time, that becomes the real challenge.

In fact, research confirms that weight maintenance really is a different ballgame for former fatties than for those who have always been at a normal weight. Researchers at Rockefeller University in New York City found that people who lost more than 10 percent of their body weight had to consume about 15 percent fewer calories simply to maintain their new, lower weight, compared to the always-been-there group. And that remained the case even when percentages of muscle mass and body fat were the same between the two groups, so it wasn't more calorie-burning muscle that gave the always-been-theres a metabolic advantage.

What's going on here? "As people lose body fat, their bodies become more conservative with energy," explains researcher Jules Hirsch, M.D., professor and senior physician at Rockefeller University. That means that they burn fewer calories doing anything, from walking the dog to watching television.

There doesn't seem to be a magic moment when the body's metabolism readjusts to your new weight, either, so you will always need to eat a bit less than you used to, Dr. Hirsch says.

But there is something that former fatties can do to even the score: exercise.

Adding as little as 90 minutes more a week of aerobic exercise to your normal activity schedule will burn enough calories to cover your new deficit. And muscle-building exercise like weight training also boosts calorie burning.

gaining all that weight problematic? To be considered a yo-yo dieter, you have to have gained and lost a bunch of weight—at least two or three times. In order for a five-foot-five-inch, 125-pound woman to gain 50 pounds in six months, she would have to consume, on average, 7,000 calories a week more than she would eat at her maintenance level (this works out to roughly 1,000 extra calories a day, or

Even if the act of yo-yo dieting isn't dangerous, isn't the act of gaining all that weight problematic?

one medium cheeseburger, an order of french fries and one vanilla milk shake over and above her regular diet every day). That adds up to approximately 185,000 extra calories in six months! And while you're carrying around all that weight, you're putting unnecessary strain on the heart, arteries, knees and back, to name just a few key body parts.

So what are you to make of all this? First, there is no evidence that it is any healthier to be chronically overweight than it is to lose and regain weight. So if you've put on more than a few extra pounds, it's still a good idea to lose some, even if you have a tendency to yo-yo. Second, keep in mind another of the NIH panel's findings: "Weight loss of as little as five to ten pounds can improve cases of high blood pressure, diabetes and high cholesterol, which often translates into better emotional as well as physical health."

After a few experiences with weight cycling, then, overweight people might do well to drop just a little bit of weight instead of trying to get thin again. This can go a long way toward reducing risk factors like elevated blood pressure. Finally, diet experts might spend more time researching how they can make fat people healthy instead of always trying to figure out how to make fat people thin.

No one should plan on becoming a yo-yo dieter. Nor should anyone revel in the fact that the act itself is not dangerous. The point is that gaining 40 pounds is not, and never was, good for you. Even Rush Limbaugh would agree with that.

PART THREE

Low-Fat Recipes of the Year

We Picked the Best!

Imagine having a friend who buys all the new low-fat cookbooks on the market, tries the recipes that look most tempting and then passes the very best of them to you, along with her comments about what makes them so special. That's exactly what our own cookbook editors have done. They looked through some 18,000 recipes from more than 50 great new cookbooks to come up with their 50 top choices.

Their criteria? Variety, easy preparation, less than one gram of fat per serving and, most of all, taste. Every one of these recipes is a winner, suited for everyday use or special occasions.

Appetizers and Snacks

Even between-meal treats and finger foods can be
healthy fare with these great recipes.

Heart-Healthy Deviled Eggs

Your next picnic will be a hit with these heart-smart appetizers from
1,001 Low-Fat Recipes by Sue Spitler. What makes them so creamy and
delicious? It's not egg yolks but a tasty mixture of cottage cheese, finely
chopped vegetables and various seasonings.

½	cup low-fat cottage cheese
¼	cup fat-free mayonnaise
¼	cup finely minced scallions
¼	cup finely minced celery
¼	teaspoon celery seeds
¼	teaspoon salt-free herb seasoning
1	teaspoon Dijon mustard
8	hard-cooked egg whites, halved
2	tablespoons minced fresh parsley

In a medium bowl, whisk the cottage cheese and mayonnaise until
fluffy. Add the scallions, celery, celery seeds, herb seasoning and mustard
and beat well.

Stuff the egg white halves with the cheese mixture, cover and refrigerate
for 20 minutes. Before serving, sprinkle with the parsley.

Makes 8 servings
PER SERVING (2 PIECES): 36 CALORIES, 0.2 G. FAT

Vietnamese-Style Spring Rolls with Ginger Soy Dipping Sauce

We couldn't resist these light and practically fat-free spring rolls from Steven Raichlen's *High-Flavor, Low-Fat Vegetarian Cooking*. They're chock-full of noodles, herbs and vegetables. And the ginger soy dipping sauce gives them just the right amount of zip.

Spring Rolls

8–10	dried Chinese black mushrooms
2	packages (1¾ ounces each) bean threads or rice vermicelli
2	medium carrots, cut into thin strips
1	cup snow peas, ends and strings removed and cut into thin strips
1	cup mung bean sprouts
16–18	9" round rice papers
24	fresh mint leaves
3	scallions, cut into thin slivers
	Salt and ground black pepper
12	large fresh basil leaves or Thai basil leaves
	Lettuce

Dipping Sauce

½	cup fresh lime juice
6	tablespoons tamari or soy sauce
¼	cup water
2	tablespoons honey
2	cloves garlic, minced
1	teaspoon minced fresh ginger
2	scallions, minced
1–3	serrano, jalapeño or Thai chili peppers, thinly sliced crosswise (wear plastic gloves when handling)

To make the spring rolls: In a small bowl, soak the mushrooms in enough hot water to cover for 20 to 30 minutes. Remove the stems and reserve the soaking liquid for another use. Slice the caps into very thin strips.

In a medium bowl, soak the bean threads or vermicelli in enough water to cover for 20 to 30 minutes, or until tender. Drain well.

In a large pot of lightly salted boiling water, cook the bean threads or vermicelli for 1 minute, or until tender but not mushy. Using a slotted spoon, transfer the noodles to a colander and rinse with cold water. Drain well and set aside.

Blanch the carrots in the remaining boiling water for 1 minute. Using a slotted spoon, transfer the carrots to a colander and rinse with cold water. Drain well and set aside.

Blanch the snow peas in the water for 1 minute. Using a slotted spoon, transfer the snow peas to a colander and rinse with cold water. Drain well and set aside.

Blanch the bean sprouts in the water for 30 seconds. Using a slotted spoon, transfer the sprouts to a colander and rinse with cold water. Drain well and set aside.

Fill a large shallow bowl with water. Soak a sheet of rice paper in the water for 1 minute. Carefully transfer the rice paper to a clean dish towel on a cutting board and let stand for 1 to 2 minutes, or until pliable.

To assemble the rolls, arrange 2 mint leaves along the bottom third of the softened rice paper. Arrange 1 tablespoon each of the noodles, mushrooms, carrots, sprouts, scallions and snow peas in a row on top. Sprinkle with salt and pepper to taste.

Carefully wrap up the rice paper to form a tight roll, folding in the sides halfway up as you would to form an egg roll. After folding in the sides, lay a basil leaf on the remaining one-third of the rice paper and finish rolling. The idea is to form a compact roll about 6″ long. Assemble the remaining spring rolls, cover and refrigerate for up to 6 hours before serving.

To make the dipping sauce: In a small bowl, combine the lime juice, tamari or soy sauce, water, honey, garlic, ginger and scallions. Add a little more water if the sauce tastes too strong. Just before serving, pour the sauce into a small bowl and float the sliced peppers on top.

Cut each spring roll diagonally in half. Line a platter with lettuce leaves and arrange the spring roll halves on top. Serve with the sauce.

Makes 12

Per serving (2 rolls): 143 calories, 0.2 g. fat

Note: Bean threads are very thin noodles made from mung bean starch. They are available in Asian grocery stores and large supermarkets.

Steamed Pork and Chicken Dumplings

Barry Bluestein and Kevin Morrissey, creators of *The 99% Fat-Free Book of Appetizers and Desserts,* cleverly substituted lean chicken for half of the fatty pork in these scrumptious little bundles.

4	ounces boneless pork tenderloin, trimmed of all visible fat and cut into chunks
4	ounces boneless, skinless chicken breast, cut into chunks
¼	cup sliced water chestnuts, finely chopped
1½	teaspoons reduced-sodium soy sauce
1	tablespoon dry sherry or nonalcoholic white wine
1	scallion, finely chopped (white part only)
¼	cup chopped fresh spinach
1	large egg white
48	square wonton wrappers
3	cups water

Place the pork and chicken in a food processor and process until finely chopped. Transfer the meat to a large bowl. Add the water chestnuts, soy sauce, sherry or wine, scallions, spinach and egg white and mix thoroughly.

Spoon 1 teaspoon of the mixture into the center of a wonton wrapper. Dab a little water around the outer edges. Gather the corners of the wrapper together and pinch them closed to form a pouch. Repeat with the remaining filling and wonton wrappers.

Fit a wok or large saucepan with a wire rack or steaming rack and fill with 1″ to 2″ of water. Bring the water to a boil over high heat, then reduce the heat to medium.

Place the dumplings in a single layer on an oven-safe plate and set the plate on the rack. Cover and steam for 4 minutes. Repeat with the remaining dumplings. Serve immediately.

Makes 48

PER DUMPLING: 30 CALORIES, 0.2 G. FAT

Notes: This recipe is easily halved for smaller occasions. But the uncooked dumplings freeze well, so why not make the larger quantity and have some on hand? Thaw them in the refrigerator before steaming.

For wonton soup, add the dumplings to defatted chicken broth.

Rumaki

Classic rumaki calls for bacon and chicken livers, two ingredients that are sky-high in fat and cholesterol. This lighter version, from *Prevention's Quick and Healthy Low-Fat Cooking Featuring All-American Food*, substitutes lean chicken breasts, pineapple and Canadian bacon. At just 0.2 gram of fat per serving, you and your guests won't be able to get enough!

2	boneless, skinless chicken breast halves (3 ounces each)
$1/4$	cup reduced-sodium soy sauce
20	pineapple chunks
20	water chestnuts
5	slices Canadian bacon

Cut the chicken breast halves into nickel-size pieces, approximately 10 per breast. In a small bowl, combine the chicken and 2 tablespoons of the soy sauce.

In another small bowl, combine the pineapple and water chestnuts with the remaining soy sauce. Let both marinate for about 15 minutes.

Preheat the oven to 500°. Coat a baking sheet with no-stick spray and set aside.

Cut each slice of Canadian bacon lengthwise into 12 strips, 4″ × ¼″ each. Wrap each water chestnut, pineapple chunk and chicken piece with a bacon strip and secure with a toothpick. Place the rumaki on the prepared baking sheet and broil for 5 minutes, turning once. Serve warm.

Makes 60

PER RUMAKI: 13 CALORIES, 0.2 G. FAT

Note: Buy rectangular rather than round Canadian bacon to ensure that the meat strips will be long enough to wrap around the chicken, water chestnuts and pineapple.

Crab and Corn Beignets

Beignet is a fancy French word for fritter. How do you make a fritter low-fat? With a little American ingenuity. These savory treats from *Prevention's Quick and Healthy Low-Fat Cooking Featuring Cuisines from the Mediterranean* use an irresistible combination of crab and corn.

¼	cup fat-free egg substitute
¼	cup skim milk
2	tablespoons unbleached flour
1	teaspoon olive oil
1	teaspoon honey
1	teaspoon Dijon mustard
½	teaspoon baking powder
½	teaspoon ground black pepper
1	cup flaked crabmeat
1	cup fresh or frozen corn
1	tablespoon minced fresh tarragon or parsley

In a medium bowl, whisk together the egg substitute, milk, flour, oil, honey, mustard, baking powder and pepper until smooth. Stir in the crabmeat, corn and tarragon or parsley.

Coat a large no-stick skillet with no-stick spray and warm over medium heat for 2 minutes. Drop scant tablespoons of the crab mixture into the pan and flatten slightly with the back of a wooden spoon or spatula to form beignets about 2″ in diameter. Cook for 2 to 3 minutes per side, or until golden. If necessary, reduce the heat to keep the beignets from getting too dark before they're cooked through.

Makes 18

PER SERVING: 27 CALORIES, 0.4 G. FAT

Cherrystone Clams
in Red Pepper Mayonnaise

Prevention's Stop Dieting and Lose Weight Cookbook comes through again! These easy seafood treats make a stunning presentation—perfect for summer gatherings. Serve the clams on the half-shell, nestled into a bed of rock salt, or on a platter lined with leaves of ornamental kale.

1   sweet red pepper, halved lengthwise
½   cup water
2   tablespoons lemon juice
1   tablespoon minced fresh tarragon or 1 teaspoon dried
2   shallots, halved
2   cloves garlic, minced
1   bay leaf
32 cherrystone clams, scrubbed
3   tablespoons fat-free mayonnaise
2   tablespoons minced fresh parsley (optional)

Remove the stem, seeds and inner membranes from the peppers. Place the halves, cut side down, on a baking sheet. Broil 5″ from the heat for about 10 minutes, or until the skins begin to blister. Place the peppers in a clean paper bag, seal the bag and set aside for 20 minutes.

Meanwhile, in a large, heavy saucepan, combine the water, lemon juice, tarragon, shallots, garlic and bay leaf. Bring to a boil over high heat, then add the clams. Reduce the heat to medium-low, cover and simmer for about 5 minutes, or until the clams open. Drain and discard the liquid and any clams that did not open. Let the clams cool until easy to handle.

Remove the clams from their shells, transfer to a bowl and cover to keep warm. Reserve 32 of the shell halves.

Using a knife, pull the skin from the peppers and discard the skin. In a food processor or blender, puree the peppers.

In a medium bowl, stir together the peppers and the mayonnaise. Add the clams and toss until coated.

To serve, place 1 clam in each of the reserved shell halves. Garnish with the parsley (if using).

Makes 32
PER SERVING (4 CLAMS): 38 CALORIES, 0.4 G. FAT
Note: Always choose fresh clams that have tightly closed shells, which indicate that they're alive. If the shells are slightly open, tap them lightly with your finger. If the clams don't close, don't buy them. Keep the clams refrigerated until you need them and use them within a day of purchase.

Soft Pretzels

For an authentic "streets-of-Philadelphia" snacking experience, eat these fat-free pretzels warm from the oven with a squirt of mustard. Or do what *All-American Vegetarian* authors Barbara Grunes and Virginia Van Vynckt suggest—slice the pretzels in half lengthwise and use them in place of bread for Swiss cheese sandwiches. With nonfat Swiss cheese, you'll have an easy fat-free lunch!

1	cup warm water (105°–115°)
1	package active dry yeast
3–4	cups bread flour
1	tablespoon malted milk powder or 2 teaspoons molasses
1	teaspoon salt
	Cornmeal
1	quart water
2	tablespoons baking soda
	Kosher or coarse salt (optional)

Coat 2 baking sheets with no-stick spray and set aside.

Pour the warm water into a large bowl. Sprinkle the yeast on top and set aside to proof for 5 minutes, or until bubbly.

Stir in the bread flour, malted milk powder or molasses and 1 teaspoon salt. Beat with an electric mixer at medium speed (or vigorously by hand) for several minutes, or until the dough is smooth and springy. Let the dough rest for a minute, then turn out onto a floured board and knead by hand for another minute or two.

Coat another large, clean bowl with no-stick spray. Add the dough. Cover the bowl and set aside to rise in a warm place for 1 to 2 hours, or until doubled in size.

Punch the dough down and divide it into 12 equal pieces. Roll each piece into a rope about 16″ long and the thickness of a pencil. To make a pretzel, lift the ends of one rope and twist them together. To complete the pretzel shape, place the twist down across the middle of the loop that has formed. Place the pretzel on the prepared baking sheet. Repeat with the remaining ropes.

Set the baking sheets in a warm place and let the pretzels rise for 40 to 60 minutes.

Preheat the oven to 425°. Sprinkle cornmeal evenly over 2 clean baking sheets and set aside.

Pour the water into a large saucepan. Add the baking soda and bring to a simmer. Add the pretzels, 2 or 3 at a time, and cook for 1 minute, turning after 30 seconds. Place the pretzels on the baking sheets sprinkled with cornmeal. Sprinkle lightly with the Kosher or coarse salt (if using).

Bake for 10 to 15 minutes, or until the pretzels are dark golden brown. Serve warm.

Makes 12

PER PRETZEL: 120 CALORIES, 0 G. FAT

Notes: For a more chewy, soft pretzel texture, add 1 tablespoon gluten flour along with the bread flour.

To make the pretzels in a bread machine, combine the ingredients in the order recommended by the manufacturer. Adjust the setting to Dough or Manual. If your machine does not have a manual setting for dough, put it on a basic bread setting, then reset or turn off the machine after the first rising. After the first rising, remove the dough from the machine and shape into pretzels. Let rise, simmer and bake as directed.

You can freeze these pretzels for up to two months. The crust will become soft, so reheat the pretzels in a 300° oven until crisp.

FAT STATS

How We Hate Fat

- Percentage of people who would rather be 50 pounds overweight than have genital herpes: 91
- Percentage who would rather be run over by a truck than gain 150 pounds: 54.3

Baked Stuffed Mushrooms

Many versions of stuffed mushrooms are packed with fatty sausage. *Prevention's Healthy Hometown Favorites* remakes this mainstay of the buffet table with a savory, low-fat bread crumb filling.

16	large fresh mushrooms (caps about 1½" in diameter)
1	tablespoon reduced-calorie butter blend
3	tablespoons dry white wine or nonalcoholic white wine
¼	cup finely chopped fresh parsley
4	teaspoons finely shredded fresh Parmesan cheese
2	teaspoons fine dry bread crumbs
1	clove garlic, minced
¼	teaspoon dried thyme, crumbled
¼	teaspoon dried oregano, crumbled
	Pinch of salt
	Pinch of ground black pepper

Preheat the oven to 375°. Coat a 13" × 9" baking dish with no-stick spray and set aside.

Gently wash the mushrooms and remove the stems. Place the mushroom caps on paper towels to drain. Finely chop the stems.

Melt the butter blend in a medium no-stick skillet. Remove the pan from the heat and stir in 2 tablespoons of the wine. Remove 1 tablespoon of the wine mixture and set aside.

Add the chopped mushrooms to the remaining wine mixture in the pan. Cook and stir over low heat until the mixture is dry.

Stir in the parsley, Parmesan, bread crumbs, garlic, thyme, oregano, salt and pepper. Stir in enough of the remaining 1 tablespoon of wine to moisten.

Spoon the mushroom mixture into the mushroom caps. Arrange the caps in the prepared baking dish. Bake for 15 to 20 minutes, or until heated through and slightly tender, basting occasionally with the remaining wine mixture. Serve hot.

Makes 16
PER MUSHROOM: 15 CALORIES, 0.9 G. FAT

Chicken Fingers
with Honey Mustard Sauce

These lip-smacking treats, from *Secrets of Fat-Free Cooking* by Sandra Woodruff, R.D., cut the fat with a crunchy cornflake crust.

Chicken Fingers

3	cups cornflakes
½	teaspoon poultry seasoning
¼	teaspoon ground black pepper
3	tablespoons fat-free egg substitute
3	tablespoons skim milk
1	pound boneless, skinless chicken breast halves, cut into strips

Honey Mustard Sauce

¼	cup + 2 tablespoons fat-free mayonnaise
3	tablespoons spicy mustard
3	tablespoons honey
2	tablespoons fresh lemon juice

To make the chicken fingers: Preheat the oven to 400°. Coat a large baking sheet with no-stick spray and set aside.

Place the cornflakes in a food processor or blender and process just until small crumbs form.

In a shallow dish, stir together the crumbs, poultry seasoning and pepper. Mix well and set aside.

In another shallow dish, combine the egg substitute and milk and stir well.

Dip each chicken strip into the egg mixture and then into the crumb mixture, coating each side thoroughly with the crumbs.

Arrange the strips in a single layer on the prepared baking sheet. Coat the tops of the strips with no-stick spray and bake for 15 minutes, or until the strips are golden and no longer pink in the center.

To make the honey mustard sauce: Combine the mayonnaise, mustard, honey and lemon juice in a small bowl. Mix well. Serve with the chicken.

Makes 20
Per serving (1 piece with 2 teaspoons of sauce): 51 calories, 0.4 g. fat

Aloha Meatballs

Cocktail party meatballs don't have to break your diet. Here, Sandra Woodruff, R.D., author of *Secrets of Fat-Free Cooking*, uses ground turkey breast and tropical ingredients to give the meatballs a bright new flavor—with a mere 0.1 gram of fat per serving.

Meatballs

1	pound ground turkey breast or extra-lean ground beef
1	cup cooked brown rice
1	can (8 ounces) crushed pineapple in juice, drained
1	can (8 ounces) sliced water chestnuts, drained
½	cup chopped scallions
1	tablespoon reduced-sodium soy sauce
1	teaspoon ground ginger

Sauce

¾	cup sodium-free chicken broth
⅓	cup ketchup or chili sauce
3	tablespoons seasoned rice vinegar
2	tablespoons brown sugar
2	teaspoons cornstarch
½	teaspoon ground ginger

To make the meatballs: Preheat the oven to 350°. Coat a baking sheet with no-stick spray and set aside.

In a medium bowl, combine the turkey or beef, rice, pineapple, water chestnuts, scallions, soy sauce and ginger. Mix thoroughly. Shape the meat mixture into 1″balls and place on the prepared baking sheet.

Bake for 25 minutes, or until cooked through. Transfer the meatballs to a chafing dish or slow-cooker to keep warm.

To make the sauce: In a small saucepan, combine the broth, ketchup or chili sauce, vinegar, brown sugar, cornstarch and ginger. Stir until the cornstarch is dissolved.

Cook and stir over medium heat until the mixture comes to a boil. Reduce the heat to low and cook and stir for 1 minute, or until the mixture thickens slightly. Pour the sauce over the meatballs and toss gently to mix.

Makes 45

PER MEATBALL: 24 CALORIES, 0.1 G. FAT

Note: To avoid the last-minute party rush, make these meatballs in advance. Prepare them without the sauce and freeze them in plastic freezer bags. The day before the party, thaw the meatballs in the refrigerator. Then make the sauce in a large saucepan and heat the meatballs right in the sauce.

Hot and Cold Soups

Serve them as a first course or a light meal. These no-fat soups are brimming with nourishment.

Chilled Peach and Nectarine Soup

This chilled fruit soup is so full of flavor that you won't believe it has less than a half-gram of fat per serving. Linda Rosensweig, author of *New Vegetarian Cuisine*, suggests using only the freshest, ripest fruits of summer. You can make the soup with just peaches, but we like the added dimension of nectarines.

1	cup peeled and thinly sliced peaches
1	cup peeled and thinly sliced nectarines
2	tablespoons lemon juice
1	tablespoon honey
1	cup low-calorie cranberry juice cocktail
1	cup apple juice
1	cinnamon stick
1	whole nutmeg
2	whole cloves
¼	cup nonfat sour cream

Place the peaches and nectarines in a food processor and process until smooth. Transfer the fruit to a large bowl and stir in the lemon juice and honey. Cover and refrigerate for 20 minutes, or until chilled through.

Meanwhile, in a medium saucepan over medium-high heat, bring the cranberry juice, apple juice, cinnamon stick, nutmeg and cloves to a boil. Reduce the heat to low and simmer for 5 minutes. Strain and discard the cinnamon, nutmeg and cloves. Set aside to cool.

When completely cool, stir the juice mixture into the fruit puree. Cover and refrigerate for at least 2 hours. Serve topped with the sour cream.

Makes 4 servings
PER SERVING: 95 CALORIES, 0.3 G. FAT

Creamy Corn Chowder

If you love thick, creamy chowders, you'll want to try Betty Rohde's scrumptious version from *More So Fat, Low Fat, No Fat.* We couldn't resist it! The potatoes and whole-kernel corn make it hearty enough to serve as a main dish.

1	package (10 ounces) frozen corn
³/₄–1	cup peeled and cubed potatoes
½	cup chopped onions
½	cup thinly sliced celery
1	teaspoon instant chicken bouillon granules
	Dash of ground white or black pepper or ground black pepper
⅓	cup water
1³/₄	cups skim milk
2	tablespoons all-purpose flour
2	tablespoons nonfat dry milk powder

In a large saucepan, combine the corn, potatoes, onions, celery, bouillon, pepper and water. Bring to a boil over high heat, then reduce the heat to low and simmer, stirring frequently, for about 10 minutes, or until the corn and potatoes are just tender.

Add 1½ cups of the skim milk and cook until the milk is hot.

In a small bowl, combine the flour and dry milk powder. Whisk in the remaining ¼ cup of skim milk until smooth. Gradually add to the corn mixture, stirring gently to avoid mashing the cooked vegetables. Stir until thickened. Cook for about 1 minute, being careful not to let the soup burn.

Makes 4 servings
PER SERVING: 166 CALORIES, 0.6 G. FAT

White Chili

Jeanne Jones, author of *Cook It Light,* calls this one of her signature recipes. You'd never guess it has less than a gram of fat per serving. It's delicious and it's a breeze to prepare. It even freezes well.

1	pound dried Great Northern beans, soaked overnight and drained
4	cups defatted chicken broth
2	medium onions, coarsely chopped (about 4 cups)
3	cloves garlic, finely chopped
1	teaspoon salt
½	cup chopped canned mild green chili peppers
2	teaspoons ground cumin
1½	teaspoons dried oregano
1	teaspoon ground coriander
¼	teaspoon ground cloves
¼–½	teaspoon ground red pepper
4	ounces shredded reduced-fat Monterey Jack cheese (optional)

In a large, heavy saucepan, combine the beans, broth, 2 cups of the onions, garlic and salt. Bring to a boil over high heat; reduce the heat to medium-low. Cover and simmer for about 2 hours, or until the beans are tender. Add more broth if the mixture begins to dry out.

When the beans are tender, add the remaining 2 cups of onions, the chili peppers, cumin, oregano, coriander, cloves and ground red pepper. Stir well and cook, covered, for 30 minutes.

To serve, spoon 1 cup of the chili into each serving bowl and top with 2 tablespoons of the Monterey Jack (if using).

Makes 8 servings
PER SERVING (WITHOUT CHEESE): 207 CALORIES, 0.9 G. FAT
Notes: It is important to use a heavy saucepan to make the chili. The liquid boils down too quickly in a lightweight pan. If too much liquid is left after the chili has finished cooking, let it stand, uncovered. As it cools, much of the liquid will be absorbed.
For a nonvegetarian entrée, add 1½ to 2 cups cooked chicken, turkey breast, rabbit, veal or drained water-packed white albacore tuna.

Pacific Rim Gazpacho

Ripe, fresh tomatoes are by far the best choice for chilled tomato soup. This zesty version of gazpacho, from *Arlyn Hackett's Menu Magic*, makes a great starter course when paired on the menu with fish.

2	cups water
1	cup no-salt-added tomato puree
½	cup rice vinegar
4	teaspoons reduced-sodium soy sauce
¼	teaspoon hot-pepper sauce
1	tablespoon frozen orange juice concentrate
1	teaspoon dark sesame oil
3	cups finely diced tomatoes
1	cup peeled, seeded and diced cucumber
1	cup finely diced green or sweet red pepper
½	cup diced scallions
2	cloves garlic, minced
½	cup sliced canned water chestnuts
¼	cup minced fresh cilantro or parsley

In a large bowl, combine the water, tomato puree, vinegar, soy sauce, hot-pepper sauce, orange juice concentrate and sesame oil. Refrigerate for 2 hours.

Add the tomatoes, cucumbers, peppers, scallions and garlic and stir until well-mixed. Refrigerate for 1 hour.

When ready to serve, ladle the gazpacho into individual serving bowls. Sprinkle the water chestnuts and cilantro or parsley over each serving.

Makes 8 servings
PER SERVING: 53 CALORIES, 0.9 G. FAT
Note: If fresh tomatoes are unavailable, replace them with drained canned Italian plum tomatoes.

Maine Clam Chowder

If a cup of thick, steaming New England clam chowder is on your list of soup favorites, you'll want to sample this ultra-low-fat version from *1,001 Low-Fat Recipes* by Sue Spitler. Don't forget the crackers!

32	littleneck clams or other fresh small clams, scrubbed
6	cups hot water
1	cup chopped onions
½	cup sliced celery
1	carrot, thinly sliced
4	potatoes (about 2 pounds), peeled and cubed
2	cups skim milk
½	cup clam juice
¼	cup all-purpose flour
¼	teaspoon ground white or black pepper

Place the clams in a large saucepan or Dutch oven and add the hot water. Cover and cook over medium heat for 5 to 10 minutes, or until the clams open. Using a slotted spoon, remove the clams and discard any that did not open. Reserve the cooking liquid.

Holding the clams over the reserved liquid, remove them from their shells; discard the shells. Chop the clams and set aside. Strain the reserved liquid through a double layer of cheesecloth or a fine mesh strainer and set aside.

Lightly coat the bottom of a large saucepan with no-stick spray. Add the onions, celery, carrots and potatoes. Cover and cook over medium heat, stirring occasionally, for 5 minutes. Add the milk, reserved clam liquid and clam juice. Cover and simmer for 25 to 30 minutes, or until the vegetables are tender.

Ladle ½ cup of the soup into a small bowl. Whisk in the flour and pepper and pour it back into the pan. Add the chopped clams. Cook and stir until slightly thickened.

Makes 8 servings
PER SERVING: 148 CALORIES, 0.8 G. FAT
Notes: Inspect the clams before cooking and discard any that are already open.

The fresh clams can be replaced with 3 cans (6 ounces each) of chopped clams. Drain the clams and reserve the juice. Mix the juice with enough hot water to equal 5 ¾ cups of liquid. If using canned clams, omit the first two steps of the directions.

Cold Zucchini Soup with Fresh Mint

This chilled soup, from Martha Rose Shulman's celebrated book *Provençal Light*, is tailor-made for summer days. Fresh mint and zucchini abound during the summer, and here they're paired perfectly for a refreshingly simple first course or light lunch.

2	cups water
2	pounds zucchini, thickly sliced
3	cups low-fat plain yogurt
1	teaspoon crushed coriander seeds
2	cloves garlic, minced (optional)
¼	cup slivered fresh mint leaves
	Salt and ground black pepper
2	tablespoons fresh lemon juice
	Fresh mint sprigs

In a medium saucepan, bring the water to a boil over high heat, then reduce the heat to medium. Arrange the zucchini in a steamer basket, place over the water and cook for 10 to 15 minutes, or until tender. Transfer the zucchini and the water to a food processor or blender and process until smooth.

Add the yogurt, coriander seeds, garlic (if using) and mint leaves. Add salt and pepper to taste. Refrigerate for several hours. Just before serving, stir in the lemon juice and garnish with the mint sprigs.

Serves 4
PER SERVING: 131 CALORIES, 0.7 G. FAT
Note: This soup must be made several hours before serving. It can be made a day ahead of time, but don't add the mint leaves until a few hours before serving.

Chilled Carrot Soup

You may think chilled carrot soup is summertime fare, but in this re-freshing version the cumin and cinnamon make it a wonderful winter dish. Leave it up to *Arlyn Hackett's Menu Magic* to do the unthinkable—and the soup has less than a half-gram of fat per serving, too!

5	large carrots, peeled and trimmed
2	cups water
½	teaspoon ground cumin
¼	teaspoon ground cinnamon
⅛	teaspoon ground red pepper
1½	cups nonfat plain yogurt
2	cups skim milk
2	tablespoons frozen orange juice concentrate
2	teaspoons reduced-sodium soy sauce
8	small sprigs fresh cilantro or mint

Grate enough of the carrots to measure ½ cup and set aside. Slice the remaining carrots into ½"-thick rounds and transfer to a medium saucepan. Add the water, cumin, cinnamon and pepper. Cover and cook over medium-low heat for 30 minutes, or until the carrots are tender. Transfer the carrots and cooking liquid to a medium bowl and refrigerate for 30 minutes, or until chilled through.

Place the carrots and cooking liquid in a food processor or blender and puree until smooth. Transfer the carrot puree to a large bowl and whisk in the yogurt, milk, orange juice concentrate and soy sauce. Refrigerate for at least 1 hour before serving.

To serve, ladle the cold soup into individual serving bowls or goblets. Sprinkle the grated carrots over each serving and garnish with the cilantro or mint.

Makes 8 servings
PER SERVING: 76 CALORIES, 0.3 G. FAT
Note: To bring out the natural sweetness of carrots, slowly simmer them over low heat rather than cooking them in rapidly boiling water.

Soupe au Pistou
(French Vegetable Soup with Basil)

One of our favorite low-fat cookbooks, *Everyday Cooking with Dr. Dean Ornish*, takes on the rich flavors of southern France with this classic summer vegetable soup. Like Italian pesto, pistou is a French herb paste used to flavor other ingredients. Here it's a savory mixture of basil, beans and garlic that's stirred into the soup at the last minute.

½   cup diced onion
½   cup diced carrots
½   cup diced celery
½   cup diced turnips
½   cup peeled and diced russet potatoes
½   cup diced leeks (white part only)
½   cup peeled and diced fresh or canned tomatoes
4   cups vegetable broth
½   cup 1″ pieces of uncooked whole-wheat spaghetti
1   can (15 ounces) navy beans
1   cup tightly packed fresh basil leaves
3   cloves garlic, minced
    Salt and ground black pepper

In a large pot, combine the onions, carrots, celery, turnips, potatoes, leeks, tomatoes and broth. Bring to a simmer over medium heat. Cover, reduce the heat to medium-low to maintain a simmer and cook for 10 minutes. Add the spaghetti and 1 cup of the beans with a small amount of the liquid. Cover and simmer for 10 to 12 minutes, or until the spaghetti is tender.

Combine the remaining beans and liquid, the basil and garlic in a food processor or blender and puree until smooth. Add the puree to the soup and stir until blended. Sprinkle with salt and pepper to taste.

Makes 4 servings
PER SERVING: 271 CALORIES, 0.9 G. FAT
Note: To store any extra fresh basil, wrap the leaves in damp paper towels and refrigerate in a resealable plastic bag. They will keep for several days.

Cream of Fresh Asparagus Soup

You don't need cream to make flavorful cream soups. Here the asparagus is pureed to give the soup a rich texture without added fat. The result is a thick and delicious side-dish soup with less than a gram of fat per serving, compliments of *Prevention's Healthy Hometown Favorites*.

2	pounds fresh asparagus, trimmed and cut into ½" pieces
1	can (14½ ounces) defatted reduced-sodium chicken broth
½	cup evaporated skim milk
½	teaspoon fresh lemon juice
⅛	teaspoon ground white or black pepper
⅛	teaspoon salt (optional)
1	tablespoon finely chopped fresh parsley

Place the asparagus pieces in a large saucepan and add the broth. Bring to a boil over high heat, then reduce the heat to medium-low. Cover and simmer for 10 to 15 minutes, or until the asparagus is very tender.

Transfer the asparagus mixture in small batches to a food processor or blender and process until smooth. Return the mixture to the saucepan. Stir in the milk, lemon juice, pepper and salt (if using). Heat the soup until warm.

To serve, ladle the soup into small soup bowls and sprinkle with the parsley.

Makes 4 servings
PER SERVING: 85 CALORIES, 0.7 G. FAT
Notes: When selecting asparagus, choose stalks that are crisp, long and slender and have tightly closed tips.

The fresh green asparagus can be replaced with white asparagus. Look for it in specialty produce markets between March and June.

Minty Cream of Butternut Squash Soup

The secret to this beautifully smooth and creamy soup, from *Jacques Pépin's Simple and Healthy Cooking*, is fresh mint and a dash of curry powder. Rich and flavorful, it makes a good first-course party dish.

1   butternut squash ($2^3/_4$ pounds), peeled, seeded and cut into 2″pieces
1   medium onion, sliced
2   cups water
$^1/_2$ teaspoon curry powder
$^1/_2$ teaspoon ground cumin
3   cups reduced-sodium chicken broth
2   sprigs fresh mint
1   medium carrot, sliced into thin strips
1   small leek or piece of leek, washed, trimmed and cut into thin strips
$^3/_4$ teaspoon salt (optional)
$^1/_4$ teaspoon ground black pepper

Place the squash, onions, water, curry powder, cumin and 2 cups of the broth in a large saucepan. If the mint sprigs have woody stems, strip off the leaves and add them to the pot; otherwise, add the whole sprigs. Bring the mixture to a full boil. Reduce the heat to low, cover and cook for 45 minutes.

Place the carrots and leeks in a medium saucepan with the remaining 1 cup of broth. Bring to a boil, reduce the heat to medium and boil for 10 minutes. Set aside.

After the squash mixture has cooked, transfer it in small batches to a food processor or blender and blend until smooth. Return the mixture to the saucepan and stir in the salt (if using), pepper, carrots and leeks. Return the mixture to a boil and serve.

Makes 6 servings
PER SERVING: 80 CALORIES, 0.3 G. FAT

Salads and Dressings

Make fresh greens the centerpiece of any meal with these creative combinations.

Crab Salad

Doris Cross, author of *Fat Free and Ultra Low Fat Recipes*, uses this versatile crab salad in sandwiches and salads and on crackers. But we think it's ideal for stuffed tomatoes—from the biggest beefsteak to the tiniest cherry.

9 ounces crabmeat, cooked
¼ cup chopped green peppers
2 tablespoons chopped pimento
1 small onion, chopped
¼ cup fat-free mayonnaise
2 teaspoons sugar
1 teaspoon lime juice
1 tablespoon chopped fresh parsley
1–2 drops hot-pepper sauce
Seasoned salt and ground black pepper

In a medium bowl, combine the crabmeat, green peppers, pimentos, onions, mayonnaise, sugar, lime juice, parsley and hot-pepper sauce. Sprinkle with seasoned salt and pepper to taste and mix well. Refrigerate for at least 20 minutes, or until ready to serve.

Makes 4 servings
Per serving: 107 calories, 0.7 g. fat

Tomato-Vinaigrette Dressing

Who says a tasty vinaigrette has to be high in fat? This fabulous salad dressing from *Jacques Pépin's Simple and Healthy Cooking* is practically fat-free. Use about 1½ to 2 tablespoons on each serving of your favorite salad greens.

1 cup reduced-sodium chicken broth
2 teaspoons cornstarch
1 tablespoon cold water
1 large ripe tomato (about 8 ounces), halved and seeded
2 scallions, trimmed and coarsely chopped (about ¼ cup)
3 tablespoons balsamic vinegar
3 tablespoons red-wine vinegar
2 tablespoons Dijon mustard
1 teaspoon paprika
½ teaspoon salt (optional)
3 cloves garlic, crushed
½ teaspoon ground black pepper
¼ teaspoon hot-pepper sauce

In a small saucepan, bring the broth to a boil. Remove from the heat.

In a cup, dissolve the cornstarch in the water. Whisk into the broth to thicken it slightly. Return the pan to the heat and bring the mixture to a boil. Set aside to cool.

Cut the tomato into 1″ chunks and place them in a food processor or blender. Add the scallions, balsamic vinegar, red-wine vinegar, mustard, paprika, salt (if using), garlic, pepper and hot-pepper sauce. Process until smooth. Add the thickened broth and process just until incorporated.

Transfer the dressing to a jar with a tight-fitting lid. Store, tightly covered, in the refrigerator for up to one week. Shake well before using.

Makes 2¼ cups
PER SERVING (2 TABLESPOONS): 10 CALORIES, 0.2 G. FAT

Macaroni-Bleu Cheese Salad

Here's a new twist on macaroni salad from Sue Spitler, author of *Skinny Pasta*. She works wonders with just 2 tablespoons of bleu cheese in the dressing. The salad has a pleasing, bright flavor and less than a gram of fat per serving.

Salad

4	ounces elbow macaroni, cooked and cooled to room temperature
³⁄₄	cup chopped sweet red peppers
¹⁄₂	cup chopped cucumbers
¹⁄₂	cup shredded carrots
¹⁄₄	cup thinly sliced scallions

Dressing

¹⁄₂	cup fat-free mayonnaise or salad dressing
2	tablespoons crumbled bleu cheese
1	tablespoon red-wine vinegar
1	teaspoon celery seeds
¹⁄₂	teaspoon salt (optional)
¹⁄₈	teaspoon ground red pepper
¹⁄₈	teaspoon ground black pepper

To make the salad: In a large bowl, combine the macaroni, peppers, cucumbers, carrots and scallions. Set aside.

To make the dressing: In a small bowl, combine the mayonnaise or salad dressing, bleu cheese, vinegar, celery seeds, salt (if using), red pepper and black pepper.

Pour the dressing over the salad, stirring well until all of the ingredients are coated.

Makes 8 servings
PER SERVING: 82 CALORIES, 0.9 G. FAT

New Potato Salad with Dill

Here's one of our favorite versions of potato salad. It's simple, flavorful and completely guilt-free. Fresh dill adds a tempting aroma that makes the salad perfect for picnics. The recipe comes from *Prevention's Quick and Healthy Low-Fat Cooking Featuring All-American Food.*

1	pound new potatoes
3	hard-cooked egg whites
⅓	cup sliced scallions
¼	cup thinly sliced radishes
2	tablespoons chopped fresh dill
⅓	cup fat-free mayonnaise
¼	cup nonfat sour cream
3	tablespoons skim milk
1	teaspoon white-wine vinegar
1	teaspoon yellow mustard

Place the potatoes in a large saucepan with enough water to cover. Bring to a boil over high heat. Reduce the heat to medium and boil for 15 to 20 minutes, or until the potatoes are tender. Drain the potatoes, rinse with cold water and let cool; do not peel them.

When the potatoes are cool, cut them into quarters and slice them. Transfer to a medium bowl. Add the egg whites, scallions, radishes and dill and toss gently.

In a small bowl, combine the mayonnaise, sour cream, milk, vinegar and mustard and mix well. Pour the dressing over the potato mixture and stir gently.

Makes 4 servings
Per serving: 151 calories, 0.2 g. fat
Note: The potato skins add fiber as well as color to the salad, but you can peel the potatoes if you prefer.

Calico Slaw with Poppyseed Dressing

Traditional coleslaw packs a wallop of fat because of the mayonnaise. This tasty alternative comes from *Prevention Magazine's Quick and Healthy Low-Fat Cooking—Healthy Home Cooking*. The citrus juices, honey and poppy seeds give it a zesty-sweet flavor, while nonfat mayonnaise adds a creamy texture.

⅓	cup fat-free mayonnaise
1	tablespoon frozen orange juice concentrate
2	teaspoons fresh lemon juice
1	teaspoon poppy seeds
½	teaspoon honey
¼	teaspoon ground black pepper
1½	cups finely shredded green cabbage
1½	cups finely shredded red cabbage
½	cup thinly sliced sweet red peppers
½	cup stringed and julienned snow peas
¼	cup coarsely grated carrots

In a salad bowl, combine the mayonnaise, orange juice concentrate, lemon juice, poppy seeds, honey and black pepper and whisk together until well-blended.

Add the green cabbage, red cabbage, red peppers, snow peas and carrots and toss until the vegetables are well-coated with the dressing.

Makes 4 servings
PER SERVING: 55 CALORIES, 0.5 G. FAT
Note: To bring out the flavor of the poppy seeds, cook them in a dry skillet over medium heat just until they smell fragrant and toasty. Immediately transfer the seeds to a plate and let them cool a bit before adding them to the dressing.

Side Dishes

Think the only no-fat veggies are salad and steamed broccoli? These taste-grabbing alternatives will convince you otherwise.

Mexican Red Rice

In the traditional version of this recipe, the tomatoes are pureed. But in Sue Spitler's version from *Skinny Mexican Cooking*, the tomatoes are chopped for added color and flavor. It's a simple adjustment—and we love it!

1	large tomato, chopped
½	cup chopped onions
1	clove garlic, minced
½	teaspoon dried oregano
¼	teaspoon ground cumin
1	cup long-grain rice
1	can (14½ ounces) defatted chicken broth
⅓	cup water
1	carrot, cooked and diced
½	cup thawed frozen peas
	Salt and ground black pepper

Coat a large saucepan with no-stick spray; heat over medium heat. Add the tomatoes, onions, garlic, oregano and cumin; cook for 3 to 5 minutes, or until the onions are tender. Add the rice. Cook and stir for 2 to 3 minutes.

Add the broth and water; bring to a boil. Reduce the heat to medium low; simmer, covered, for about 20 minutes. Add the carrots and peas; cook for 5 minutes, or until the rice is tender. Sprinkle with salt and pepper.

Makes 6 servings

PER SERVING: 146 CALORIES, 0.4 G. FAT

Pennsylvania Dutch Potato Dressing

From the heartland of Pennsylvania, here is a mashed potato casserole with a rich, buttery taste. This dish, from *Prevention's Healthy Hometown Favorites*, is called "dressing," not "stuffing," because it is cooked in its own dish instead of inside a bird.

    8   medium potatoes (about 2½ pounds), quartered
    2   stalks celery, chopped
    1   small green pepper, chopped
    1   medium onion, chopped
    ½   cup reconstituted butter-flavor mix
    1   cup + 2 tablespoons plain stuffing croutons,
         slightly crushed
    ⅛   teaspoon salt
    ⅛   teaspoon ground black pepper
    1   can (5 ounces or ⅔ cup) evaporated skim milk
    ½   cup skim milk
    3   teaspoons reduced-calorie tub-style margarine

Place the potatoes in a large saucepan with enough water to cover. Bring to a boil over high heat, then reduce the heat to medium, cover and gently boil for about 20 minutes, or until tender.

Meanwhile, in a medium no-stick skillet, combine the celery, peppers, onions and butter-flavor mix. Cook and stir over medium heat for about 10 minutes, or until the celery is tender. Remove from the heat and stir in the croutons. Set aside.

Preheat the oven to 325°. Coat a 1½-quart baking dish with no-stick spray and set aside.

Drain the potatoes. Use a potato masher to mash the potatoes or beat with an electric mixer at low speed. Add the salt and black pepper. Gradually beat in the evaporated milk and skim milk until smooth.

Gently stir the vegetable mixture into the potato mixture, then transfer to the prepared baking dish. Dot the top with the margarine, using ½-teaspoon portions. Bake for about 1 hour, or until the mixture appears lightly browned.

Makes 14 servings
PER SERVING: 103 CALORIES, 0.9 G. FAT

Note: Butter-flavor mix is sold in packets and is often found with condiments and spices at supermarkets. The mix is packaged dry but is used in liquid form in most recipes. Follow the package directions for the exact amounts of water to be used when reconstituting it.

Baked Stuffed Tomatoes

Garlic, parsley and basil combine deliciously with the natural sweetness of tomatoes. Add some fat-free mayonnaise for texture, a bit of balsamic vinegar for zip and you have an irresistible side dish—with less than a gram of fat per serving! These tasty tomatoes come from *Prevention's Quick and Healthy Low-Fat Cooking Featuring Pasta and Other Italian Favorites.*

4	plum tomatoes
1	cup fresh bread crumbs
¼	cup chopped fresh Italian parsley
2	tablespoons fat-free mayonnaise
2	teaspoons balsamic vinegar
1	clove garlic, minced
	Salt and ground black pepper
2	tablespoons chopped fresh basil

Coat a small baking sheet with no-stick spray. Slice the tomatoes in half lengthwise and remove and discard the seeds and pulp, leaving the shells intact. Place on the prepared baking sheet.

In a small bowl, combine the bread crumbs, parsley, mayonnaise, vinegar and garlic and add salt and pepper to taste. Fill the tomato shells with the bread crumb mixture.

Bake at 350° for 15 to 20 minutes, or until the tomatoes are soft and the stuffing is heated through. Sprinkle with the basil just before serving.

Makes 4 servings
PER SERVING: 67 CALORIES, 0.9 G. FAT
Note: You can replace the plum tomatoes with 2 large garden tomatoes, halved crosswise. Increase the baking time to 25 to 30 minutes, then check for doneness. Allow one half per person.

Scalloped Root Vegetables

Lynn Fischer, author of *Healthy Indulgences*, gets fat down to a minimum in this winter casserole—without sacrificing flavor. She uses evaporated skim milk and nonfat mozzarella for a creamy texture.

1	large rutabaga, thinly sliced
3	medium potatoes, thinly sliced
3	medium leeks (white part only), thoroughly rinsed and thinly sliced
10–12	shallots, chopped
3	tablespoons all-purpose flour
½–1	teaspoon salt (optional)
	Ground black pepper
3	tablespoons grated nonfat Parmesan cheese
¼	cup Madeira wine or apple cider
1	can (12 ounces) evaporated skim milk
1	tablespoon Dijon mustard
3	cloves garlic, minced
¼	cup fat-free egg substitute
2	teaspoons chopped fresh thyme or parsley
2	tablespoons shredded nonfat mozzarella cheese

Preheat the oven to 375°. Line an 8″ springform pan with foil and coat with no-stick spray. Arrange one-third of the rutabagas on the bottom of the pan. Add one-third of the potatoes, one-third of the leeks and one-third of the shallots. Coat the vegetables with no-stick spray and sprinkle with 1 tablespoon of the flour, one-third of the salt (if using), pepper and 1 tablespoon of the Parmesan. Repeat the layers two more times.

In a medium bowl, mix together the wine or apple cider, milk, mustard, garlic, egg substitute and 1 teaspoon of the thyme or parsley. Pour over the vegetables and sprinkle with the mozzarella. Cover the pan with foil and bake for 1 hour. Remove the foil and place the pan under the broiler for about 4 minutes, or until the top is lightly browned. Sprinkle with the remaining thyme or parsley. Set aside to cool for 15 minutes; remove from the pan and slice into 8 wedges. Serve immediately.

Makes 8 servings
PER SERVING: 159 CALORIES, 0.5 G. FAT

Barbecued Beans

Tangy, flavorful and very low in fat, these beans from *100% Pleasure* by Nancy Baggett and Ruth Glick go wonderfully with barbecued chicken. Or make them the centerpiece of a vegetarian meal with rice and a salad.

1	cup dry Great Northern beans, sorted and rinsed
1	cup dry black-eyed peas, sorted and rinsed
1	medium onion, chopped
1	clove garlic, minced
3	quarts water
1	can (15 ounces) tomato sauce
1	cup ketchup
1	tablespoon light brown sugar
1	teaspoon dried thyme
1	teaspoon mild chili powder
$\frac{1}{2}$	teaspoon mustard
$\frac{1}{8}$	teaspoon ground cinnamon
	Pinch of ground cloves
3	drops hot-pepper sauce (optional)
	Salt and ground black pepper

Place the beans and peas in a Dutch oven or other large heavy pot. Cover with 2" of water and bring to a boil over high heat. Reduce the heat to medium-low and boil for 2 minutes. Remove the pot from the heat, cover and let stand for 1 hour. Drain the vegetables.

Return the beans and peas to the pot. Add the onions, garlic and water and bring to a boil over high heat. Reduce the heat to medium-low and simmer for 1¼ to 1½ hours, or until tender. Drain well in a colander.

Return the mixture to the pot. Add the tomato sauce, ketchup, sugar, thyme, chili powder, mustard, cinnamon, cloves, hot-pepper sauce (if using) and salt and pepper to taste. Gently stir to mix well.

Simmer, stirring frequently, for 20 to 25 minutes, or until the flavors are well-blended.

Makes 6 servings
PER SERVING: 197 CALORIES, 0.8 G. FAT

Main Courses

With these flavor-packed, no-fat entrées, there are no more excuses for boring dinners.

Old-Fashioned Chicken and Dumplings

Here's a traditional stick-to-your-ribs supper from Doris Cross's *Fat Free and Ultra Low Fat Recipes*. This satisfying version of chicken and dumplings cuts the fat by using a light broth and dumplings made with reduced-fat cottage cheese. Try it on cold winter nights to warm your soul.

Chicken and Broth

4	boneless, skinless chicken breasts, cut into chunks
2	cans (14 ounces each) defatted chicken broth
3	cups water
1	medium onion, chopped
¼	teaspoon garlic powder
½	cup finely chopped celery
¼	teaspoon poultry seasoning
1	teaspoon parsley
	Salt and ground black pepper

Dumplings

3	egg whites
½	cup nonfat cottage cheese
2	tablespoons water
	Pinch of salt
1	cup all-purpose flour
	Imitation butter sprinkles (optional)

To make the chicken and broth: Coat a large pot with no-stick spray. Add the chicken and cook over medium heat, stirring occasionally, until browned. Add the broth, water, onions, garlic powder, celery, poultry seasoning, parsley and salt and pepper to taste. Reduce the heat to medium-low and simmer, uncovered, for 30 minutes.

To make the dumplings: Meanwhile, in a large bowl, combine the egg whites and cottage cheese. Using an electric mixer, beat at medium speed until well-blended. Add the water and salt and mix well. Add ½ cup of the flour and mix by hand until well-blended. Add the remaining ½ cup of flour and mix by hand until it forms a soft dough.

Bring the chicken broth to a rolling boil over high heat. Drop the dough into the broth a tablespoon at a time. After all of the dough has been added, reduce the heat to medium, cover and cook for 15 minutes. (If a thicker, richer broth is desired, uncover and cook a bit longer.) Sprinkle with imitation butter sprinkles (if using).

Makes 8 servings
PER SERVING: 123 CALORIES, 0.9 G. FAT

Roasted Eggplant and Sweet Onion Tart

If you like pizza, you'll love this pizzalike tart from *Lynda's Low-Fat Kitchen* by Lynda A. Pozel. Even folks who aren't crazy about eggplant will ask for seconds.

Filling

1	medium eggplant (about 12 ounces)
½	teaspoon salt
1	teaspoon dried oregano
1	large sweet onion, halved and sliced
½	cup dry sherry or nonalcoholic white wine
5	cups sliced mushrooms
2	roasted sweet red peppers, coarsely chopped

Crust

1	cup warm water (105°–115°)
1	teaspoon honey
2	packages (¼ ounce each) active dry yeast
2¼	cups all-purpose flour
½	teaspoon salt (optional)

To make the filling: Preheat the broiler. Cut the eggplant in half lengthwise and place it cut-side down on a broiler pan. Broil 4″ from the heat for 5 minutes, or until the pulp is soft and the skin blisters and blackens. Place the eggplant in a clean paper bag, seal the bag and set aside for 3 minutes.

Remove the eggplant flesh with a knife and discard the skin. Transfer the flesh to a food processor or blender and puree until smooth. Add the salt and ½ teaspoon of the oregano. Set aside.

In a large no-stick skillet over medium heat, cook the onions in the sherry or white wine for about 4 minutes, or until the onions are soft and the liquid has partially evaporated. Stir in the mushrooms and the remaining ½ teaspoon of oregano. Cook for 10 minutes, or until the mushrooms are soft and the liquid has evaporated. Set aside.

To make the crust: Preheat the oven to 400°. Lightly coat a 12″ pizza pan or baking sheet with no-stick spray.

In a large bowl, combine the water and honey. Sprinkle the yeast on top and set aside to proof for 2 minutes. Stir to dissolve the yeast.

Stir in 2 cups of the flour and the salt (if using). Gradually add the remaining flour until the dough feels smooth and elastic and not too sticky.

Turn the dough out onto the prepared pan and, with well-floured or oiled hands, shape to within an inch of the edge of the pan. Set aside in a warm place for 10 minutes, or until the dough rises slightly.

To assemble, spread the pureed eggplant over the dough. Spoon the onion mixture on top, covering the eggplant completely. Arrange the roasted peppers on top and bake for about 25 minutes, or until the crust is lightly browned. Carefully transfer the tart to a mesh pizza screen or oven rack and bake for 5 minutes to crisp the bottom of the crust. Remove from the oven and cool for 5 minutes before serving.

Makes 8 servings

PER SERVING: 175 CALORIES, 0.6 G. FAT

Notes: The eggplant can be cooked and pureed up to 3 days in advance and refrigerated until needed.

You can use jarred roasted red peppers or make your own. To roast them, preheat the oven to 450°. Lightly coat a baking sheet with no-stick spray. Cut 2 sweet red peppers in half lengthwise, then remove and discard the stems, seeds and membranes. Arrange the peppers, cut side down, on the baking sheet and spray the skins with no-stick spray. Bake for 20 to 35 minutes, or until the skins just begin to blister. Remove the peppers from the oven and cool slightly. When the peppers are cool enough to handle, remove and discard the skins.

Microwave Orange Roughy with Port Sauce

Sue Spitler's *1,001 Low-Fat Recipes* contributes this tasty sauce.

Port Sauce

3	scallions, sliced
1½	cups nonfat lemon yogurt
1	tablespoon lemon rind
3	tablespoons port wine or apple cider
⅛	teaspoon ground white or black pepper
⅛	teaspoon dried tarragon

Orange Roughy

1¼	pounds orange roughy fillets, cut into 4 equal pieces
2	tablespoons port wine or apple cider
2	tablespoons minced fresh chives

To make the port sauce: Coat a small no-stick skillet with olive oil no-stick spray. Add the scallions and cook over medium heat, stirring occasionally, for 4 minutes, or until tender. Transfer to a small bowl. Add the yogurt, lemon rind and wine or apple cider. Stir in the pepper and tarragon and mix well. Cover and refrigerate until ready to serve.

To make the orange roughy: Coat a microwave-safe baking dish with olive oil no-stick spray. Place the fish in the baking dish; if necessary, tuck the thin ends of the fillets under the thicker ends to make the fish an even thickness. Sprinkle with the wine or apple cider and chives. Cover tightly with plastic wrap.

Microwave on high power for 3 to 4 minutes. If the fish is not completely cooked, continue cooking for 30 seconds at a time until it is opaque and flakes easily with a fork. Remove the dish from the microwave and remove the plastic wrap carefully to avoid escaping steam.

Serve the fillets with equal amounts of the port sauce.

Makes 4 servings
PER SERVING: 184 CALORIES, 0.8 G. FAT

Rice-Stuffed Bell Peppers

These simple peppers are from *Everyday Cooking with Dr. Dean Ornish*.

8	large sweet red peppers
2½	cups vegetable broth
½	teaspoon salt
¼	teaspoon ground black pepper
1	cup diced mushrooms
½	cup finely diced onions
½	cup finely diced celery
2	cups basmati rice
½	cup canned diced tomatoes
1	teaspoon cumin seeds
1	cup fresh or thawed frozen peas

Make caps for the peppers by slicing about ⅓" off the top of each one. Set the caps aside. Carefully remove the seeds and ribs from each pepper.

In a large pot of salted water, boil the peppers for 5 to 7 minutes, or until tender. Drain the peppers and plunge them into a large pot of ice water. When cool, drain again and pat dry. Set aside.

In a large saucepan, bring the broth to a simmer. Add the salt, pepper, mushrooms, onions and celery. Cook for 5 minutes, or until the vegetables are tender.

Add the rice, tomatoes and cumin seeds. Return to a simmer. Cover, reduce the heat to the lowest setting and cook for 18 minutes. Uncover and place the peas on top, but do not stir. Cover the pan again and remove from the heat. Let stand for 7 minutes to allow the peas to cook through. Transfer the mixture to a large bowl and fluff with a fork.

Preheat the oven to 425°. Stuff each pepper with about 1 cup of the rice mixture and top with the caps. Arrange them in a 9" × 13" baking dish (if they won't stand up, lay them gently on their sides). Bake, uncovered, for 20 minutes, or until the peppers are heated through.

Makes 8 servings
PER SERVING: 229 CALORIES. 0.7 G. FAT
Note: The stuffing alone makes a delicious rice pilaf. On a busy evening, serve the pilaf with soup and a salad.

Lemon-Pepper Horseradish Shrimp

Nobody knows shrimp better than Cajuns. In this recipe, from *Enola Prudhomme's Low-Fat Favorites*, the shellfish is marinated in a tangy blend of seasonings and served chilled. The zesty flavors of lemon, pepper, horseradish and hot-pepper sauce will take you straight to the bayous of Louisiana.

1	cup water
8	ounces medium shrimp, peeled and deveined
1	teaspoon salt
1	cup nonfat mayonnaise
¼	cup liquid from canned baby corn
3	tablespoons finely chopped onions
2	tablespoons finely chopped scallions
2	teaspoons prepared horseradish
2	tablespoons salt-free lemon-pepper seasoning
1	tablespoon reduced-sodium Worcestershire sauce
1	tablespoon lemon juice
1	teaspoon garlic powder
½	teaspoon Dijon mustard
½	teaspoon hot-pepper sauce
1	can (4 ounces) baby corn, cut in half

In a large skillet, bring the water to a boil over high heat. Add the shrimp and salt. Cook and stir for 3 minutes, or until the shrimp are cooked through. Using a slotted spoon, remove the shrimp and set aside to cool. Remove ¼ cup of the cooking liquid and set aside to cool.

In a medium bowl, combine the mayonnaise, corn liquid, onions, scallions, horseradish, lemon-pepper seasoning, Worcestershire sauce, lemon juice, garlic powder, mustard, hot-pepper sauce and the reserved cooking liquid. Refrigerate for 1 hour. Add the corn and shrimp and toss gently to combine.

Makes 4 servings
PER SERVING: 240 CALORIES, 0.8 G. FAT

Orange-Rosemary Roasted Turkey Breast

Next time the holidays roll around, consider making this low-fat, no-fuss turkey breast from *Prevention's Stop Dieting and Lose Weight Cookbook*. You'll save time and be blessed with white-meat-only leftovers.

1	fresh or frozen bone-in turkey breast (4–5 pounds)
1	small bunch fresh Italian parsley, finely chopped
1	small bunch fresh thyme, finely chopped
1	small bunch fresh rosemary, finely chopped
2	oranges
1	lemon
	Pinch of ground black pepper
	Pinch of paprika

If using a frozen turkey breast, thaw it. Rinse and pat dry with paper towels.

Preheat the oven to 325°.

In a medium bowl, combine the parsley, thyme and rosemary. Grate the rind from the oranges and lemon, then set the oranges and lemon aside. Add the grated rind to the herb mixture and toss until combined.

Rub the herb mixture over the skin of the turkey. Place the turkey on a rack in a large roasting pan.

Cut the oranges and lemon in half and squeeze their juices over the turkey. Sprinkle with the pepper and paprika. Insert a meat thermometer in the thickest part of the breast.

Roast, uncovered, for 2¼ to 2½ hours, or until the thermometer registers 170° to 175°. Baste frequently with the pan juices. (If necessary, loosely cover the turkey with foil during roasting to avoid overbrowning.)

Let stand for at least 15 minutes before carving. Remove and discard the skin before serving. Cover and refrigerate the remaining turkey for another use.

Makes 12 servings

PER SERVING (3 OUNCES): 125 CALORIES, 0.8 G. FAT

Poached Turkey
with Lemon-Caper Mayonnaise

This light, cool dish from *Prevention's Quick and Healthy Low-Fat Cooking Featuring Pasta and Other Italian Favorites* makes the perfect summer meal. Try it served on a bed of dark leafy greens and garnished with lemon wedges.

Turkey

2	turkey breast tenderloins (about 8 ounces each)
8	cups defatted chicken broth
2	stalks celery, halved crosswise
2	carrots, halved crosswise
1	small onion, studded with 15 cloves
2	cloves garlic

Mayonnaise

½	cup fat-free mayonnaise
½	cup nonfat plain yogurt
1	tablespoon lemon juice
1	tablespoon chopped fresh tarragon
1	teaspoon chopped fresh oregano
1	teaspoon drained capers
	Salt and ground black pepper

To make the turkey: In a large saucepan, cover the turkey with the broth (add water if necessary so that the meat is covered with liquid). Add the celery, carrots, onion and garlic. Bring to a boil, cover and simmer for 20 to 25 minutes, or until the meat is no longer pink when sliced with a knife.

Remove the turkey and cool for 15 minutes. Or, if preparing this dish ahead, let the turkey stay in the broth, cool to room temperature and refrigerate, covered, until ready to use.

To make the mayonnaise: In a small bowl, stir together the mayonnaise, yogurt, lemon juice, tarragon, oregano and capers; add salt and pepper to taste.

To serve, slice the turkey. Spoon the mayonnaise evenly over the slices.

Makes 4 servings

PER SERVING: 171 CALORIES, 0.8 G. FAT

Pasta with Smoked Chicken and Pea Pods

This remarkably quick meal, from Barry Bluestein and Kevin Morrissey's *The 99% Fat-Free Cookbook*, uses just a bit of smoked poultry for a notably rich, smoky taste—and less than a gram of fat per serving.

9	ounces thin pasta
1	cup thinly sliced white onions
1	tablespoon water
3	cloves garlic, coarsely chopped
1	large sweet red pepper, seeded and thinly sliced
4	ounces snow peas, ends and strings removed
3	ounces skinless smoked chicken breast, thinly sliced
1/4	cup coarsely chopped fresh basil
1/8	teaspoon salt
1/8	teaspoon ground black pepper
1	cup defatted chicken broth

In a large pot of boiling water, cook the pasta until just tender (3 to 4 minutes for fresh pasta; 8 to 10 minutes for dry). Drain well and set aside.

In a large no-stick skillet over medium heat, cook the onions in the water, stirring occasionally, for about 4 minutes, or until wilted. Add the garlic, peppers and peas. Cover and cook for 2 minutes. Add the chicken, basil, salt and pepper. Cover and cook for 5 minutes.

Meanwhile, transfer the pasta to a large pot and add the broth. Cook and stir over medium to medium-low heat until most of the broth is absorbed. Remove from the heat and add the chicken mixture. Toss gently and serve.

Makes 6 servings
PER SERVING: 211 CALORIES, 0.9 G. FAT

Broccoli Pizza
with Quick and Easy Crust

Sarah Schlesinger, author of *500 Fat-Free Recipes*, has made homestyle pizza synonymous with healthy fast food. The crust is made with beer, and it requires no separate rising time.

Sauce

¼	cup water
1	clove garlic, minced
½	cup finely chopped onions
¼	cup chopped fresh parsley
¼	cup finely chopped green peppers
1½	cups reduced-sodium tomato sauce
3	tablespoons reduced-sodium tomato paste
½	teaspoon dried oregano
½	teaspoon dried marjoram
½	teaspoon sugar
	Pinch of ground black pepper

Dough

2	cups unbleached all-purpose flour
1	cup whole-wheat flour
1	tablespoon baking powder
12	ounces beer

Topping

1½	cups shredded nonfat mozzarella cheese
¼	cup grated nonfat Parmesan cheese
½	cup sliced mushrooms
¾	cup broccoli florets, steamed
½	cup chopped scallions

To make the sauce: In a medium saucepan, heat the water over medium heat. Add the garlic and onions. Cook and stir for 5 minutes, or until the onions are tender. Add more liquid, if necessary.

Stir in the parsley, peppers, tomato sauce, tomato paste, oregano, marjoram, sugar and pepper. Bring to a boil, then reduce the heat to medium-low and simmer, uncovered, for 10 minutes. Set aside.

To make the dough: Preheat the oven to 425°.

In a large bowl, combine the all-purpose flour, whole-wheat flour, baking powder and beer. Mix until a soft dough forms, then turn out into a 9″ × 13″ pan. Using your hands, flatten the dough to fit the bottom of the pan.

To assemble, spread the sauce over the dough. Sprinkle the mozzarella and Parmesan on top. Add the mushrooms, then the broccoli and scallions.

Bake for 25 minutes, or until the crust is crisp and golden. Cut into 6 wedges.

Makes 6 servings

PER SERVING: 272 CALORIES, 0.7 G. FAT

FAT STATS

Obstacles to Eating Right

- Percentage of Americans who don't want to give up favorite foods: 36
- Percentage who say it takes too much time: 21
- Percentage who say health information is contradictory: 21
- Percentage who say it's important only for those with health risks: 15
- Percentage who say there are too few healthy alternatives: 9
- Percentage who don't understand health guidelines: 8

Delta Beef and Rice

A true taste of the South, this casserole, from *Prevention's Healthy Hometown Favorites*, features the "holy trinity" of onions, celery and peppers.

1½	pounds extra-lean ground round
1	cup sliced scallions
1	cup chopped celery
½	cup chopped green peppers
1	large clove garlic, minced
1	tablespoon + 1 cup defatted reduced-sodium beef broth
1	can (16 ounces) no-salt-added tomato sauce
1	can (15 ounces) no-salt-added tomato puree
¼	cup chopped fresh parsley
1	tablespoon dried oregano
1	tablespoon dried basil
1	tablespoon Worcestershire sauce
¼	teaspoon seasoned salt
¼	teaspoon ground black pepper
3	cups cooked brown rice
¾	cup finely shredded reduced-fat sharp Cheddar cheese (optional)

Preheat the oven to 350°. In a large no-stick skillet, cook the beef, stirring occasionally, until browned. Drain the beef in a strainer or colander, then transfer to a large plate lined with paper towels. Blot the top of the beef with additional paper towels and set aside.

Wipe the skillet with paper towels. Add the scallions, celery, green peppers, garlic and 1 tablespoon of the broth. Cook and stir over medium heat for about 8 minutes, or until the celery is tender. Stir in the beef, tomato sauce, tomato puree, parsley, oregano, basil, Worcestershire sauce, salt, pepper and the remaining broth. Add the rice. Stir until combined.

Coat a 9" × 13" baking dish with no-stick spray. Add the beef mixture and cover with foil. Bake for 30 minutes, or until heated through. Sprinkle with the Cheddar (if using) and bake for 5 minutes.

Makes 8 servings
PER SERVING: 141 CALORIES, 0.8 G. FAT

Desserts

Make your grand finale lean and luscious with these tempting recipes.

Pears in Red Wine

Succulent pears steeped in a tasty combination of red wine and lemon juice, compliments of *Jacques Pépin's Simple and Healthy Cooking*.

5   medium to large Bartlett pears (about 1$^{1}/_{2}$ pounds), peeled, quartered and cored
1$^{1}/_{2}$ cups hearty red wine or nonalcoholic red wine
$^{1}/_{3}$ cup sugar
   Grated rind of 1 lemon
$^{1}/_{4}$ cup lemon juice

In a large saucepan, bring the pears, wine, sugar, lemon rind and lemon juice to a boil. Reduce the heat to medium-low, cover and boil gently for about 25 minutes (less if the pears are very ripe, more if they are hard). Pierce the pears with a sharp knife to determine tenderness. Use a slotted spoon to transfer the pears to a serving bowl.

You should have about 1$^{1}/_{4}$ cups of liquid remaining. Bring the liquid to a boil and cook until it is reduced to about $^{2}/_{3}$ cup. Add to the pears and cool to room temperature. (The liquid should become syrupy.)

Divide the pear quarters among 6 small, deep dessert dishes. Spoon on some of the syrup and serve.

Makes 6 servings
Per serving: 152 calories, 0.5 g. fat
Note: If you use unripe pears or you use a Seckel or Bosc variety, they may have to cook for as long as an hour to become tender.

Classic Cheesecake

Don't miss this dessert! It's a simple, old-fashioned cheesecake that really satisfies—without expanding your waistline. The geniuses behind this cake are Barry Bluestein and Kevin Morrissey, authors of *The 99% Fat-Free Book of Appetizers and Desserts*. They replaced the basic mixture of cream cheese and baker's cheese with a combination of nonfat cream cheese, nonfat ricotta cheese and nonfat yogurt cheese.

Crust

¼	cup nonfat cream cheese
½	cup confectioners' sugar, sifted
¼	cup fat-free egg substitute
1	teaspoon vanilla
½	teaspoon grated lemon rind
1	cup + 2 tablespoons all-purpose flour, sifted
	Pinch of salt

Filling

2	cups nonfat vanilla yogurt cheese
1¼	cups nonfat ricotta cheese
1½	cups sugar
1¼	cups fat-free egg substitute
2	tablespoons all-purpose flour
1	teaspoon grated lemon rind
2	teaspoons vanilla
⅓	cup evaporated skim milk

To make the crust: Preheat the oven to 350°. Coat a 9″ springform pan lightly with no-stick spray. Use your fingers to spread the oil completely over the surface. Set aside.

In a medium bowl, combine the cream cheese, confectioners' sugar and egg substitute. Using an electric mixer, beat at medium speed for about 30 seconds, or until the sugar is incorporated. The mixture may still be lumpy.

Add the vanilla, lemon rind, flour and salt. Beat at low speed for about 15 seconds, or until the mixture forms a crumbly dough. Transfer the dough to the prepared pan. With lightly floured hands, press it down evenly to cover the bottom.

Bake on the center oven rack for 10 to 12 minutes, or until golden. Place on a wire rack to cool.

Reduce the heat to 325°. Fill a cake pan three-quarters full of water and place on the bottom rack of the oven.

To make the filling: In a large bowl, combine the yogurt cheese and ricotta. Using an electric mixer, beat at medium speed until smooth. Add the sugar and beat until well-blended. Add the egg substitute, $^1/_4$ cup at a time, beating after each addition until well-incorporated. Add the flour, lemon rind, vanilla and milk and beat at low speed.

Pour the batter over the crust and set the pan on a baking sheet. Place it on the center oven rack and bake for 1 hour and 20 minutes, or until the cake is golden and firm in the center.

Cool on a wire rack for at least 2 hours. Cover and refrigerate for at least 4 hours before serving.

Makes 12 servings
Per serving: 220 calories, 0.3 g. fat
Note: To make 2 cups of nonfat vanilla yogurt cheese, spoon $2^1/_3$ cups of nonfat vanilla yogurt into a strainer lined with cheesecloth or a paper coffee filter. Let drain for 20 minutes, or until the resulting yogurt cheese equals 2 cups.

Glazed Cinnamon Rolls

And you thought cinnamon rolls were off the menu? Evelyn Tribole, R.D., author of *Healthy Homestyle Cooking*, has created wonderful and guilt-free sweet rolls with just a few changes. She uses skim milk and egg whites in the dough and corn syrup instead of butter in the cinnamon filling. And the sweet glaze is, well, the icing on the cake.

Sweet Dough

2–2½	cups all-purpose flour
2	cups whole-wheat flour
1	package (¼ ounce) active dry yeast
2	teaspoons ground cinnamon
½	teaspoon salt
1	cup skim milk
⅓	cup sugar
4	egg whites, lightly beaten

Cinnamon Filling

3	tablespoons light corn syrup
½	cup sugar
3	teaspoons ground cinnamon

Glaze

½	cup confectioners' sugar
¼	teaspoon vanilla
2–3	teaspoons skim milk

To make the sweet dough: In a large bowl, combine 1 cup of the all-purpose flour, 1 cup of the whole-wheat flour, the yeast, cinnamon and salt. Set aside.

In a small saucepan, combine the milk and sugar. Heat and stir until very warm (120° to 130°). Stir the milk mixture into the flour mixture, then add the egg whites. Using an electric mixer, beat at low speed just until blended. Then beat at high speed for 3 minutes. Gradually stir in the remaining 1 cup of whole-wheat flour. Then stir in enough of the remaining all-purpose flour to make a soft dough.

Sprinkle 1 tablespoon of the all-purpose flour evenly on a work surface. Place the dough on the surface and knead for 6 to 8 minutes, incorporating as much of the remaining all-purpose flour as needed to produce a dough that's smooth and elastic. Shape the dough into a ball.

Coat a clean, dry, large bowl with no-stick spray. Place the dough in the bowl and lightly coat the top with no-stick spray. Cover and let rise in a draft-free place for about 1 hour, or until doubled in size.

Punch down the dough and divide it in half. Cover and let rest for 10 minutes. Meanwhile, coat two 9″ round baking pans with no-stick spray and set aside.

Sprinkle 1 tablespoon of the all-purpose flour evenly on a work surface. Place half of the dough on the surface and roll into a 12″ × 10″ rectangle. Repeat with more flour and the remaining dough.

To make the cinnamon filling: Brush each piece of dough with 1¹/₂ tablespoons of the corn syrup. In a small bowl, mix the sugar and cinnamon. Sprinkle it evenly over the dough pieces.

Roll up each piece of dough, starting at a long side, to form a cylinder. Pinch the seams together to seal. Cut each roll into 12 equal pieces. Divide the pieces between the prepared pans, placing the rolls cut side down.

Cover and let the rolls rise in a draft-free place for about 30 minutes, or until nearly doubled in size. Meanwhile, preheat the oven to 375°.

Uncover the rolls and bake for 20 to 25 minutes. Cool the rolls in their pans for 5 minutes, then invert them onto wire racks and remove the pans. Cool slightly.

To make the glaze: In a small bowl, stir together the sugar, vanilla and enough milk to make a glaze of the desired consistency. Drizzle the glaze over the warm rolls and serve.

Makes 24
PER ROLL: 132 CALORIES, 0.4 G. FAT
Note: If you want to freeze the baked rolls, do not top them with the glaze. Cool the rolls completely, then tightly wrap them in heavy foil and freeze. To thaw, place the foil-wrapped rolls in a 300° oven for about 20 minutes. Remove the foil and drizzle the glaze over the rolls before serving.

Strawberry Meringue Torte

This simple dessert is the perfect conclusion to a spring supper. Lynda A. Pozel, author of *Lynda's Low-Fat Kitchen*, uses egg whites, strawberries and chocolate in an elegant, flavorful finale that has less than a gram of fat per serving.

Meringue

3	large egg whites, at room temperature
¼	teaspoon cream of tartar
½	teaspoon almond extract
½	cup sugar

Strawberry Sauce

1	package (10 ounces) thawed frozen sweetened strawberries
2	teaspoons cornstarch
2	teaspoons water
2	cups fresh whole strawberries, hulled

Chocolate Sauce

¼	cup semisweet chocolate chips
1–2	teaspoons water or milk

To make the meringue: Preheat the oven to 300°. Line a baking sheet with parchment paper or a brown paper bag that has been cut to fit. Set aside.

In a medium bowl, using an electric mixer, whip the egg whites with the cream of tartar and almond extract until soft peaks form. Add the sugar, 1 tablespoon at a time, beating after each addition until the sugar is dissolved. Beat until stiff peaks form.

Spread the meringue on the prepared baking sheet to form a 9″ circle and make a rim around the edge.

Bake for 45 minutes, then turn off the oven but do not open the oven door. Allow the meringue to stand in the oven for 1 hour.

Remove the meringue from the oven and carefully remove the paper. Place the meringue on a serving platter and set aside.

To make the strawberry sauce: Place the thawed strawberries in a small saucepan and bring to a boil.

In a cup, combine the cornstarch and water. Stir into the strawberries and boil for 1 minute. Remove from the heat and cool completely.

Pour the cooled sauce onto the meringue shell. Arrange the whole strawberries on top and set aside.

To make the chocolate sauce: In the top of a double boiler over gently boiling water, melt the chocolate chips. Add enough water or milk to thin the mixture to a pourable consistency. Drizzle the sauce over the berries and serve.

Makes 8 servings
PER SERVING: 94 CALORIES, 0.6 G. FAT

Note: If you don't have a double boiler, melt the chocolate chips in the microwave. Place them in a bowl or cup and microwave on high power for 1 to 2 minutes, stopping every 15 seconds to stir the chips. Avoid overcooking, because the chips will become pasty and difficult to work with.

FAT STATS

Our Giant Sweet Tooth

- Per person, average amount of chocolate consumed in the United States each year: 16.3 pounds
- America's top three chocolate treats, in order: Snickers, M&M's, Hershey's Almond.
- Per person, average amount of ice cream consumed in the United States each year: 23 quarts
- Elvis's last snack: four scoops of ice cream and six Chips Ahoy! cookies.

Chocolate-Hazelnut Meringue Kisses

These melt-in-your-mouth kisses are a godsend. Created by Nancy Baggett in *Dream Desserts*, these treats contain less than a gram of fat each—compared to 6 or 8 grams in traditional chocolate-nut cookies.

¼	cup hazelnuts
½	ounce unsweetened chocolate, grated
¼	cup unsweetened cocoa powder
3	tablespoons cornstarch
½	cup confectioners' sugar, sifted
½	teaspoon instant coffee powder or granules
½	teaspoon hot water
¾	teaspoon vanilla
⅛	teaspoon almond extract
3	large egg whites, at room temperature
⅛	teaspoon salt
⅔	cup granulated sugar

Preheat the oven to 350°. Line several large baking sheets with parchment paper and set aside.

Spread the hazelnuts in a baking pan. Place in the oven and toast, stirring occasionally, for 15 to 17 minutes, or until the hulls loosen and the nuts are browned. Set the nuts aside to cool. Reduce the heat to 275°.

Remove and discard any loose bits of hull from the cooled hazelnuts by rubbing them between your hands or in a clean kitchen towel. Using a sharp knife or a food processor, finely chop the nuts.

Transfer the nuts to a large bowl. Add the chocolate, cocoa powder, cornstarch and confectioners' sugar. Stir until well-blended. Set aside.

In a cup, combine the coffee, hot water, vanilla and almond extract. Stir until the coffee dissolves. Set aside.

In a large, clean bowl, using an electric mixer, beat the egg whites at medium speed until very frothy. Increase the speed to high and add the salt. Beat just until very soft peaks begin to form. Immediately add the granulated sugar, 2 tablespoons at a time, continuing to beat until all of the sugar is incorporated and the mixture is stiff, smooth and glossy, about 3 minutes.

Beat the coffee mixture into the meringue until smooth. Using a rubber spatula, fold the nut mixture into the meringue just until evenly blended. Do not overmix.

Drop the mixture by small rounded teaspoonfuls about $1^1/_2''$ apart on the prepared baking sheets.

Bake the cookies on the center oven rack for 17 to 20 minutes, or until they are firm on the outside and slightly soft inside. Remove from the oven and set aside until completely cool. Carefully peel the cookies from the paper. Store in an airtight container for 3 or 4 days, or freeze for longer storage.

Makes about 35
Per cookie: 32 calories, 0.8 g. fat
Note: For more elegant kisses, use a pastry bag fitted with a $1/_2''$-diameter plain tip. Pipe into $1^1/_4''$-diameter kisses.

Chocolate-Banana Brownies

Dr. Marvin A. Wayne and Dr. Stephen R. Yarnall stumbled upon a winner with this recipe from *The New Dr. Cookie Cookbook*. Bananas and chocolate create a deliciously moist brownie that pairs pefectly with a glass of cold milk.

1	cup quick-cooking oats (not instant)
1	cup boiling water
4	large egg whites
$^3/_4$	cup packed brown sugar
$^1/_2$	cup granulated sugar
2	tablespoons canola oil
1	teaspoon vanilla
$1^1/_2$	cups mashed ripe bananas (about 3)
1	cup unbleached all-purpose flour
1	teaspoon baking soda
$^1/_2$	teaspoon salt
4	tablespoons cocoa powder

Preheat the oven to 350°. Coat a 9″ × 13″ baking pan with no-stick spray and set aside.

In a small bowl, mix the oats with the water and set aside for about 5 minutes, or until the water is absorbed.

In a large bowl, combine the egg whites, brown sugar, granulated sugar, oil, vanilla and bananas. Using an electric mixer, beat at medium speed until smooth. Add the flour, baking soda, salt, cocoa powder and soaked oats. Beat until well-mixed. Pour the batter into the pan.

Bake for 20 to 25 minutes, or until a toothpick inserted in the center of the brownies comes out clean. Cool completely in the pan. Cut into 48 squares and store in the refrigerator until ready to serve.

Makes 48

PER BROWNIE: 50 CALORIES, 0.8 G. FAT

Note: The brownies are much easier to cut if you place the cooled brownies, still in the baking pan, into the freezer for about 20 minutes.

Carrot Cake
with Cream Cheese Frosting

Wouldn't it be great to dig into a rich and moist carrot cake that isn't loaded with fat? You can! This incredibly moist cake, from *Everyday Cooking with Dr. Dean Ornish*, cuts the fat with carrot puree, crushed pineapple and nonfat cream cheese.

Carrot Cake

2	cups grated carrots
½	cup sugar
1	can (4 ounces) crushed pineapple (with juice)
1	jar (4 ounces) carrot puree
½	cup egg whites or fat-free egg substitute
2	teaspoons vanilla
¼	teaspoon salt
1¼	cups sifted cake flour
1¼	cups oat bran
2	teaspoons baking soda
1½	teaspoons ground cinnamon

Cream Cheese Frosting

8	ounces nonfat cream cheese, softened
¼	cup sugar

To make the carrot cake: Preheat the oven to 425°. Coat a 9″ pie pan with no-stick spray. Set aside.

In a large bowl, combine the carrots, sugar, pineapple (with juice), carrot puree, egg whites or egg substitute, vanilla and salt. Whisk until well-blended.

In another bowl, stir together the flour, oat bran, baking soda and cinnamon. Add the dry ingredients to the carrot mixture and fold in gently.

Pour the batter into the prepared pan. Bake for 30 minutes, or until lightly browned and firm to the touch. Cool in the pan, then unmold and frost.

To make the cream cheese frosting: In a medium bowl, beat the cream cheese and sugar until smooth and creamy. Spread evenly over the cake.

Makes 12 servings
PER SERVING: 118 CALORIES, 0.9 G. FAT

Old-Fashioned Chocolate Cake with Chocolate Frosting

This is a real old-time chocolate cake. And there's almost no fat, thanks to buttermilk, applesauce and cocoa powder. Barry Bluestein and Kevin Morrissey, authors of *The 99% Fat-Free Book of Appetizers and Desserts*, create a light, crumbly texture by beating in each egg white individually.

Chocolate Cake

$1^3/_4$ cups all-purpose flour
$^1/_2$ cup + $1^1/_2$ teaspoons unsweetened Dutch-processed cocoa powder
1 teaspoon baking soda
$^1/_2$ teaspoon salt
$^1/_2$ cup natural unsweetened applesauce
3 tablespoons light corn syrup
1 cup sugar
3 large egg whites, at room temperature
1 cup buttermilk

Chocolate Frosting

1 tablespoon light corn syrup
3 tablespoons unsweetened Dutch-processed cocoa powder
$1^1/_2$ cups confectioners' sugar
$^1/_4$ cup boiling water

To make the chocolate cake: Preheat the oven to 350°.

In a medium bowl, sift together the flour, $^1/_2$ cup of the cocoa powder, the baking soda and salt. Set aside.

In a large bowl, combine the applesauce and corn syrup. Using an electric mixer, beat at medium speed until blended. Gradually add the sugar.

Increase the speed to high and add the egg whites, one at a time. Beat at high speed until the mixture is light and frothy.

Reduce the speed to medium and beat in half of the flour mixture, then $^1/_2$ cup of the buttermilk. Beat until well-blended. Beat in the remaining flour mixture and the remaining ½ cup of buttermilk. Scrape down the sides of the bowl occasionally with a rubber spatula.

Lightly coat two 8″ round, no-stick cake pans with no-stick spray. Dust each pan with ¾ teaspoon of the remaining cocoa powder.

Pour the batter into the prepared pans. Bake for 25 to 30 minutes, or until a toothpick inserted into the center of each cake comes out clean.

Transfer the pans to a wire rack and cool for 15 minutes. Remove the cakes from the pans and cool completely.

When the cakes are cool, frost with the chocolate frosting. Let stand for 1 hour before serving.

To make the frosting: In a medium bowl, combine the corn syrup, cocoa powder, confectioners' sugar and 1 tablespoon of the boiling water. Using an electric mixer at low speed, beat in the remaining boiling water, a tablespoon at a time, until the mixture is fluffy and glossy.

Makes 12 servings
PER SERVING: 230 CALORIES, 0.9 G. FAT

Chocolate-Almond Biscotti

These Italian chocolate cookies make great gifts for chocolates-lovers. The Dutch-processed cocoa and toasted almonds give you a double hit of flavor without a lot of fat. These irresistible goodies are from Anne Casale's *Lean Italian Meatless Meals*. And they're really pretty easy to make.

$^3/_4$ cup natural whole almonds
2 cups unbleached all-purpose flour
$^3/_4$ cup sugar
$^1/_3$ cup unsweetened Dutch-processed cocoa
2 teaspoons instant espresso coffee powder
2 teaspoons baking powder
2 large eggs, at room temperature
3 large egg whites, at room temperature
$1^1/_2$ teaspoons vanilla

Preheat the oven to 350°. Place the almonds on a small baking sheet and toast on the center oven rack for about 9 minutes, or until the skins are a deep golden color. Cool slightly. Using a sharp knife or a food processor, coarsely chop the almonds and set aside. Keep the oven on.

Line a 14″ × 17″ baking sheet with parchment paper and set aside.

In a large bowl, combine the flour, sugar, cocoa, coffee and baking powder. Stir until well-combined.

In a small bowl, whisk together the eggs, 2 of the egg whites and the vanilla. Add to the flour mixture. Using an electric mixer, beat at low speed until the dough becomes crumbly, about 30 seconds. Stir in the almonds.

Turn the dough onto a well-floured work surface (the dough will be soft and sticky). With well-floured hands, gently knead the dough 2 or 3 times, or until it begins to hold together in a ball.

Divide the dough into 3 equal pieces. Shape each piece into a rope about 11″ long. Place the ropes 3″ apart on the prepared baking sheet. With your fingers, gently flatten each into a log $^1/_2$″ high, $2^1/_2$″ wide and 13 inches long.

Lightly beat the remaining egg white and brush it on the logs.

Bake the logs for about 20 minutes, or until firm to the touch. Place the baking sheet on a wire rack to cool for 5 minutes.

Reduce the heat to 325° and transfer the logs to a cutting board. Leave the parchment paper on the baking sheet. With a serrated knife, cut the logs crosswise at a slight diagonal into ½"-thick slices. Place half of the slices cut-side down on the baking sheet, spacing them ½" apart. Bake for about 7 minutes on each side, or until the surfaces are dry to the touch. Transfer the biscotti to a wire rack to cool completely. Line the baking sheet with fresh parchment paper and bake the remaining slices. Store the biscotti in a tin lined with wax paper for up to 3 weeks.

Makes 60
PER BISCOTTO: 40 CALORIES, 0.9 G. FAT

Blackberry Zabaglione

Graham Kerr notes that the Italian custard zabaglione was created when a seventeenth-century chef accidentally poured wine into an egg custard. Ever since, this dessert has been made with a variety of liquors. But in *Graham Kerr's Best*, you'll find this recipe for a delicious zabaglione without added alcohol—or fat.

2½ cups thawed frozen unsweetened blackberries
2 tablespoons cornstarch
1¾ cups nonalcoholic white wine
3 tablespoons maple syrup
¼ teaspoon almond extract
¼ teaspoon vanilla
1 cup fat-free egg substitute
½ cup superfine sugar

Using 1½ cups of the blackberries, fill six 6-ounce wine glasses about half-full. Puree the remaining 1 cup of blackberries in a food processor or by pressing them through a sieve.

In a cup, mix the cornstarch with ¼ cup of the wine. Set aside.

In a small saucepan, bring the remaining 1½ cups of wine to a boil. Add the maple syrup, almond extract and vanilla. Stirring constantly, add the cornstarch mixture and return to a boil. Remove from the heat and set aside.

In the top of a double boiler over gently boiling water, combine the egg substitute and sugar. Whisk until the mixture is thick and creamy, like a frothy pudding.

Slowly whisk in the syrup mixture. Add 6 tablespoons of the blackberry puree and whisk until well-blended.

Pour the custard over the blackberries in the wine glasses. Top with the remaining blackberry puree. Serve warm.

Makes 6 servings
PER SERVING: 149 CALORIES, 0.3 G. FAT
Note: To give egg whites an additional boost in volume and texture, use a copper bowl as the top part of your double boiler.

Credits

"How Much We Spend" on page 10, portions of "What We Eat" on page 58, "Who's Losing" on page 125, "How We (Don't) Exercise" on page 169, "Celebrity Size-Up" on page 209 and "The Price of a Pound" on page 222 are adapted from "What Price Diet?" by Laura Fraser and Valerie Fahey in *Mademoiselle* magazine. Copyright © 1995 by Laura Fraser and Valerie Fahey. Reprinted by permission.

What the Experts Eat" on page 19 is adapted from an article of the same name by Laura Flynn McCarthy that originally appeared in *Cooking Light* magazine. Copyright © 1996 by Laura Flynn McCarthy. Reprinted by permission.

"Stop Beefing and Eat Up" on page 25 is adapted from "The New Healthy Meat" by John Sedgwick, which originally appeared in *Self* magazine. Copyright © 1995 by John Sedgwick. Reprinted by permission.

The table "And the Meat Goes On" on page 28 is adapted from *Self* magazine. Sources: USDA Handbook 8; American Ostrich Association, *Self* research. Copyright © 1995 by the Condé Nast Publications, Inc. Courtesy *Self*.

"Dieter's Dream or Marketer's Ploy?" on page 46 is adapted from an article of the same name that originally appeared in *Consumer Reports on Health*, July 1995. Copyright © 1995 by Consumers Union of the U.S., Inc., 101 Truman Ave., Yonkers, NY 10703-1057. Reprinted by permission. For more information, write to the above address.

"Olestra: Procter's Big Gamble" on page 54 is adapted from an article of the same name by Myra Karstadt and Stephen Schmidt that originally appeared in *Nutrition Action Healthletter*. Copyright © 1996 by the Center for Science in the Public Interest. Reprinted by permission.

"Good-Bye, Mr. Goodbar" on page 59 is adapted from an article of the same name by Stephen P. Gullo, Ph.D., that originally appeared in *Self* magazine. Copyright © 1995 by Stephen P. Gullo. Reprinted by permission.

The quiz "Put Your Diet to the Test" on page 64 was developed by Elizabeth Ward, R.D., and is adapted from *Walking* Magazine. Copyright © 1995 by *Walking* Magazine. Reprinted by permission.

"Low-Fat French? *Mais Oui!*" on page 94 and "The Too-Busy-to-Eat-Right Low-Fat Plan" on page 138 are adapted from *Low-Fat Living* by Robert K. Cooper, Ph.D., with Leslie L. Cooper. Copyright © 1996 by Robert K. Cooper, Ph.D., and Leslie L. Cooper. Reprinted by permission.

"Fiber's Back—And It's a Fat-Fighting Superstar" on page 99 is adapted from

"Mother Nature's Weight-Loss Secret" by Jennifer Rapaport, which originally appeared in *McCall's* magazine. Copyright © 1995 by Gruner & Jahr USA Publishing. Reprinted by permission of *McCall's*.

"The Biology of a Pig-Out" on page 118 is adapted from an article of the same name by Judith Mandelbaum-Schmid that originally appeared in *Self* magazine. Copyright © 1995 by Judith Mandelbaum-Schmid. Reprinted by permission.

"The New Scoop on Liquid Calories" on page 127 is adapted from "Liquid Calories" by Dawn Margolis, which originally appeared in *American Health* magazine. Copyright © 1995 by Dawn Margolis. Reprinted by permission of *American Health*.

"More Low-Fat Time-Savers" on page 140 is adapted from *Quick and Healthy Recipes and Ideas* by Brenda J. Ponichtera, R.D. Copyright © 1991 by Brenda J. Ponichtera, R.D. Reprinted by permission.

"And The Winners Are . . ." on page 155 is adapted from "Winning at Losing" by Patricia Long, which originally appeared in *Health* magazine. Reprinted from *Health*. Copyright © 1996.

"Escape Your Shape" on page 168 is adapted from an article of the same name by Beth Tomkiw that originally appeared in *Self* magazine. Copyright © 1996 by the Condé Nast Publications, Inc. Courtesy *Self*. The photographs by Kenji Toma on pages 171–79 also originally appeared in *Self*.

"The 30-Minute Fat-Burning Workout" on page 180 is adapted from an article of the same name by Dana Sullivan that originally appeared in *Self* magazine. Copyright © 1995 by the Condé Nast Publications, Inc. Courtesy *Self*. The photographs by Terry Doyle on pages 182–85 also originally appeared in *Self*.

"The 24-Hour Workout" on page 186 is adapted from an article of the same name by Teryl Zarnow that originally appeared in *Ladies Home Journal*. Copyright © 1995 by Teryl Zarnow. Reprinted by permission.

"Metabolism: How Calories Burn" on page 188 is adapted from an article of the same name by Ilene Springer that originally appeared in *Ladies Home Journal*. Copyright © 1995 by Ilene Springer. Reprinted by permission.

"Tips for Overweight Walkers" on page 196 is adapted from *Walking* Magazine. Copyright © 1995 by *Walking* Magazine. Reprinted by permission.

"Dieting: When Your Friends Want You to Fail" on page 224 is adapted from an article of the same name by Michele Meyer that originally appeared in *Lose Weight and Stay Fit*, a *Women's Day* special. Copyright © 1995 by Michele Meyer. Reprinted by permission.

"The Ups and Downs of Yo-Yo Dieting" on page 227 is adapted from an article of the same name by Curtis Pesmen that originally appeared in *Self* magazine. Copyright © 1995 by the Condé Nast Publications, Inc. Courtesy *Self*.

"Yo-Yo Dieting Is Bad for Your Head" on page 228 is adapted from *Women's Health Letter*. Copyright © 1995 by Soundview Communications. Reprinted by permission.

The recipes for Heart-Healthy Deviled Eggs on page 233, Maine Clam Chowder on page 250 and Microwave Orange Roughy with Port Sauce on page 270 are adapted from *1,001 Low-Fat Recipes* by Sue Spitler. Copyright © 1995 by Surrey Books, Inc. Reprinted by permission.

The recipe for Vietnamese-Style Spring Rolls with Ginger Soy Dipping Sauce on page 234 is adapted from *High-Flavor, Low-Fat Vegetarian Cooking* by Steven Raichlen. Copyright © 1995 by Steven Raichlen. Used by permission of Viking Penguin, a division of Penguin Books USA Inc.

The recipes for Steamed Pork and Chicken Dumplings on page 236, Classic Cheesecake on page 280 and Old-Fashioned Chocolate Cake with Chocolate Frosting on page 292 are adapted from *The 99% Fat-Free Book of Appetizers and Desserts* by Barry Bluestein and Kevin Morrissey. Copyright © 1996 by Barry Bluestein and Kevin Morrissey. Used by permission of Doubleday, a division of Bantam Doubleday Dell Publishing Group, Inc.

The recipe for Soft Pretzels on page 240 is adapted from *All-American Vegetarian* by Barbara Grunes and Virginia Van Vynckt. Copyright © 1995 by Barbara Grunes and Virginia Van Vynckt. Reprinted by permission of Henry Holt & Co., Inc.

The recipes for Chicken Fingers with Honey Mustard Sauce on page 243 and Aloha Meatballs on page 244 are adapted from *Secrets of Fat-Free Cooking* by Sandra Woodruff, R.D. Copyright © 1995 by Sandra Woodruff. Reprinted by permission of Avery Publishing Group.

The recipe for Creamy Corn Chowder on page 247 is adapted and reprinted with the permission of Simon & Schuster from *More So Fat, Low Fat, No Fat* by Betty Rohde. Copyright © 1996 by Betty Rohde.

The recipe for White Chili on page 248 is adapted with permission of Macmillan Reference USA, a Division of Simon & Schuster, from *Cook It Light: Pasta, Rice and Beans* by Jeanne Jones. Copyright © 1994 by Jeanne Jones.

The recipes for Pacific Rim Gazpacho on page 249 and Chilled Carrot Soup on page 252 are adapted from *Arlyn Hackett's Menu Magic* by Arlyn Hackett. Copyright © 1995 by Arlyn Hackett. Reprinted by permission of Hastings House.

The recipe for Cold Zucchini Soup with Fresh Mint on page 251 is adapted from *Provençal Light* by Martha R. Shulman. Copyright © 1994 by Martha R. Shulman. Used by permission of Doubleday, a division of Bantam Doubleday Dell Publishing Group, Inc.

The recipes for Soupe au Pistou (French Vegetable Soup with Basil) on page 253, Rice-Stuffed Bell Peppers on page 271 and Carrot Cake with Cream Cheese Frosting on page 291 are adapted from *Everyday Cooking with Dr. Dean Ornish* by Dean Ornish, M.D. Copyright © 1996 by Dean Ornish, M.D. Reprinted by permission of HarperCollins Publishers, Inc.

The recipes for Minty Cream of Butternut Squash Soup on page 255, Tomato-Vinaigrette Dressing on page 257 and Pears in Red Wine on page 286 are adapted from *Jacques Pépin's Simple and Healthy Cooking* by Jacques Pépin. Copyright © 1994 by Jacques Pépin. Reprinted by permission.

The recipes for Crab Salad on page 256 and Old-Fashioned Chicken and Dumplings on page 266 are adapted from *Fat Free and Ultra Lowfat Recipes* by Doris

Cross. Copyright © 1995 by Doris Cross. Reprinted by permission of Prima Publishing, 3875 Atherton Road, Rocklin, CA 95765

The recipe for Macaroni-Bleu Cheese Salad on page 258 is adapted from *Skinny Pasta* by Sue Spitler. Copyright © 1994 by Sue Spitler. Reprinted by permission of Surrey Books, Inc.

The recipe for Mexican Red Rice on page 261 is adapted from *Skinny Mexican Cooking* by Sue Spitler. Copyright © 1996 by Sue Spitler. Reprinted by permission of Surrey Books, Inc.

The recipe for Scalloped Root Vegetables on page 264 is adapted from *Healthy Indulgences* by Lynn Fischer. Copyright © 1995 by Lynn Fischer. Reprinted by permission of William Morrow & Co., Inc.

The recipes for Roasted Eggplant and Sweet Onion Tart on page 268 and Strawberry Meringue Torte on page 284 are adapted from *Lynda's Low-Fat Kitchen* by Lynda A. Pozel. Copyright © 1995 by Lynda A. Pozel. Reprinted by permission of Chariot Publishing, Inc.

The recipe for Lemon-Pepper Horseradish Shrimp on page 272 is adapted from *Enola Prudhomme's Low-Fat Favorites* by Enola Prudhomme. Copyright © 1994 by Enola Prudhomme. Reprinted by permission of William Morrow & Co., Inc.

The recipe for Pasta with Smoked Chicken and Pea Pods on page 275 is adapted from *The 99% Fat-Free Cookbook* by Barry Bluestein and Kevin Morrissey. Copyright © 1994 by Barry Bluestein and Kevin Morrissey. Used by permission of Doubleday, a division of Bantam Doubleday Dell Publishing Group, Inc.

The recipe for Broccoli Pizza with Quick and Easy Crust on page 276 is adapted from *500 Fat-Free Recipes* by Sarah Schlesinger. Copyright © 1994 by Sarah Schlesinger. Reprinted by permission of Villard Books, a division of Random House, Inc.

The recipe for Glazed Cinnamon Rolls on page 282 is adapted from *Healthy Homestyle Cooking* by Evelyn Tribole, R.D. Copyright © 1994 by Evelyn Tribole. Reprinted by permission.

The recipe for Blackberry Zabaglione on page 287 is adapted and reprinted by permission of the Putnam Publishing Group from *Graham Kerr's Best* by Graham Kerr. Copyright © 1995 by Graham Kerr.

The recipe for Chocolate-Hazelnut Meringue Kisses on page 288 is adapted from *Dream Desserts* by Nancy Baggett. Copyright © 1993 by Nancy Baggett. Reprinted by permission of Stewart, Tabori & Chang, Inc.

The recipe for Chocolate Banana Brownies on page 290 is adapted from *The New Dr. Cookie Cookbook* by Marvin A. Wayne and Stephen R. Yarnall. Copyright © 1994 by Marvin A. Wayne and Stephen R. Yarnall. Reprinted by permission of William Morrow & Co., Inc.

The recipe for Chocolate-Almond Biscotti on page 294 is adapted from *Lean Italian Meatless Meals* by Anne Casale. Copyright © 1995 by Anne Casale. Reprinted by permission of Ballantine Books, a division of Random House, Inc.

Index

Note: **Boldface** page references indicate primary discussion of topic. <u>Underscored</u> references indicate boxed text. *Italic* page references indicate illustrations and photographs.